Contents

P9-BYX-347

ABOUT THE AUTHOR

At the age of 6, Clotilde picked up the needle and hasn't stopped sewing since. She creates her own clothing and many garments for her family. Clotilde and her husband now live in Fort Lauderdale, Fla. Clotilde enjoys touring the United States giving seminars at universities, fabric stores and wherever people who sew might gather together. She also has a passion for traveling the world in search of new experiences, quality products and treasures to offer in the Clotilde mail-order catalog.

Clotilde is a graduate of Miami University, Oxford, Ohio. After graduation, she worked for 20th Century Fox in the wardrobe department. She sewed commercially for boutique shops in Beverly Hills, learning many custom sewing techniques. Her curiosity about "how expensive designer clothes are sewn" was satisfied while making alterations on these garments. From this experience came many of the professional tips found in *Sew Smart*.

Clotilde taught adult sewing classes for an exclusive fabric store in Woodland Hills, Calif.,

for seven years—covering all facets of sewing, from basic sewing to tailoring to working with Ultrasuede fabric. She conducted seminars for sewers and teachers in the United States, England and Australia.

A love of antiques and sewing culminated in combining the two areas by collecting antique sewing items. She has an extensive collection, some of which are shown in this book.

When *Sew Smart* was first published, Clotilde collaborated with Judy Lawrence. Judy had previously authored two widely accepted books, *Sewing Knits* and *Sewing Knits Menswear*.

Well known as an author and lecturer, Judy worked as a consultant for a national sewing machine company, taught classes and conducted seminars all over the country. She met Clotilde at a workshop in the Los Angeles area in 1970, and their friendship and professional experiences developed into the co-authoring of the original version of this book—*Sew Smart*.

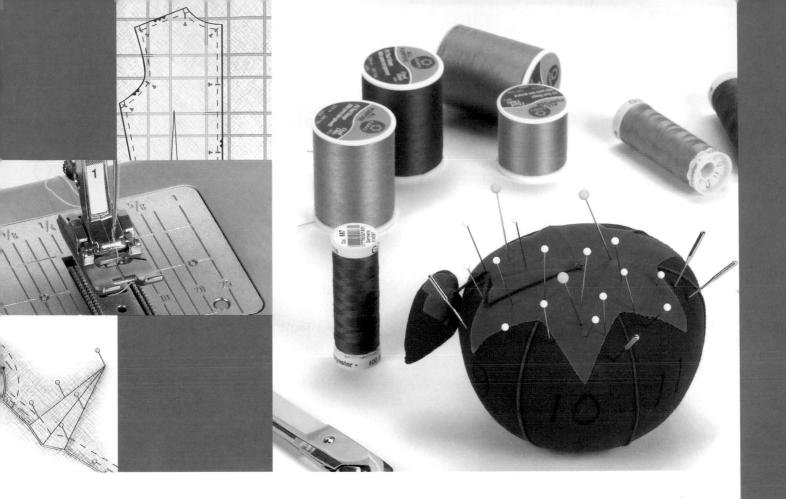

GETTING IT TOGETHER

1

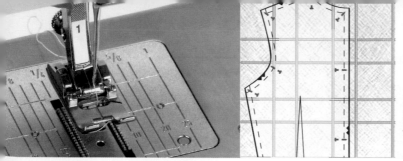

Chapter 1: Getting It Together

BEFORE YOU BEGIN each new sewing project, you should spend an adequate amount of time in the planning process so that you choose a good workable fabric/pattern combination. Some fabrics are not suitable for certain patterns; for example, a plaid fabric will not match along a raglan sleeve line, and a long A-line skirt would require almost twice the amount of yardage if a napped fabric is used. Not all fabrics can be used for all types of garments. A fabric that ravels easily will not hold up in children's playwear or for sports clothes. Firmly woven fabrics are not suitable for draped or gathered styles.

Achieving the proper fabric/pattern combination becomes easier as you gain more experience. We want to hurry that process along by giving you some guidelines for choosing and cutting your fabric. Spend some time thinking about the finished garment before you make a purchase, and then spend more time thinking about the pattern layout so that you use your fabric to its best advantage. One little slip-up during the layout and cutting process, on certain fabrics, can ruin the whole garment or send you back to the fabric store for more yardage.

Plan before you buy—plan before you cut. The time you spend at the beginning is well worth it, in order to create a garment of professional quality. Simple patterns or plain fabrics won't require much planning, but detailed patterns, using fabrics that must be matched, can take as much time for the planning process as for the whole sewing process.

FABRIC TYPES

There are three basic types of fabrics used by home sewers today: wovens, knits and nonwovens, such as felt and synthetic suedes. Each type has many subtypes, which is what makes the world of fashion so interesting. Each type also has its own characteristics and problems. These should be understood so that you can handle each fabric the best way.

Woven Fabrics

Woven fabrics are made from many natural and synthetic fibers. They come in different weaves, weights and combinations of yarns. Woven fabrics have been the mainstay of the fashion scene for many, many years and will always have a large part of the fabric market. A few of the problems found with woven fabrics follow.

- Woven fabrics tend to fray along cut edges, some fabrics more than others. Fraying edges require seam finishes of some kind.

- Some fabrics are woven "off-grain." This means that the lengthwise and crosswise threads are not at right angles. Off-grain fabrics will not hang properly and cannot be matched at the seams. Check grain line on fabrics you plan to purchase by folding the fabric crosswise so that the selvages line up. The crosswise thread and/or pattern should run along the length of the fold. A little variance is acceptable, but if the thread or pattern dips down more than 1/2", save yourself some problems and don't buy the fabric.

GOOD

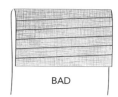
BAD

- Some off-grain woven fabrics can be straightened by pulling on the bias and pressing. Permanent-press fabrics are an exception, since they are heat or chemically set during the finishing process. However, the straightening process isn't always permanent, and after the garment is washed you are right back where you started.

- Permanent-press fabrics have a firm finish that makes them difficult to ease or drape. Keep this in mind when choosing patterns that require these techniques. These fabrics also tend to be nonabsorbing, which can make them feel warm.

- Woven fabrics don't have give, like knits, and so need more ease, making the garment appear somewhat larger. Knits are more suitable for active sportswear.

Knit Fabrics

Knits are the miracle fabric of our time, and we all love their easy care and the simplified sewing techniques. They are not without problems, though, and you should be aware of these problems so that you will have success with your sewing.

- The crosswise grain of most knit fabrics is not at right angles to the lengthwise rib (grain), because many of them are made on circular knitting machines, which produce a crosswise line that spirals up around the tube of fabric. It is impossible to straighten this crosswise line. Instructions will be

given later on that will help you overcome this problem during the cutting process.

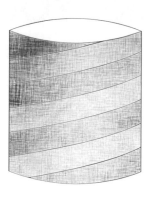

- Some printed, striped and solid-colored knits will be pressed during the finishing process in such a way that the crosswise grain is "off" more than it should be. Perhaps you have seen plaid or printed knits with the pattern dipping down as it approaches the center fold. There isn't any way you can use this fabric unless you buy extra and throw away the crooked part, or you cut only nonvisible, facing pieces from the crooked section. Unless you just have to have that fabric, you are better off leaving it in the store.

FOLD LINE

- Single knits tend to roll after they have been preshrunk. The rolling edges can be somewhat controlled by spraying with fabric finish or starch and then pressing.

- Most interlock knits will run like a nylon stocking in one direction. This tendency has nothing to do with the quality of the fabric. Find out the direction of the run by gently pulling across both cut edges of the fabric. Position the pattern pieces so that the runs go **up** the garment. This will prevent runs from forming at the neckline and shoulder seams. You can discourage runs at the bottom edges of hems and sleeves by straight stitching or zigzagging 1/4" from the edge of the fabric. Fortunately, manufacturers do check the direction of the run and print one-way prints in the correct direction.

- The lengthwise grain on a knit fabric is marked by the rib of knit loops that run the length of the fabric. The crosswise grain is more difficult to identify, but it is also marked by a line of knit loops that run across the fabric.

- Many knit fabrics have a permanent crease down the center. This must be avoided during pattern layout.

Nonwoven Fabrics

Matted fabrics, such as felt and polyester fleece, nonwoven vinyls, and nonwoven synthetic suedes, such as Ultrasuede, are relatively new to the home sewer. They are easy to work with because they do not fray, and one can take advantage of simple seam and construction techniques.

- Synthetic suedes have a nap, and require a nap layout so that you won't get different color shades on various parts of the garment.

Ultraleather is a wonderful synthetic looks-like-leather fabric. It is easy to sew and so practical. No one will believe it is not the "real thing"—until you throw it into the washing machine. Ultraleather has all the benefits of real leather, such as suppleness, beauty and comfort, but none of the negatives—such as expensive leather cleaning bills! When stretched, it recovers perfectly, collar points lie flat, skirts don't "bag out" in the hip area.

- Ultraleather has no nap. Save fabric by using a "without nap" layout when cutting out the pattern.

Ultraleather has good crosswise stretch, but unlike Ultrasuede and Ultrasuede Lite, it also stretches lengthwise. This stretch in both directions makes it super-comfortable to wear.

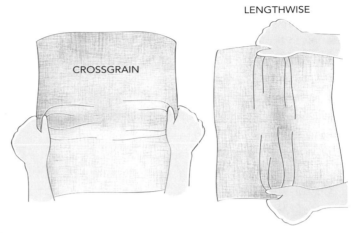

LENGTHWISE

CROSSGRAIN

Fabrics are usually folded and rolled so that the right side is to the inside. This is done to keep the fabric clean and also to avoid fading. However, not all fabrics are handled this way. If you are confused as to which is the right or wrong side, choose the side that appeals most to you. If anyone ever questions your choice, just say, "That's the way I like it!" Remember, there are no mistakes, only designer touches.

You can tell the right side of a knit fabric by gently stretching the crosswise edge. The fabric will roll to the right side.

Often fabric looks the same on both sides. If you have to look hard to determine the right side, use either side, but be consistent and use the **same** side as the right side. Mark the wrong side of confusing fabrics with strips of transparent or drafting tape, or use tailor's chalk or a sliver of soap. This will help you put the garment together properly.

Carefully examine all fabrics for flaws before you have them cut from the bolt. As you well know, not all fabrics are perfect, and it is better to find the flaws at the store, rather than after you get home.

Check fabrics again, after they have been preshrunk. Sometimes the flaw is in the dye, and won't show up until it has been washed.

Don't hesitate about returning unsatisfactory fabric to the store, or refusing to buy inferior fabrics. Most fabric stores want to handle only quality goods, and appreciate your help in catching poor merchandise.

Preshrinking Fabric

Most fabrics should be preshrunk before they are cut. This removes any fiber shrinkage and allows the fabric to relax. After all, it has been stretched on a bolt for a fair amount of time and needs to regain its natural size.

Preshrinking also removes any excess finishing materials in the fabric. Finishing chemicals can have a disagreeable odor, and they can also coat the machine needle, causing it to skip stitches.

Use the same method to preshrink the fabric that you will use to clean the finished garment. If you are going to machine wash and machine dry the finished garment, then preshrink the fabric using the same water temperature and dryer setting.

Cotton knits tend to shrink quite a bit, and more than once. We suggest that you preshrink them twice, using hot water and the highest setting on your dryer, even if you don't plan to do this afterward. This will guarantee maximum shrinkage before the yardage is cut.

Many other knits, including polyester double knits, will have a small amount of continued shrinkage if they are always dried in the dryer. Prevent this problem by drip-drying the garments, or just partially drying them in the dryer.

Woolens, woven fabrics or knits should be preshrunk with steam, unless they are labeled "needle-ready." Send the yardage to a professional dry cleaner, or do it yourself by running the fabric through a coin-operated dry-cleaning machine.

Small amounts of wool can be conveniently preshrunk at home, in the dryer. Place the dry wool yardage in the dryer with some damp clothes. Run the dryer for about 10 minutes. The heat and moisture will remove the shrinkage. Lay the moist yardage on a flat surface to dry.

Ultraleather is 48" wide and definitely should be preshrunk. Ultraleather doesn't shrink in the washing machine but the dryer heat does cause shrinkage.

Other fabrics that are going to be used for dry-cleanable garments don't usually have to be preshrunk. However, it's best to spread them out on a flat surface overnight to allow them to relax before cutting.

If you find it necessary to press your fabric after it has been preshrunk, run the iron along the lengthwise grain rather than across the fabric. This will result in a smooth finish and not stretch the fabric out of shape.

Measure your yardage before and after preshrinking. Make note of the amount of shrinkage, and keep this information handy when purchasing similar fabric.

To avoid the "high-water" pant look, hem all slacks 1/4" to 3/8" longer than you want them to be, thus compensating for the residual shrinkage that occurs after a dozen or more launderings. Men's ready-to-wear slacks should be hemmed a bit longer also, as residual shrinkage occurs even in dry cleaning. (Now you know why so many men walk around with high-water pants. They didn't buy them that way, they gradually became shorter after repeated washing or dry cleaning—and you thought it was the cheap dry cleaners' fault!)

SHRINKAGE MAY CAUSE HIGH-WATER LOOK

Fusible interfacing should be preshrunk to be on the safe side; however, **not** in the washer and dryer! Place the fusible interfacing, neatly folded, in the kitchen sink. Cover with hot tap water and allow it to soak for 10 minutes. Gently press out the water; don't wring, as you don't want to wring in wrinkles. Spread out flat and allow it to dry naturally.

Silk fabric **can** be washed by hand. This saves expensive dry-cleaning bills, and you will have a super bonus in that water spots are eliminated as the whole garment has become one big water spot! (If in doubt about washing silk, remember that the Chinese have had silk for thousands of years and there were no dry cleaners then!) However, first of all, consider the pattern. Is it going to be difficult to iron? If so, let the dry cleaner press it. As a tailored shirt takes only about 10 minutes to iron, multiply those 10 minutes by the dry-cleaning cost and it's very tidy ironing wages.

Always test-wash and test-iron a 2" or 3" square of silk fabric. Check for shrinkage. Has the texture been altered? Has the color run? Usually a print with a white background should be dry-cleaned because one color may run, ruining the garment.

Wash by hand in lukewarm water using Ivory, Bubble Jet Rinse or Orvus soap. Rinse in lukewarm water, squeeze gently (do not wring). Roll in several bath towels to remove excess moisture, hang on a padded hanger to air-dry for 15 minutes. Iron silk while it is very damp as you don't want to iron in wrinkles. When using an Iron Safe or Magic Slipper Iron Shoe, silk can be ironed from the right side; otherwise, iron from the wrong side.

If the wash water turns color, help set the dye by adding several tablespoons of white vinegar to the wash and rinse water every time. Vinegar acts as salt does to help set the dye. (Don't worry, you won't smell like a vinegar bottle by the time it's ironed!) Add the vinegar to the final rinse of white silk blouses also, as it is the soapy residue that yellows white silk.

WHICH SIZE

Most women sew from too large a pattern, because they have taken their full bust measurement. The result is a garment with sleeves that fall off the shoulders and have gaping necklines that are comparable to a man wearing a size 16 shirt when he should be wearing a size 15 shirt. Instead, take two measurements: the full bust measurement as well as the high bust measurement. Hold the tape above the bust and high up under the arms. Pull the tape snug.

If the difference between the two measurements is 2" or more, use the high bust measurement to correspond to the measurement on the pattern. If the difference is less than two inches, use the full bust measurement. There is not much correlation between ready-to-wear sizes and pattern sizes. The more expensive the clothes are, the smaller the size. They're just flattering your ego!

Be aware that misses patterns are made for a B cup and half-size patterns are made for a C cup. If you have a C cup, you don't have to be limited to half-size patterns, merely slash and spread the bodice to accommodate your larger bust, see Dart Placement in Chapter 3. Always use the **bodice** measurement to determine the correct pattern size. The garment hangs from the neck and shoulders, where fit is most important, and it is the most complicated

area to adjust on the pattern. One must adjust the depth of the armhole, the width of the neck and possibly the collar length as well as the width of the bodice front and back. It is much simpler to have the pattern fit the bodice and to slash and spread the skirt pattern to accommodate the larger waist or hipline. When buying a slacks or skirt-only pattern, use the hip measurement.

Patterns have four categories: fitted, semi-fitted, loose-fitting and very loose-fitting. All are the same size pattern, but the designer ease varies considerably. This chart shows the considerable difference in designer ease.

Average Ease Allowances in Commercial Patterns				
Dress, Shirt, Vest		**Jacket**	**Coat**	**Skirt, Slacks**
	(at bust)	(at bust)	(at widest area)	(at hips)
Fitted	3" to 4"	3 3/4" to 4 1/2"	5 1/4" to 6 3/4"	2" to 3"
Semi-fitted	4" to 5"	4 3/8" to 5 3/4"	6 3/4" to 8"	3" to 4"
Loose-fitting	5" to 8"	5 7/8" to 10"	8" to 12"	4" to 6"
Very Loose-fitting	more than 8"	more than 10"	more than 12"	more than 6"

Designer ease as well as the choice of fabric can make all the difference in the fit of the garment. The photograph in the pattern book may look fantastic—but will it look fantastic on you? Read the pattern description, the required notions and the suggested suitable fabrics. The wrong fabric for the pattern can result in a disaster. Imagine a deep dolman-sleeve dress pattern made out of Ultrasuede fabric. The pattern called for a soft, lightweight fabric but it was made in Ultrasuede. It happens! A trial garment in brushed denim or corduroy would have shown how wrong the pattern was for the Ultrasuede fabric.

Before cutting into an expensive piece of fabric for that gorgeous-looking suit, make up a trial garment or a "muslin" to be sure the finished jacket will look as you expect it to look. It may need to be lengthened or shortened—or maybe forgotten!

For the trial jacket, buy cuts of suit-weight fabric from the remnant table. Brushed denim is an inexpensive fabric for a trial jacket. If the trial jacket looks great, finish sewing it for a bonus jacket. (If the trial jacket is made out of muslin, it can't be finished and worn.)

If you don't plan on wearing the trial jacket, merely cut the fronts, back, under collar and one sleeve. With a pen, draw on the pockets, the lapel roll line, the waistline mark as well as the buttonhole placement. Trim off the lapel seam allowances, pin up the hem, pin in the shoulder pads the thickness called for in the pattern and try it on. Now you can see how the jacket looks on you. Trying on pinned-together tissue paper pattern just doesn't give a realistic evaluation of the pattern.

Note: *Use the shoulder pad size called for in the pattern as the pattern maker has allowed for that size pad. You may use a thinner pad if desired, but you must stitch a deeper shoulder seam allowance at the armscye to compensate for the difference; also adjust the sleeve cap ease so that it will fit into the smaller armscye. Here again, the trial garment shows what adjustments need to be made.*

As mentioned, there is much confusion and frustration between pattern sizes and ready-to-wear sizes. Included below, with Rosalie Lemontree's permission, is a reprint from her *Fashion Sewing Journal* that addresses this issue.

FABRIC EASE
Why Don't Patterns Fit Like Ready-To-Wear (RTW)?

We've been asked this question many times and the answer is both simple and complex. Essentially it is because the pattern companies use one set of measurements consistently and each ready-to-wear (RTW) manufacturer uses the measurements that suit him at the moment.

We raise this question in connection with dress forms because the dress form and its measurements is an essential part of the garment industry. It determines how the end product will fit, whether the product is a home sewing pattern or a RTW garment. The big four pattern companies and the ready-to-wear industry all buy their dress forms from Wolf and/or Superior. The pattern companies order their dress forms made to body measurements based on government research. Each RTW manufacturer orders his dress forms made to his particular measurements, which are different from his competitors and different from the home sewing industry.

The U.S. Department of Agriculture does the research on which the pattern industry depends. Periodically,

thousands of women are measured to see if the average American female has changed. The last changes came over 15 years ago and they were a big undertaking. Not only were dress forms and patterns changed, but tons of printed information and books published by the pattern companies and others had to be updated. The most recent changes—a lower bust position and a slightly larger waistline—hardly caused a ripple of concern.

The big four pattern companies all use the same basic body measurements. If you compare the charts in the back-of-the-counter catalogs, they are the same. A size 10 is a size 10 is a size 10 whether it's Vogue, Butterick, McCall's or Simplicity. If the patterns from one company seem to fit you better than another, it is because the designer ease differs, not the basic body measurements. Even when the companies buy a design from 7th Avenue, the pattern is drafted to the pattern company measurements, not the designer's RTW measurements.

On the other hand, RTW uses whatever body measurements a manufacturer finds work for him and has his dress forms made to those measurements. There is no consistency. You've probably noticed you can wear a size 10 from one house but need a size 12 when buying from his competitor. You may even have discovered that clothes from one manufacturer fit differently this year than they did last year.

RTW thinks nothing of changing their basic measurements if it seems indicated. "Indicated" is typically something like the manufacturer had lots of complaints and returns from stores because a skirt was tight through the hips. That passes for research in the garment industry and to them means American women have bigger hips this year than they did last year. You can bet the dress forms for the following season will be made with bigger hips! Yes, RTW does change their measurements and dress forms frequently. Every dress form has a date stamped on the front along with the size so there is no mistake.

Even Wolf and Superior do not use the same measurements for the standard forms they sell to you and me. Wolf makes their standard form with a 38 1/2" bust; Superior makes theirs with a 39" bust and the form for the pattern companies has a 36" bust no matter who makes it!

Rather than indulge in this mass confusion, the pattern companies stick to their government research. At least they are consistent and you know you must make the same adjustments each time you make a garment. It is too bad the home sewing industry and RTW are so far apart, but we hope you see why it is unlikely that the two will ever meet.

PATTERN LAYOUT

Once you have selected your pattern and preshrunk the fabric, you are ready for one of the most important steps in the process of making a beautiful garment—cutting out. No matter how expert your sewing techniques or how perfect your fit, you will have the "loving hands at home look" if your pattern layout and cutting procedure don't match your other skills. We're not just talking about cutting a straight line; there is more to it than that.

Take a look at designer clothes in an exclusive dress shop or nice department store. You will notice that grain lines are perfect, stripes and plaids match, and even the pockets on patterned or striped fabric are cut and sewn so that they match the garment perfectly. Patterned fabric is cut so that the design flatters the figure—no big roses on the bust or derriere. Great care is given to the cutting of small detail pieces, so that they add interest to the garment.

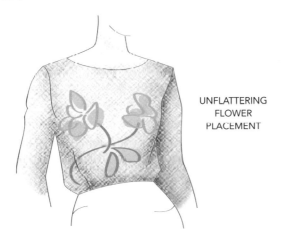

UNFLATTERING
FLOWER
PLACEMENT

Since your paper pattern has been designed without any specific fabric in mind, the only help you receive in the layout process is an economical placement of pattern pieces, with grain lines in the proper position. Many times this is all you need, but some fabrics require careful positioning of various pieces so that you get a custom look rather than a homemade look.

Place fabric with the right sides together, as it keeps the fabric cleaner and makes marking darts and buttonholes easier. Exception: Heavily napped fabrics such as

corduroy and velvet should be cut **wrong** sides together to keep the layers from shifting. Use a small piece of soap to mark an arrow in the direction of the nap on the wrong side of the fabric. (Use plain soap, as complexion soap may leave an oily residue.) Now, when cutting additional pieces from leftover fabric, you know instantly which is the right side and in which direction it was cut.

Some of the fabrics that require extra planning are: napped fabrics such as corduroy and Ultrasuede, plaids and stripes, diagonally printed or woven fabrics, and patterned fabrics that have a definite repeat or large motif.

There are some layout rules that pertain to all fabrics. Let's consider them first.

General Layout Guidelines

- Separate needed pattern pieces, and place the remaining ones back in the pattern envelope so that they won't get mixed up.

- Trim away excess pattern tissue. However, it isn't necessary to cut out pattern pieces exactly.

- Press all pattern pieces with a dry iron to remove wrinkles. This makes cutting more accurate.

- Make any necessary alterations to the paper pattern before pinning it to the fabric.

- Extend the grain line on all pattern pieces from the top to bottom edge. This makes it easier to place them on grain.

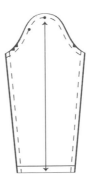

- Make a rough layout of all pattern pieces before you permanently pin them in place, or do any cutting. This lets you know if you are short of yardage while there is still time to do something about it.

- The pattern grain line should run parallel to the fabric grain line. This is absolutely necessary for a properly hanging garment.

- The distance from the pattern grain line to the fabric fold or edge should be the same at the top and bottom of the pattern piece. Use a ruler or yardstick to help measure it exactly.

- Permanently pin pattern pieces in place only after grain lines are perfect and you are sure you have enough fabric.

- Pattern pieces can be placed right or wrong side up if the fabric is folded double. If you are cutting one layer at a time, cut one piece with the pattern printing right side up, and the other piece with the pattern printing right side down. This makes sure you end up with a left and right garment piece.

- The selvage edge can be used only if it lies flat and does not pucker after preshrinking. It can be used on any straight-grain seam, such as the center back seam of a skirt. This gives more stability to the seam line and reduces the sit-out problem in the seat area. Use the selvage edge along one side of waistbands. This reduces bulk, since you won't have to turn under a raw edge on the inside of the garment.

- Some fabrics will have a faded line along the fold, which is caused by gas fumes in the fabric store—not direct sunlight. Gas fumes are due to the formaldehyde used in the finishing process at the mill. These fumes cause your eyes to smart if you ever happen to be in a fabric store just as they open up a new shipment of fabric. Check your fabric for a faded fold, and cut around it, or return it to the store.

- Use a nap layout for napped fabrics, uneven plaids or stripes, and all knits. Place the pattern pieces on the fabric so that the tops all face the same direction.

- Save Ultraleather fabric by cutting out slacks without a nap layout.

Short on Fabric

Sometimes the most careful planning fails, and you find yourself short of fabric. Check through the following list of suggestions to see if you can find the help that saves a trip to the store.

- Cut facings and/or pockets, flaps and cuffs from another fabric. Many times you see contrasting fabric used for collar, cuff and placket facings on ready-made shirts and jackets.

- For garments that have a straight front edge, overlap the garment front and front-facing pattern pieces until the seam lines meet, and cut as one. This gives you two more seam widths of fabric, which is sometimes all you need.

- Change the grain lines of collars, yokes, pockets, flaps and cuffs so they are cut on the bias. This adds interesting detail, as well as saves fabric.

- Change the sleeve length to a shorter style.

- Face hems with another fabric, rather than making the usual turned-up hem.

Napped Fabrics

Napped fabrics have some sort of surface interest that influences the way light rays are reflected from the fabric. Even though a garment is made from one piece of napped fabric, it can look as though two different shades of fabric were used if the pattern pieces are not placed on the fabric so that all tops face in the same direction. You are probably most familiar with this problem on corduroys and velvetlike fabrics.

Knits and some woven fabrics have a naplike effect because of the way they are constructed. Knits are made up of continuous rows of loops, with the tops facing in one direction. The closed ends of the loops reflect light differently from the open ends. This makes for shading problems at seam lines if all pattern pieces are not cut using a nap layout. The same thing happens with textured wovens if ridges or other surface interest are not symmetrical.

Many fabrics have subtle color variations that are not apparent at first glance and all too often aren't noticed until after the garment has been completed. Use this simple drape test if you aren't sure. Drape the uncut yardage from one shoulder to the other, letting as much hang down toward the floor as possible. Stand in front of a full-length mirror, in a well-lighted room, or have a friend go out into the sunlight with you. If the fabric on one side of your figure looks slightly darker than the fabric on the other side, you have a napped fabric, and **must** use a nap layout when pinning the pattern to the fabric.

DRAPE TEST

Check the fabric **before** it is cut off the bolt to determine if there is any color variation. You may need to buy 3/8 to 1/2 yard more fabric to enable cutting it with a nap layout.

Corduroy and velvet are examples of obvious nap variations.

Most patterns have a nap layout in the cutting guide, and it usually requires extra yardage. If your pattern doesn't tell you how much extra yardage is needed, find out by laying all pattern pieces on a cutting board, keeping them within the same measurement as the fabric you will use. Many fabric stores will let you lay your pattern pieces out on the actual fabric you have chosen so that you purchase just the right amount.

Check the direction of the nap by running your hand over the surface. Short-pile fabrics, such as velvet and velveteen, should be cut so that the pile runs up the garment. This gives a dark, rich color. Long-pile fabrics should be cut so that the pile runs down the garment.

Most napped or naplike fabrics can be cut double. However, you will find that fabrics with quite a bit of pile, such as velvet or fake furs, handle more easily when cut one layer at a time. Doing this makes each garment piece accurate in size and shape. Remember to cut one piece with the pattern printing right side up, and the other piece with the pattern printing right side

down. This makes sure you end up with right and left garment pieces.

Care must be taken when cutting fabric pieces for collars and pocket flaps that turn down on the garment. These pieces should be cut so that the nap lies in the same direction as the fabric that they will lie against. You won't have to worry about this problem if commercial pattern pieces are placed on the fabric so the printing all faces one direction.

Plaids

The correct use of plaids can make a stunning garment, but you must be aware of the careful planning required to match up everything. A little extra time spent in the layout process can eliminate most of the sewing problems. Keep the following points in mind when choosing your pattern and fabric.

Patterns of simple design, with a minimum of intricate detail, work best with plaids. Some patterns just aren't suitable, which is usually stated somewhere on the pattern envelope. Avoid patterns with darts placed at angles, rather than on the horizontal or vertical line. Long curved darts, or seams that require some easing, such as princess lines, will also give matching problems.

Patterns cut from plaid fabrics require more yardage than other fabrics. Yardage requirements are given on the pattern envelope, or you will find the statement, "extra fabric needed for matching plaids." Small plaids need approximately 1/2 yard extra fabric, while large plaids require more, sometimes up to 1 1/2 yards. Plaids repeat at regular intervals, and it is this repeat factor that determines the extra yardage. Large distances between repeats require more extra yardage than small distances between repeats.

There are basically two types of plaids: even and uneven. Even plaids have strong horizontal and vertical lines that repeat at regular intervals. This plaid is symmetrical in design. It looks the same from the top or the bottom, or from side to side.

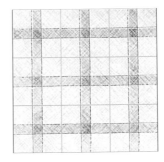

Uneven plaids can be asymmetrical in either the horizontal or vertical direction, or in both directions. The design will not appear the same if viewed from top or bottom, or from one side or the other. Uneven plaids require more extra yardage than even plaids, and are a bit more difficult to cut and match.

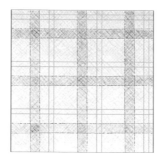

An easy way to tell if a plaid is even or uneven is to turn back a corner of the fabric, making sure that the selvage edge is parallel to a horizontal plaid line. Even plaids can be matched up along the diagonal fold, so that the design looks continuous. You are unable to do this with an uneven plaid.

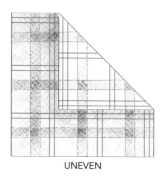 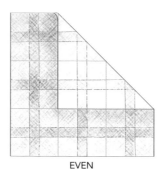

UNEVEN   EVEN

Careful thought should be given to the relationship of the plaid to the body.

- Avoid having a strong, dominant plaid line fall at the bust or hipline if you have a full figure.

- Plan to have a dominant horizontal line of the plaid fall at the hemline. This gives balance to the finished garment.

- Tall figures should have the dominant vertical lines centered on either side of the center front and center back lines. Short figures can wear the dominant vertical line on the center front and back.

Carefully position pattern pieces for a front-closing garment on the fabric so that the plaid matches when the garment is buttoned. This is done by placing the center front lines on the same vertical stripe.

Match plaids on pattern pieces from the bottom up. The section of garment above the bust darts will not match, but the rest of the garment will.

Make all length adjustments on your paper pattern before pinning it to the fabric so that you can tell exactly where hemlines will fall on the plaid.

Uneven plaids require a nap layout. Even plaids do not. If you are in doubt about your plaid, then cut using the nap layout, just to be safe.

You should match **seam lines**, not cutting lines, when you pin the pattern pieces to the fabric. Use notches and other construction marks as key points for matching.

Place main front pattern piece on the fabric first, and then place other pieces to match its placement.

Plaid fabric is cut more accurately if it is cut one layer at a time. We're sure you know how difficult it is to fold a plaid fabric so that the plaid lines match up underneath each other. You really save cutting time if you work with a single layer of fabric.

Position the main pattern piece as you want it on the fabric, then lay the adjoining piece next to it so that the seam lines match. Pin and cut. Flip these pieces over so that the fabric rather than the pattern is up, and position them on the fabric so that the plaid lines up exactly. Pin and cut. You now have exactly matching right and left garment pieces.

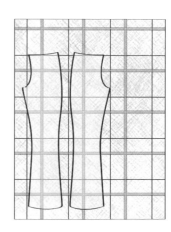

Another method is to mark plaid lines on the paper pattern, and then use these lines as a guide for cutting the matching piece.

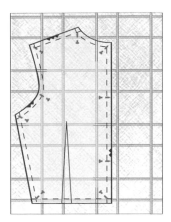

Plaids should match across all vertical seam lines, including center front, sides and center back.

Set-in sleeves can be matched only at the front armhole. Use sleeve dots and notches as guides remembering that you are matching **seam lines** rather than cutting lines. Raglan sleeves cannot be matched. Kimono sleeves will match only below the shoulder notch. Other things that should match are, if possible, the center back of the collar to the center back of the garment; pockets and flaps; and the joining line of two-piece outfits.

Design details, such as pockets, flaps, tabs, yokes or stitched-on belts, can be cut to match the garment exactly, or cut on the bias for effect. If you want to match these details, it is suggested that they be cut after all the main pattern pieces have been cut and construction marks transferred.

Place small-detail pattern pieces on the garment section in the proper position. Pin in place, and carefully trace plaid lines onto the paper pattern. Pin this pattern to the fabric, matching up plaid lines, and cut. You will get a perfect match every time.

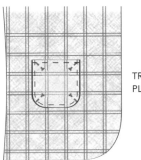

TRACE
PLAID LINES

Now that the cutting out has been accurate and well thought out, sewing should be a snap.

Checks

Follow the same basic rules for cutting plaids as when working with checked fabrics. It is usually not necessary to match up checks, 1/4" or smaller, unless it will be very obvious in the finished garment.

Consider cutting detail pattern pieces, such as collars, cuffs and yokes, on the bias for an interesting effect. This also eliminates the need for matching.

Stripes

Stripes are fun to work with, and they can add lots of zip to your wardrobe. They present fewer cutting and sewing problems than plaids, and most of them can be solved by proper pattern selection and pattern layout. The following points should be kept in mind when cutting striped fabrics.

Did you know that corduroy and twill fabrics are considered to be striped fabrics, just the same as printed or woven stripes?

Not all patterns are suitable for striped fabrics. This information is usually given on the pattern envelope. Design lines of some patterns can conflict with the stripes and make a very unattractive combination. A rule to follow here is: the busier the fabric, the simpler the pattern.

There are two basic kinds of striped fabrics—balanced and unbalanced. Balanced stripes are like even plaids in that they are symmetrical and can be cut in either direction.

Unbalanced stripes are like uneven plaids and require a nap layout and usually more yardage.

Examine your fabric before cutting to decide if there is a dominant stripe that should be placed in a particular position on the figure. Refer back to the plaid section for help with this problem.

Remember to match **seam lines**, not cutting lines, when placing pattern pieces on the fabric. Use notches and construction marks as guides for matching.

Balanced and unbalanced horizontal stripes should match at all side seams, and at the front of the armhole. Start matching from the bottom of the pattern piece, and remember that stripes above the bust dart will not match.

A dominant stripe should fall at the hemline except when the pattern has a very curved hem, or if such placement will cause another dominant stripe to fall at the bust or hipline.

Plan the cutting of vertical stripes so that the dominant stripe falls where you want it to on your figure. Stripes on flared skirts will form a chevron effect along the side seams. This effect is very striking when matched perfectly, so take care when laying these pattern pieces out on the fabric.

Diagonal stripes are not very common, but they do show up occasionally and present a few problems of their own. Many patterns state that they are not suitable for diagonal stripes or weaves, so watch out for this. Lapels on jackets will not balance when they are cut from a diagonally striped or woven fabric.

Chevron seams on flared skirts are impossible to achieve with some diagonals and difficult with others. It is suggested that the fabric be cut so that the diagonal runs around the figure, with no attempt at creating a chevron.

Printed Fabrics

Printed fabrics are always very popular, and while many are just as easy to cut and sew as solid-colored fabrics, some have to be matched, or cut with a nap layout,

while others have large motifs that have to be carefully arranged on the garment.

Consider the different colors in your print. Which color do you want next to your face? Lay your pattern pieces on the fabric to get the desired effect.

How will the print best fit onto the finished garment? When cutting collars and cuffs, plan which bit of color or print will show on the finished side. A turtleneck pattern piece should be placed on the fabric so that the "show" section of the collar features the print or color you want.

Carefully cut patch pockets so that they exactly match the fabric on which they are being placed. This is a touch you will always see on expensive, designer clothes.

Border prints are fun to wear and can be used for many exciting trims. They are usually easy to match; just remember to start at the bottom. Use the border design to trim waistbands, cuffs and necklines.

Knits

We all love the sewing and wearing ease of knits, yet they are not without their own set of layout problems. Some are caused by the way the fabric is constructed, while others are due to poor finishing procedures. You can't do much about the fabric construction, but you can, and should, refuse to buy poor-quality fabric. No matter how good your sewing skills, you can't make bad fabric look good.

Have you ever purchased striped T-shirt fabric and then been unable to get the stripe at right angles to the lengthwise rib? No matter how hard you try to straighten the fabric, pin and push, you still can't do it. Well, don't get upset, because you are trying to do the impossible.

T-shirt knits, as well as many other knit fabrics, are made on circular knitting machines, which make a tubular fabric. Some of the fabrics are left in the tube form when they are sold in fabric stores, while others are split open along the joining line and finished flat. This joining line looks like a big vertical flaw when the fabric is in the tube form.

Whatever the finished form, circular knits are all constructed so that the crosswise run of yarn spirals up the tube. When the tube is split open, crosswise yarns or stripes will not be at right angles to the lengthwise rib.

Properly finished fabric will be "off" just a small amount. Poorly finished fabric can be really crooked. Carefully examine all knits to see how much off-grain they are.

The amount of off-grain is determined by folding the fabric along the crosswise grain until the selvage edges meet. Check the pattern or crosswise yarn along the fold. It should be as nearly parallel to the fold as possible. Anything up to 1/2" is workable. A fabric off much more than that is going to create lots of problems.

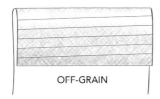

OFF-GRAIN

Because of this off-grain problem, we suggest that you cut all knits that have to be matched in a single layer. This saves time in the long run and guarantees a perfect match along the seam lines.

Use an expanded rather than a half pattern when cutting pieces that have to be placed on a fold. Duplicate the pattern on a large piece of folded paper, and cut it out while the paper is still folded. This gives you an expanded pattern

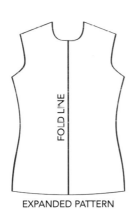

FOLD LINE

EXPANDED PATTERN

In working with woven fabrics, placing pattern pieces on grain is extremely important. When cutting knits, however, the grain line can be ignored in favor of the print or stripe. This is one place where the finished look takes precedence over the grain line. Use the following guidelines to help place pattern pieces correctly.

- Place the pattern on horizontally striped fabrics so that the pattern grain line is at right angles to the stripe. Check this by folding down the pattern at the underarm points. The fold should be on or parallel to a stripe. Make sure you position the garment front, back and sleeves so the underarm points all lie on the same stripe.

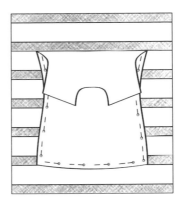

- Some printed fabrics can have the pattern printed crooked on the fabric. Again, ignore the grain line, and position the pattern so that the print or design looks straight.

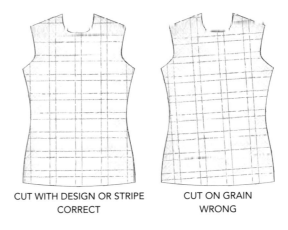

CUT WITH DESIGN OR STRIPE
CORRECT

CUT ON GRAIN
WRONG

- Cut solid-color knits with the lengthwise grain of the pattern on the lengthwise rib of the fabric.

- Many solid color velours have what we call an "invisible horizontal stripe." This is probably caused by a variance in yarn color and is really just a periodic, subtle change of color across the fabric. Treat this invisible stripe like a real one when you position the pattern on the fabric.

Other things to keep in mind when cutting knit fabrics are listed below:

- Cut knit fabric so that the greatest stretch goes around the body. This gives the most wearing comfort.

- Don't let the end of the fabric hang over the edge of the table when pinning the pattern in place and cutting the fabric. This will stretch the fabric and adversely affect the size of the cut pieces.

- Knits should be cut with a nap layout in order to prevent color changes at seam lines.

- Be aware of the permanent crease that runs the length of the fold on some knit fabrics. You know it is permanent if it is still there after the fabric has been preshrunk. Avoid putting it down the front or back of a garment, unless you have some nice trim to cover it. The crease can be used down the center of sleeves.

CUTTING TIPS

Secure pattern pieces to the fabric with enough pins to hold them in place, but not so many that the pattern begins to wrinkle. Many times pattern weights can be used in place of pins. They can save lots of time.

Always use a sharp pair of bent-handled shears, at least 8" to 10" long, when cutting fabric. Dull ones chew up the fabric and tire your hands. If you are left-handed, use a pair of left-handed shears.

Make long cuts rather than short snips when cutting. This makes for more accurate cutting. When cutting around curves, keep the shears constantly moving.

Do not overcut. This means you should cut just around the pattern edges and not make cuts extending out into the fabric at each corner. You may need some of that extra fabric, so leave it intact!

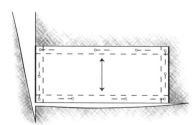

DON'T EXTEND CUTS

Be aware of the width of the cutting line on your paper pattern. Some of them seem to be very wide, and, depending upon where you cut, they can affect the size of the garment. If you think you have a problem, measure the width of the seam allowance to see just where the cutting line should be.

Do not cut out fabric with pinking shears. This makes it very difficult to judge seam widths when sewing and can easily add or subtract 1/8" from the seam edges. Use your pinking shears after seams have been sewn to help reduce fraying.

If you ever have to enlarge a pattern piece, we suggest that you actually expand it with a piece of paper, rather than trying to rely on your memory when cutting.

Cut accurately! A carelessly added 1/8" on each seam results in a garment being 1" or more too large. Then you wonder why the pattern doesn't fit. **Stitch accurately!** If the shoulder and center-back seams are carelessly stitched with "cheater" 1/2" seam allowances instead of 5/8" seam allowances, a total of 3/4" has been added to the neckline and, of course, the collar will not fit.

Cutting and sewing silk chiffon can really cause you to lose your religion. It constantly moves with every breath of air. My solution is to sew with a gauze surgical face mask tied on—honestly, it works!

WHERE TO CUT? FLOOR? BED? TABLE?

The "cutting backache" can ruin the urge to sew. Most women cut on the dining room table, worse yet, on the floor. The result is the cutting backache. The solution is to raise the table to a comfortable height. Using four empty tall juice cans, fill the bottom half with sand, and the top half with plaster of paris. Before the plaster of paris has set, countersink a furniture coaster in the top. Now place a can under each table leg, thus raising the table 7 inches. (To build up muscles, you may prefer to use concrete building blocks as table raisers!)

Cutting boards can be made from many materials. A hollow-core door from the lumberyard can be placed on sawhorses over an infrequently used guest bed. Celotex or ceiling tile can be used as a lightweight cutting board. Raise the ironing board to its highest level, place the cutting board on top. Hold the board in place by puncturing two holes in the board and securing it to the ironing board with a piece of elastic.

For a deluxe cutting table, cover a 6' x 8' sheet of plywood with 1/8" rolled cork. The cork top keeps slippery fabrics from sliding off the table and makes for easier pin-marking the fabric as pins can be inserted straight into the cork for precise marking. Support the plywood board on one end with a chest of drawers that holds sewing tools and supplies. The other end can be supported by another chest or by three file cabinets, which make excellent storage space for patterns and household records. The kneehole opening in the center accommodates a bar stool for sit-down work.

Without a cork-topped table, slippery fabrics can be controlled by covering the table with a bed sheet, which keeps the fabric from shifting; or pin the slippery fabric to sheets of tissue paper. Cut both the fabric and the paper. The tissue paper supports the fabric, making it so much easier to cut accurately.

MARKING FABRIC

Once the cutting job has been completed, your next step is to transfer construction marks to the fabric. This can be done using various methods, and we always favor the easiest and most accurate.

Outside Construction Marks

Construction marks that fall along the outside edges of the pattern are easily marked with small clips into the seam allowance. A 1/8" clip is all that is necessary, and it doesn't weaken the seam allowance.

Use the clip method to mark the following construction marks:

Notches: Clip each notch, including all the points of multiple notches.

No designer workroom ever cuts out notches, as they are too inaccurate and too time consuming. If you choose to cut out notches, please remember to trim them off before wearing the light-colored garments. The notches scream "homemade" as they shadow through the dress.

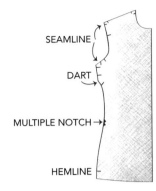

Hemlines: Mark the hem fold on each side of the pattern piece.

Seam Lines: Mark if desired. This is not necessary if you have a seam guide on the throat plate of your sewing machine.

Dart Ends: Clip each end of the dart.

Zipper Openings: Clip the end of zipper openings.

Sleeves and Armscyes: Clip the dot at the top of the sleeves and the dots around the sleeve cap and armscye.

Other Details: Clip all other outside marks, such as pockets that go in a seam, special circles marking the end of stitching lines, center front and center back on garment and facing pieces, lapel notches and also sections to be eased.

Inside Construction Marks

Inside details, such as pocket and flap locations, dart ends, pleats and trim lines, can be marked with a pencil, fabric marker or some sort of chalk. Fold fabric right sides together, this helps keep it clean and makes marking easier.

While pattern is still pinned to the fabric, insert pins through all inside construction marks as shown. Always make sure the point the pin enters the fabric is the desired marking point or stitching line. It helps to use a cutting board so that the pins have something to hold them firmly in place.

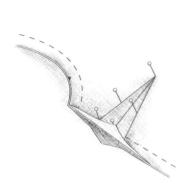

Unpin the edges of the pattern and carefully separate the fabric layers until you come to the marking pins. Place a mark on the wrong side of both layers of fabric where the pins pierce through.

Garment pieces that are going to be interfaced, and have inside construction marks, should be marked **after** the interfacing has been fused or stitched in place.

Construction marks that have to be used on the right side should be marked as described above. Transfer them to the right side just before you have to use them or they easily disappear!

Do this by running a short thread through the fabric at the exact center of the mark. This method is more accurate than tailor's tacks.

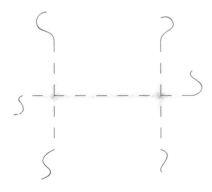

CLEANING TIPS

A word of caution before using any new treatment, **always** test the treatment on a piece of fabric first. Be sure the fabric is colorfast, that it will wash, that the marking pen **does** come out, and that the tracing paper **does** wash out. When trying to remove spots, first duplicate the spot on a scrap of fabric, or in a seam or hem allowance. Work on the test spot **before** working on the actual garment.

- For prespotting washable garments, use a solution of:

      1/3 liquid soap
      1/3 ammonia
      1/3 water

- Don't throw away scraps of soap; you're throwing away money! Put the scraps in a plastic container, add enough water to make it the consistency of Jell-O. Use this with a fingernail brush for prespotting clothes before washing. Leftover soap slivers can also be put in the blender; add a bit more water, blend and refill the liquid-soap dispensers.

- To remove ring-around-the-collar, rub chalk over the stain. The chalk absorbs the oil and washes out in the laundry.

- Use a cotton swab to check for colorfastness of fabric or ready-to-wear garments before washing them and ending up with a disaster when the colors run. Touch the water-moistened cotton swab to the fabric. If it picks up color, **don't** wash it—dry-clean it.

- To whiten tattletale gray underwear and socks, soak them in a **plastic** container in a mixture of:

      1 cup dishwasher detergent
      1/4 cup powdered chlorine bleach
      1 gallon **hot** water

- Whiten yellowed silks by soaking in a mixture of:

      2 ounces of 3 percent hydrogen peroxide
      1 gallon cool water

- Remove dog stains from the carpet by using a solution of 8 parts club soda to 1 part vinegar.

- Orvus soap is excellent to use to wash woolens and silks as well as old quilts. Use for machine or hand washing. For wool and silk, it is important to maintain a constant temperature (95 to 100 degrees) in the wash and the rinse water. Any change in temperature causes shrinkage. My authority also said that Orvus is excellent for washing dogs that constantly scratch even when there are no fleas!

- Rubbing alcohol removes ballpoint ink marks from garments, and leaves no watermark. Hair spray is often recommended but it may remove the color. Fray Check can be removed with alcohol **before** it drys. Once it is dry it is set.

- Polyester "silkies" are woven polyester fabrics with the weight and hang of silk, but not the cost or care of silk. However, avoid using fabric softener sheets when drying silkies, as the contact of the softener sheets may leave greaselike marks on the fabric. These marks can be removed with repeated washing but it's scary to see these marks on the blouse you've spent hours sewing.

SEWING EQUIPMENT

The quality and variety of your sewing equipment greatly influences the look of your finished garment, and they can make the construction process simple or difficult. Having the right tools for each specific job is as important in the sewing room as any other place. A list of recommended sewing equipment is given below. Each item serves a definite purpose and makes sewing easier.

SEWING TOOLS

Of course, your sewing machine is the most important piece of sewing equipment you own. It really doesn't make too much difference what kind of machine you own, just as long as it is kept clean, well oiled and in good repair.

Study your machine instruction book so you know how to use and care for your machine. It doesn't hurt to review it often just to remind yourself about certain points. One of the most important things contained in the instruction book is cleaning and oiling information. Perform these jobs frequently. We recommend a thorough cleaning and oiling of the bobbin area before each

sewing session. Give your machine the proper care, and it will serve you long and well.

A secretary's chair is a good choice for the sewing room. It gives good back support and can have the seat height adjusted. It is also handy because it rolls and turns.

Make sure your machine area is well lighted. A draftsman's lamp can be clamped onto the machine cabinet or sewing table; this is a must if you sew a lot at night.

Mount a small bulletin board over the sewing machine if you have a sewing room or fixed place for your sewing equipment. This is handy for pinning up pattern instruction sheets.

Machine Needles

Machine needles are almost as important as the sewing machine. Perfect stitching requires the proper size and type of needle, and a needle that isn't damaged or dull.

Needle sizes are marked by number. Machine needle thickness increases as size increases (size 18 is thick).

European	American
60	8
65	9
70	10
75	11
80	12
90	14
100	16
110	18

Machine needles also have different point shapes. Each kind is used for a certain type of fabric.

Universal Point: This needle pierces the fabric threads and is used for woven fabrics.

Stretch Needle: The needle slides along the threads of the fabric until it finds a gap to get through, rather than piercing the fabric threads. It is used for knits, which can run or develop holes if a sharp needle severs a thread.

Leather Needle: This needle has a wedge point for leather or leatherlike fabrics. It has a small, sharp edge that cuts through leather. **Do not** use for Ultraleather, as the wedge point will leave holes.

The needle chart below will help you choose the proper size and type of needle for your particular fabric.

Fabric Weight	Fabric	Needle Size	Point Type
Sheer	Chiffon, Organza Lace, Voile, Crepe, Batiste	9–10	Sharp
	Sheer Tricot	9–10	Stretch
Medium Sheer	Wool Crepe, Jersey, Gingham, Challis, Coated nylon outerwear, Ultrasuede, Ultraleather	11–12	Sharp
Medium	Seersucker, Flannel, Muslin, Gaberdine, Poplin, Broadcloth, Velveteen, Permanent press	14	Sharp
	Heavyweight knits, Sweater fabrics, Velour	14	Stretch
Heavy	Denim, Quilted fabrics, Fake fur, Terry cloth, Heavy woolens	16	Denim
Heavy	Upholstery fabric, Canvas, Duck, Sailcloth, Double-faced wool	16	Denim
Leather	Kidskin, Patent, Cabretta, Calfskin, Upholstery vinyl	14–16	Leather

Check your machine needles often for damaged points or dullness. A needle with a bent, dull or rough point will have difficulty penetrating the fabric, and it can cause fabric damage, such as holes, snags or pulled and broken threads.

Run your fingernail over the point of the needle to see if it is bent over or rough. Check for dullness by looking directly down on the point. A dull needle will have a flat, shiny spot on the top.

It is possible to bend a needle out of the straight by hitting a pin or some part of the throat plate. Do not sew over pins; you are just asking for trouble. They can damage or break your needle. Pulling the fabric through the machine can cause the needle to hit the throat plate. Bent needles cause skipped or uneven stitches; replace them.

Coated needles can interfere with perfect stitching. Chemicals used in the fabric-finishing process can build up on the needle. Preshrink your fashion fabrics to remove excess finishing chemicals and prevent the coating problem. Stitching through tape can also coat the needle. Change to a new needle if you have this problem.

Check and change your machine needles often. It is much cheaper to use a new needle than ruin a garment using a dull or damaged needle.

Use a new needle for each garment sewn out of silk-like or silk fabric. A dull needle can snag the delicate, tightly woven fabric. However, the "slightly used" needle is still usable for heavier fabrics such as denim or corduroy. Mark off a pin cushion for various sizes of used needles. No need now to reach for the magnifying glass to determine the size of the slightly used needle.

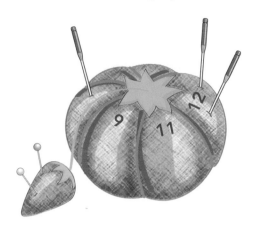

Thread

Choose the proper thread for your fashion fabric. Polyester and cotton-polyester threads can be used for nearly any fabric. They are available in a lightweight for sheer and lingerie fabrics, a medium-weight for most dressmaking fabrics, and a heavyweight for heavy-duty clothes and outerwear.

Heavy polyester thread is designed for topstitching and buttonholes. It replaces silk buttonhole twist and is much more practical because it is colorfast and has a much larger color range.

Always use the same thread on the top and bobbin of the machine. Mismatched thread (cotton on the top and polyester on the bobbin) is apt to cause stitching difficulties.

Match the thread size to the needle size. Thread that is too thick will break or fray.

Thread should be stored at a temperature of about 70° F (21° C) and a 65 percent humidity. Breakage can result with thread that is too moist or too dry. Thread also deteriorates with age. Don't expect thread that has been in your sewing room for four years to perform like fresh, new thread.

When selecting thread, choose a color one shade darker than your fashion fabric. Use a different color thread on the top and bobbin when stitching plaid or striped or printed fabrics. This makes the stitches less visible. Use a contrasting thread for machine or hand bastings.

Eliminate the problem of long tangled thread ends on stored spools by securing thread ends to the spool with small pieces of transparent tape. Use Thread Wrap or 1" x 3" strip of Amazing Wonder Tape to wrap around the spool to keep it from unwinding.

Static electricity causes skipped stitches. Commercial sewing machines have silicone cups that keep the thread static-free. Our home sewing machines don't have such contraptions. Use a silicone lubricant to eliminate the problem. On each new spool of thread, draw a vertical stripe of silicone. Allow it to dry overnight. As the thread is used, the silicone lubricates the tension discs as well as the eye of the needle, eliminating static electricity.

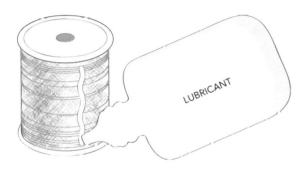

LUBRICANT

Thimble

A thimble is a must for hand sewing. Buy one that comfortably fits your finger, and learn to use it. It feels awkward at first, but it prevents wear and tear on your fingertip.

Try a leather thimble if you don't like a conventional metal one. If you have gorgeous, long fingernails, use a thimble without a top.

Needle Puller

A Needle Puller is a wonderful tool to pull your needle through the fabric. Once you have loaded stitches on to it, slide the eye of the plunger over the needle. Depress the plunger with your thumb and pull the needle instantly out of the fabric.

NEEDLE PULLER

CUTTING TOOLS

Many people feel that cutting out is the hardest or least pleasant part of making a garment. It needn't be if you use the proper tools.

Shears

Every seamstress should own a good, sharp pair of bent-handled shears. They should be 8" to 10" long. Buy left-handed shears if you are left-handed, don't try to make do with right-handed shears.

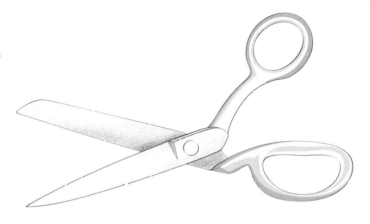

Keep shears sharp! Dull ones chew up your fabric and give you very tired hands. Have them sharpened as necessary, and hide them under your mattress so no one else can use them.

A small pair of shears about 6" long is best to keep at the sewing machine for small clipping and trimming jobs. Hide these too. Kids think the small size was made just for them and their paper projects.

Invest in a good pair of pinking shears. These are available with either a zigzag or scalloped edge. They are a good item to put on your Christmas or birthday wish list. (Don't use your pinking shears for cutting out!)

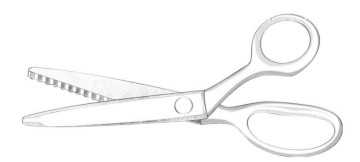

Thread nippers are helpful to keep at the machine for ripping seams, clipping into curves and cutting sewing thread when machine stitching. These are used by industrial machine operators to clip threads. They work best when the third finger, (not your thumb), is inserted into the opening.

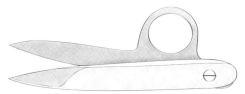

Pins, Pincushions and Pattern Weights

Long, thin pins with glass or plastic heads are the most versatile in the sewing room. They are fine enough for your most delicate fabrics, and long enough to be used on thick or bulky fabrics. Weave them into fabrics and they won't fall out. The large head makes them easy to find in your fabric (the heads don't bury down and get lost), and on the floor. Always test pins in a scrap of fabric to be sure they don't leave snags or holes. If your pins can't pass the "snag-free" test when pinned into a piece of silk, discard them or pin only in the seam allowances. Pins wear out, just like needles, so throw away all damaged, bent or dull pins.

Don't *ever* pin into real leather, as every pinhole remains forever.

A wrist pincushion is one of the handiest tools in your sewing room. Get used to using it and you won't want to be without it. The style with plastic sides and a sturdy band gives the best protection from pin pricks.

Pattern weights can be used in place of pins to hold your pattern to the fabric. They are available at most fabric stores, or you can make your own from lead sinkers, or a collection of table knives and salt shakers.

MARKING AND DRAFTING TOOLS

A collection of various types of rulers and measuring devices makes pattern alteration and layout and garment construction easier.

Yardstick

Use a metal rather than a wooden yardstick. It is more accurate and doesn't develop rough edges that can snag fabrics.

See-Through Ruler

A see-through, plastic ruler is a great help for making pattern alterations. Use the kind made of thin, flexible plastic that has the surface completely marked off in red lines. It is truly accurate and is easier to use than the wide ruler with slots.

Curved or Design Rulers

Curved rulers are available to help you alter curved pattern lines, such as armholes, hip and crotch curves. They are made of see-through plastic or metal.

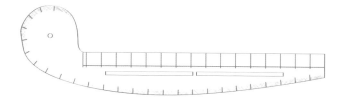

Tape Measure

Buy a good reinforced polyester tape measure with metal-tipped ends that is marked in inches on one side and millimeters on the other. Cheap paper tape measures stretch or tear and are not always accurate. A 60" tape is the recommended size.

Tape measures are also available with a fiberboard piece attached to one end. This is used to measure inseams; the fiberboard piece is placed up against the crotch.

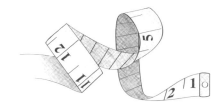

Stick-on, Mylar tape measures are handy when attached to the front edge of your sewing cabinet or sewing table. Take care not to stretch them when sticking them in place so they remain accurate. Check the measurement with a yardstick to be sure.

Hem Gauge

A hem gauge is a 6"-long ruler with a sliding marker. It is used to accurately measure and mark hems.

HEM GAUGE

Marking Devices

Pattern construction marks and seam lines can be marked with dustless chalk, tailor's chalk, a sliver of hand soap, a pencil or marking pen.

Always make a test mark on a scrap of your fashion fabric with your marking tool to see if it is visible and can be easily removed without leaving any marks. Important: Wash the test fabric to be sure it will come out.

Choco-Liner: A screw-on cap makes this chalkwheel marker refillable. It NEVER skips and the marks easily wash or brush away.

Dustless Chalk: Ordinary dustless, blackboard chalk can be sharpened in a pencil sharpener to a fine point. These chalk marks can be brushed off most fabrics. A metal chalk holder can be purchased to keep your fingers clean when using the chalk.

Tailor's Chalk: There are two kinds of tailor's chalk. One resembles ordinary chalk, except it won't mark unless it is moistened with the tongue or a small sponge. The soap-type of tailor's chalk is easier to use and comes in a handy, flat square. It disappears when touched with a warm iron.

Sliver of Soap: Save those small pieces of hand soap. They can be used to mark fabrics. Their sharp edge helps you mark accurately. Soap marks can usually be removed with a warm iron.

Pencil and Water- or Air-Erasable Pens: These can be used to mark darts and other small construction details.

Pocket Curve Template: Use a pocket curve template for perfect, identical curves. Place the desired curve on the seam line of the pocket piece. Hold the seam allowance in place with clip portion. Press and let cool. Trim seam allowance to 1/4". Now position on garmet and topstitch in place.

POCKET CURVE

Pattern Paper

Pattern paper is available in a 30" to 36" width, marked off in one-inch squares. It is useful for designing your own patterns and for pattern alterations.

A new product now on the market is a roll of 3"-wide pattern paper that is marked off in half-inch sections. It is handy for lengthening pattern pieces. Just tape or glue to the separated pattern pieces, using the marks to help you get things straight.

PRESSING TOOLS

For information on pressing tools, see Chapter 2.

MISCELLANEOUS SEWING EQUIPMENT

The following items are things we have found useful in our own sewing. You probably have some favorites that are not on this list, and you may find things listed that don't interest you. Use whatever ones work best for you.

Tape

A roll of Magic Transparent Tape and 1/2"-wide drafting tape should be kept in the sewing room. Use the Magic rather than plain transparent tape because it can be written on, and won't leave a sticky residue on your fabric. Buy drafting tape, rather than ordinary masking tape (even though they look alike), because it is less sticky. A word of caution: Always remove tape from fabric as soon as possible. It is sometimes difficult to remove if left in place too long, and it can leave a mark.

Use the above tapes to mark wrong sides of fabric, to hold zippers in place for stitching and to mark buttonhole locations.

Special sewing tapes are now on the market that can be used for basting and topstitching guides. Always follow the manufacturer's instructions when using these tapes.

Double Faced Wash-A-Way Wonder Tape is used to hold zippers in place before stitching, and for basting together leather and Ultrasuede fabric seams. This tape can be stitched through.

Do not stitch through any of the above tapes, as they may coat your needle with a sticky substance and cause stitching problems.

Point Turner

There are a variety of small devices available to help turn neat points and get into hard-to-reach areas. Use a Point Turner for collars and cuffs and a Purple Thang or Quill Stiletto for smaller narrow spaces found on pointed belts or trims.

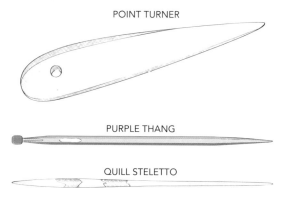

POINT TURNER

PURPLE THANG

QUILL STELETTO

Beeswax or Thread Heaven

Run hand-sewing threads through beeswax or Thread Heaven. Thread Heaven was developed for beaders. It eliminates tangles and drag on metallic threads. It is perfect for all hand sewing. This stiffens the threads and keeps them from tangling and knotting. Polyester thread builds up static electricity, which causes thread to tangle and knot. Beeswax or Thread Heaven helps to eliminate this problem.

Glue Stick

Use a glue stick for holding trims in place and seams together before stitching. Use standard all-purpose craft glue sticks found in office supply stores. Let dry 10 minutes before stitching. When glue is dry, it does not gum up the needle. It washes or dry-cleans away. (Fabric glue sticks found in fabric stores at twice the price are the same products only with different packaging.)

Glue-Baste-It

This liquid fabric glue holds appliqués of any fabric together with tiny controlled drops of glue. A long 1 3/4" nozzle gets into the smallest corners. It is 100 percent water soluble.

Scotch-Gard Spray or Fabric Guard

This spray is used on finished garments to give them a water-repellant finish. Follow the manufacturer's instructions.

Large Bobby Pin, Turn-A-Bout and Fasturn

These items help turn narrow tubing for spaghetti straps.

Seams Great

Clean-finish raw edges with this sheer nylon tricot seam finish. It eliminates raveling and creates no additional bulk. Also use it to draw in the fullness of set-in sleeves.

Steam A Seam 2®

Make instant no-sew hems and appliqué with this fusible tape. It's machine washable or dry cleanable. Simply finger-press the tape in place then peel off the paper backing and fuse with steam for a permanent bond. It cn be sewn through without gumming up the needle.

SEWING CASES

In the 19th century, sewing cases were called etui or a "Lady's Companion," as they were compact traveling cases for ladies' sewing and embroidery tools. These cases contained many items such as needlecase, thimble, stiletto, bodkin, tweezer, a sheet of ivory used as a memo pad (called an aide memoir), a small knife for cutting seams, pencil and other small personal items.

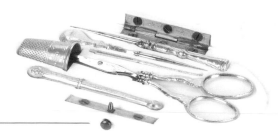

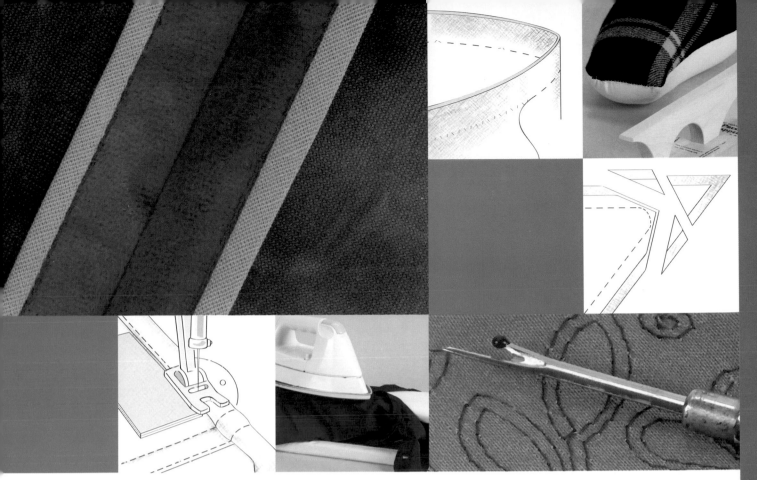

PERFECT SEAMS & PROPER PRESSING

2

Chapter 2: Perfect Seams & Proper Pressing

SEAMS are basically used to hold your garment together. However, the sewing process requires more than just feeding the fabric through the sewing machine.

The type of seam or seam finish used on a particular garment is determined by the fabric, the garment's use and the pattern design. Professionally finished garments need perfect seams and proper pressing, and this section contains the information needed to help achieve this.

MACHINE STITCHING

THE BASIC SEAM

The basic seam is made by stitching two pieces of fabric together with a given seam width. Use the seam guide that is marked on the throat plate of your machine to help keep the seam width even. If your machine doesn't have a seam guide, purchase a seam guide attachment, or make your own with a wide strip of adhesive tape following the instructions below.

Place tape alongside the presser foot, and mark a 1/4" seam, **measuring from the needle**. Continue marking off 1/8"-wide seams, up to 1".

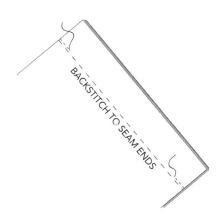

BACKSTITCH TO SEAM ENDS

important if you are using the "zigzag" throat plate when stitching on lightweight knits and woven fabrics.

See Stitching Tips of this chapter for using a "security blanket" when stitching seams. Press seam in the flat position to set the stitches, and then press the seam allowance open. Use a seam roll to prevent a seam allowance impression from showing on the right side, or place strips of paper between the fabric layers to avoid an imprint.

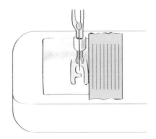

Position the needle in the fabric 1/8" in from the cut edge, along the given seam line. Backstitch to the fabric edge and then stitch forward to make the seam, backstitching at the end. **Note:** *If the seam allowance is to be trimmed, do the backstitching at the point where the seam lines cross. This prevents the seam from pulling apart after trimming.*

Hold the thread ends as you start stitching so they don't pull down into the needle hole. This is especially

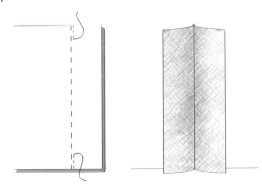

Seams can be lockstitched at the beginning and end instead of backstitched, if preferred. Do this by setting the stitch-length regulator at "0", then stitch up and down a few times in the same place. Remember to hold the thread ends at the beginning so they won't get jammed.

SEAM FINISHES

Many fabrics require seam finishes to keep the cut edges from fraying. The method you choose is determined by the fabric's characteristics.

Knit fabrics seldom need seam finishes since they don't fray. However, loosely knit fabrics look neater if the seam edges are overcast. A Hong Kong finish can be used on an unlined knit jacket for a neater inside appearance.

Pinked Seam

Using sharp pinking shears, pink the seam edges after the seam has been pressed in the flat position, but before it is pressed open. This method can be used on most firmly woven fabrics.

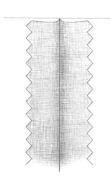

Overcast Seam

Overcast the seam edges with a wide machine zig-zag or by hand. Use this finish on loosely woven fabrics. Overcasting may leave an impression on the right side of some lightweight woven fabrics unless care is taken during the pressing process. Use a seam roll or paper strips (see page 2-21) to prevent seam impressions on the right side.

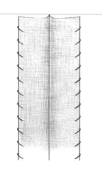

Turned-and-Stitched Seam

Turn under a narrow hem, about 1/8", on the seam edge and edge-stitch. Use this method only on light-weight, firmly woven fabrics.

Bound Seam

Enclose the seam edge in a piece of bias fabric for a bound seam finish. Use either a purchased, double-fold bias tape, Seams Great or cut your own bias strips from lining fabric and apply as for the Hong Kong finish. Use the bound seam finish for medium- to heavyweight fabrics.

Hong Kong Finish: Apply a 3/4"-wide strip of bias lining fabric to the right side of the seam allowance with a 1/8" seam.

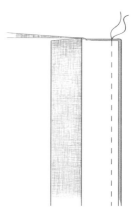

Wrap the bias strip out over the seam edge to the wrong side. Baste in place and secure by stitching in the ditch.

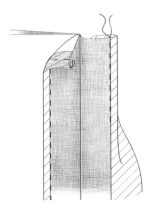

side of the garment. Make the basic seam with right sides together if you want the overlap on the inside.

Trim one seam allowance to a scant 1/4" and then press both to one side as shown. Fold under the wide seam allowance, and position it so that it covers the narrow seam allowance. Edge-stitch along the fold of the wide seam allowance.

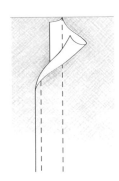

ADDITIONAL SEAMS

Welt Seam

This seam is used on heavier fabrics for extra strength. It is also used as a decorative seam on many sports clothes. It consists of a basic seam that is then topstitched from the outside.

Make a basic seam, but trim one seam allowance to 1/4" before pressing. Press the seam flat and then open. Now press both seam allowances to one side, covering the narrow seam allowance with the wide one. Turn the garment right side out and topstitch, catching the wide seam allowance in place. Trim the wide seam allowance close to the stitching line if you are working with a white or pastel-colored fabric. This prevents a wide seam allowance from showing through to the right side.

French Seam

A French seam is used on sheer fabric to prevent raw seam edges from showing through to the right side. It can also be used for the side and underarm seams of blouses and shirts. This makes a strong seam because it is double-stitched, and it also serves as a seam finish.

Stitch a basic seam, except position the fabric wrong sides together, and stitch just half the given seam width. Trim the seam to 1/8". Press the seam open and then to one side. Fold the fabric right sides together, and stitch 3/16" from the folded edge.

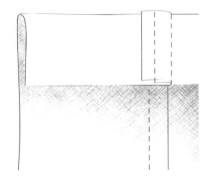

Flat-Felled Seam

A flat-felled seam is a strong seam used for sports and children's clothes, especially those that have to be machine washed often. It can be sewn so that the overlapped portion appears on the right side, or inside, of the garment. Make your basic seam with the wrong sides together if you want the overlap to show on the right

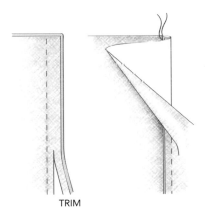

TRIM

Lap Seam

A lap seam can be used on nonwoven fabrics, such as felt, synthetic suedes and real leathers. Firmly woven fabrics, such as blanket cloth and wool melton, can also use a lap seam in order to reduce bulk in the seam area.

Trim the seam allowance from one side of the garment, then lap this side over the other piece until the cut edge meets the seam line. Baste in place and topstitch with two rows of stitching 1/4" apart. Trim the seam allowance on the underside close to the stitching line.

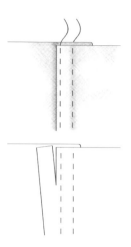

SEAM TECHNIQUES

Seams on various areas of the garment require certain construction techniques. The following information helps make seams perfect.

Points and Curves

Shorten the stitch length as you stitch around all points and curves. This strengthens these seams so they don't fray away after they have been trimmed. It also gives you better control of your stitching because the machine is moving at a slower rate. Keep the machine moving at all times when stitching around curves. This guarantees a smooth stitching line.

Always take one or more diagonal stitches across corners and points to allow for turning room. This eliminates "rabbit ears" at the corners. Thick fabrics need more diagonal length than thin fabrics.

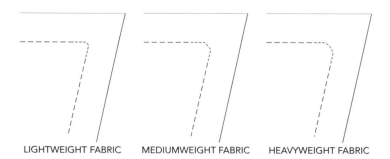

LIGHTWEIGHT FABRIC   MEDIUMWEIGHT FABRIC   HEAVYWEIGHT FABRIC

Enclosed Seams

Enclosed seams, such as the ones found on collars, cuffs, pocket flaps and facings, should be graded, trimmed and clipped as necessary to allow them to lie flat.

Grading: This technique is used to reduce bulk when seam allowances are turned back on each other. The various layers of seam allowance are trimmed to different widths so they don't all end at the same level. This is to prevent a distinct ridge from showing on the right side of the garment.

Trim the seam allowance to 1/4" on average-weight fabrics and 1/8" on heavyweight fabrics. Cut each layer a different width, leaving the seam allowance longer that is directly under the visible part of the garment. This is usually the garment seam allowance. But it will be the facing seam allowance, (in the lapel area only), on garments with a turned-back lapel. Nonfusible interfacing should be trimmed close to the stitching line.

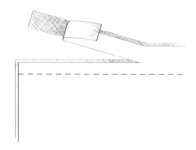

Bulky fabrics can have all the seam allowances graded in one cut, at the same time, if the shears are held at an acute angle to the fabric. This results in a beveled edge, which is what grading is all about.

Trimming: Corners should be trimmed so they can be turned with reduced bulk.

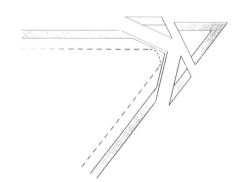

Clipping and Notching: Curved seams need to be clipped or notched in order to release the curve. Clip convex curves to the seam line at regular intervals. Notch concave curves in order to reduce bulk when the seam is turned and pressed. Pinking shears can be used for notching.

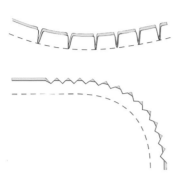

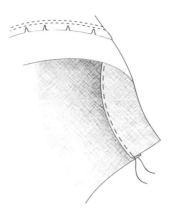

Finally, turn the facing to the finished position and press, rolling the seam slightly to the facing side.

Pressing: Press enclosed seams open before turning the facing to the right side. Use a point presser to help you press difficult-to-reach areas.

Seams can also be pressed open with the garment in the flat position. With the facing side up, press open the seam allowance with the tip of the iron.

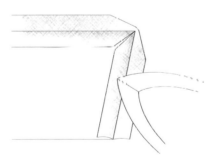

Understitching: Facing seams are understitched to help keep them in place. Understitching also gives a firm edge on which to turn and press the facing. Understitch all facing seams except for very short ones, as found on collar edges, or seams that might possibly show, such as the front facings of jackets or coats. The turned-back portion of the lapel can be understitched if you aren't topstitching the garment edges.

With the garment right side up, pull the facing out to the side and stitch along the facing edge, catching all the seam allowances.

Stay Stitching

Curved and bias-cut edges should be stay-stitched to keep them from stretching out of shape. Stitch along the seam line for deeply curved edges, such as neckline and armhole curves. Stitch 1/8" from the seam line, within the seam allowance, for all other areas. Use a regular stitch length.

Easestitching

Easestitching is a technique used to ease a long piece of fabric to fit a shorter piece of fabric, without visible gathers. It can be used around sleeve caps, backs of shoulders, elbows, flared hems and the bust-curve of princess-line garments.

Easestitching is accomplished by holding your thumb, or the eraser end of a pencil, on the fabric behind the presser foot as you stitch using a regular stitch length. Let the fabric pile up for a bit, release, and then place your thumb or pencil back in position. You are hampering the normal feeding of the machine, therefore, the fabric tends to bunch up along the seam, but doesn't actually gather. Do the stitching just **outside** the seam line so that the easestitching won't show on the finished garment.

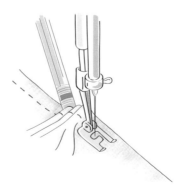

Some fabrics ease in better then others, so it is a good idea to make a test run on a scrap of fabric before stitching on the garment. If it seems to be easing in too much, release the fabric periodically, and let some feed through unhampered, or break the easestitching threads at intervals necessary to give the proper amount of ease. If it doesn't seem to be easing enough, take up some of the excess after the stitching has been completed by pulling up the bobbin thread at even intervals.

Stitching in the Ditch

Stitching in the ditch is sometimes referred to as stitching in the "seam well." It is a technique used to finish waistbands, secure facings, complete the backs of bound buttonholes and hold edge finishes in place. Practice the technique on fabric scraps until you get the feel of it. Some people find a zipper foot, rather than a regular foot, helps make the stitching easier to do, as you can really see the ditch. Try both to see which works best for you.

Stitch in the ditch (or seam well) on the right side of the garment. Shorten the stitch length so the machine runs slowly. This also helps the thread to bury down into the fabric so the stitches won't show. There are various special feet available that make this easier to do.

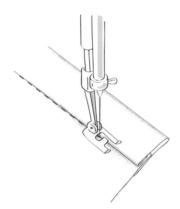

Eased Seams

Seams that require one layer to be eased to another should be stitched with the eased section on the bottom, and with the smaller section on the top. The machine feed dog tends to ease in fabric, and this helps make the seam smooth.

Curved Seams

Curved seams, such as the ones found on princess-line garments, should be stay-stitched before they are sewn together.

Clip the convex seam almost to the stitching line to release the curve before pinning the two garment pieces together. Easestitch concave edges and then notch the seam allowance to allow it to lie flat when it is pressed open.

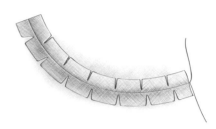

Corner Seams

Corner seams should be reinforced with stay stitching before being sewn to the adjoining piece.

Stitch for about 1" on both sides of the corner, next to the seam allowance. Use a short stitch length, and pivot fabric around the needle at the corner. Clip to stitching line. Next pin the garment pieces together for the final stitching so you can see what you are doing.

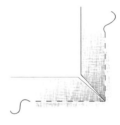

Intersecting Seams

Press open and trim all seams before crossing them with another. This reduces bulk in the seam area.

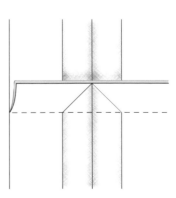

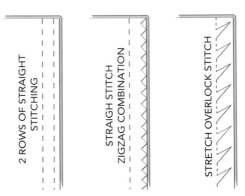

STRETCH OVERLOCK STITCH

STRAIGH STITCH ZIGZAG COMBINATION

2 ROWS OF STRAIGHT STITCHING

Unpicking Seams

Even the best seamstress has to unpick occasionally, and, "God loves a cheerful ripper!" There are various ways of doing it. Try some of the following techniques and see if they don't make the process easier.

Stitches are sometimes difficult to see in dark fabrics. Run a piece of dustless chalk down the seam line; it makes the stitches stand out. The chalk can be brushed away when stitches are gone.

Secure garment under the presser foot of the machine when unpicking a long seam. This holds the fabric securely so it can be pulled taut, which makes the unpicking process easier.

Break a thread every four or five stitches for the length of the seam. Do this on the top rather than the bobbin-thread side of the seam. Turn the garment over and easily pull the bobbin thread out.

BOBBIN THREAD

Bulky fabrics that tend to hide stitches should be carefully unpicked with thread nippers. Nippers are safer than a seam ripper. They are less apt to slip and cause fabric damage.

SPECIAL FABRICS

Special fabrics require slightly different seam techniques.

Knits

Make seams that can "give" with the fabric. Use a stretch stitch, small zigzag or stretch the fabric slightly as you sew while using a regular straight stitch. Synthetic threads are the best choice for knits as they are strong and have some built-in give. Press open knit seams if the fabric will hold a press. Fabrics that tend to roll should have the seam allowances trimmed to a scant 1/4" and edge-stitched together, using one of the illustrated seams.

Short-Pile Fabrics

Corduroys, velvets and velveteens sew more easily when stitched in the direction of the nap. Hand basting is suggested to keep the layers of fabric from shifting during the stitching process. Velvet should be hand-basted because it "creeps." Use a zipper foot or the narrow, straight-stitch foot to help reduce this creeping problem. However, there is now available the Velvet "V" Foot that is a copy of a foot used in the garment industry. On its underside, is a narrow V-shaped ridge that is the only point of contact with the fabric. Available in low shank, Singer slant and snap-on models, it truly does eliminate the creeping problem.

Fake Fur

Fake furs need a long stitch length, and they should also be stitched in the direction of the nap. Stitch a very narrow 1/8"- to 1/4"-wide seam allowance using a long (3) stitch. Use all-purpose thread with very loose tension. Zigzag edges using a 2 width and 3.5 length. Your presser foot should have light pressure so fabric will feed through. The goal is to have as narrow a seam as possible to avoid bulk.

Leather

Stitch leather with a special wedge-point needle. Do not use pins to hold seams together; use paper clips, double-faced tape or leather glue, as pins **will leave** permanent marks. However, pins can be used in the seam allowance. Use lap or welt seams on leather garments, or hold pressed-open seam allowances flat with leather glue or topstitching.

Ultraleather

Stitch seams right sides together using a longer stitch (6–8 stitches per inch). Stitch carefully so that stitches don't have to be ripped out as machine stitching may leave holes. Hold seam allowances flat by finger-pressing both to the wrong side, then edge-stitching them. Or use a glue stick from an office supply store to hold the seam layers in place and topstitch them using one or two rows of stitches. (Glue washes away after the first washing.)

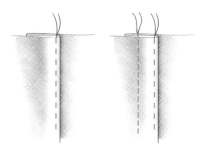

Ultrasuede

See Chapter 8 for specific instructions.

Bias-Cut Fabrics

When joining a bias-cut fabric to a straight-cut section, always stitch on the straight-cut fabric. This keeps the bias from stretching out of shape and gives a smooth seam.

Coated Fabrics

Use a medium-size ballpoint needle when stitching on coated fabrics such as ciré, (used for rainwear). Use a longer-than-regular stitch length, and hold the fabric taut in front and behind the needle. Stitch carefully so you don't have to unpick seams, since needle marks will remain. If your machine has difficulty feeding coated fabrics, sandwich the two layers of fabric between tissue paper. Tear away the paper after completing the seam. Another solution is to spray the presser foot area with silicone lubricant to eliminate resistance. Wipe off the excess. **Do not** use WD-40 as it has an oil base.

Stripes and Plaids

Making perfectly matched seams on striped or plaid fabric is necessary for a custom-finished garment. This can cause some problems, but the majority can be eliminated when cutting the fabric. Making sure the **seam lines** match when cutting out the fabric is half the battle. Use one of the following matching methods when stitching the garment together.

#1 Pin the seams together at 1" intervals. Make sure the pin enters the top layer of fabric and leaves the bottom layer of fabric **exactly** on the edge of a stripe or plaid line. Leave the pins in the fabric until just before the needle comes to them. Important, stitch very slowly.

Use Wash-A-Way Wonder Tape to hold fabric securely, eliminating all pinning or basting. It completely dissolves away in the first washing. And, it can be stitched through without gumming up the needle.

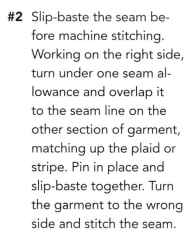

#2 Slip-baste the seam before machine stitching. Working on the right side, turn under one seam allowance and overlap it to the seam line on the other section of garment, matching up the plaid or stripe. Pin in place and slip-baste together. Turn the garment to the wrong side and stitch the seam.

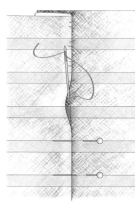

SLIP-BASTE FROM RIGHT SIDE

#3 The offset technique works nicely on thick fabrics and knits. Make a test seam on fabric scraps to see how much you have to offset the stripes to get them to match in the final seam. This works because the feed dog feeds the bottom layer of fabric through the machine faster than the upper layer.

With right sides together, position the stripe of the top layer behind the matching stripe of lower layer.

The amount of offset is determined by the test scrap. Stitch a short section, checking to make sure the fabric is matching up. This technique may take a few tries to get used to, but it surely goes fast once you get everything working properly.

STITCHING DIRECTION

OFFSET TECHNIQUE

Sequined Fabric

To avoid a "razor sharp" edge to side seams try this technique.

Sequin fabric is available in several ways. The least expensive, has sequins sewn flat onto the backing fabric. The more expensive type has "strings or cords" of sequins "meandering" all over the fabric. (The sequins have been first stitched onto a base cord.)

Always cut with the sequins running down to the hem. ("Pet" the fabric and see which direction is the smoothest.)

#1 After cutting out the pattern (using 5/8" seam allowance) and working on the wrong side of the fabric, cut the chain stitch that holds the sequin "strings" in place. Release them 1" to 15/8" back away from the cut edge.

#2 Next, sew side seams together while holding the "strings" back away from your stitching line. Check the fit as you don't want to alter it later. Trim the seam allowances to 1/4" and serge or overcast the edges. Finally, hand-sew the sequin "strings" back in place covering the side seams so that it looks as though you were "poured" into your dress.

This is the technique used to sew the multi-thousand dollar gowns you see worn by movie stars.

#3 Note that top-quality sequin fabric has a 4" to 5" border on each side that has no sequins on it. This plain fabric is used to make the facings at necklines, hems, armholes and to face the shoulder straps. (If the sequin fabric was turned back for a hem or facing, you would itch to death and have runs or snags in your stockings!) Always face all areas that touch your body.

Hold sequins in place with 17/8" flat-head flower pins. Use patterns without darts and as few seams as possible (avoid princess seams).

Cover narrow shoulder straps by hand-sewing on a sequin string.

MACHINE BASTING

Use the longest stitch length on your machine when doing machine basting. Loosening the top thread tension makes the basting stitches easier to remove. Pull on the top thread at the end of the seam line and it easily pulls right out of the seam. Just remember to readjust the tension before starting your regular stitching.

If you don't want to play with the tension, make basting removal easier by clipping a bobbin stitch every couple of inches, then pull out the small sections of bobbin thread.

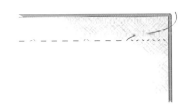

Use contrasting thread when machine basting so it will be easier to see.

TOPSTITCHING

Topstitching is used mainly for decoration, but it also serves to hold facings in place and seams flat. Topstitched seams always stay neatly in place after repeated washings. This is perfect for washable woven fabrics, knits as well as Ultraleather.

Always make sure the machine tension is balanced so that you get a good stitch. It is a good idea to test-stitch some scraps of your fabric to see how they handle the thread and needle combination you have chosen for your topstitching. Stitch through four to six layers of fabric so that you get a true picture of the topstitching results.

Topstitching can be done with regular or special polyester topstitching thread. The special thread is heavier than regular thread and stands out nicely on the finished garment. If you don't have topstitching thread, you can achieve the same heavy look by threading two regular threads through the machine needle. Just make sure you use a needle with a large enough eye to handle the two threads.

Also, try threading two threads on to the bobbin. When winding the bobbin, thread both threads through a large-eye needle to control them as they wind. Position the needle between the bobbin and winding guide. **Note:** *Using a double bobbin thread makes it unnecessary to break your thread at the roll line of a garment with a turn-back lapel.*

Topstitching thread requires a size 14 or 16 needle. Experiment a bit to see which one works best for you. Some machines cannot handle topstitching thread on both the top and bobbin. Use regular thread on the bobbin if you have stitching troubles. Sometimes tightening the top tension will also help.

Topstitching should always be done with a long stitch length. You can get the look of a broken line of topstitching, seen so often on ready-to-wear, by using a darker color thread on the bobbin. Straight, even rows of stitching are necessary for a professional look. Use one of the following methods to help achieve this.

- Use the seam guide on the throat plate of the machine as a guide for the edge of the fabric.

- Use the edge of the presser foot to help you measure equal distances between multiple rows of topstitching.

- Use the right or left needle position to help measure topstitching widths. Right position gives a 1/8" seam; left needle position gives a 3/8" seam.

- Topstitching lines that are to be stitched far in from the garment edge, can be marked with chalk or a sliver of soap. Use a ruler to ensure the lines are straight. Chalk marks brush off, and soap marks disappear when touched with a warm iron.

- Use a Satinedge/Topstitch by Creative Feet. This

special foot has adapters that let it fit **all** machines. A guide butts next to the edge of the garment so that you simply position the needle at the desired width and stitch.

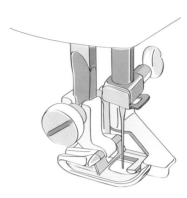

When topstitching a jacket, the right side of the presser foot rides on the trimmed seam allowance; the foot isn't level, often resulting in a drunken stitching line. Remedy this by placing a 1" x 12" cardboard strip under the **left** side of the presser foot, thus leveling it. Now stitch along the cardboard edge for a straight topstitching line. The cardboard levels the presser foot and acts as a stitching guide.

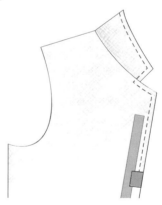

- When topstitching on Ultraleather, the fabric definitely resists feeding smoothly underneath the presser foot. The result is a distorted, stretched-out look. The solution is to use a walking foot.

If a walking foot is not available, use a silicone lubricant on the needle and the underside of the presser foot. Experiment with what is best for your machine.

- Eliminate the "dragged" look in topstitching on a jacket by placing Wash-A-Way Wonder Tape or glue stick **between** the fabric layers on the inside of the jacket. The tape holds the fabric securely, thus eliminating the shifting that causes the "drag."

Always do topstitching on the right side of the garment. A turn-back lapel should be topstitched on the garment side below the roll line, and on the facing side above the roll line. Change the stitching where the lapel breaks above the top button. Insert thread ends through a hand needle and pull them to the inside, between garment and facing; tie them in a knot or secure with a few invisible stitches.

Topstitching around the collar and lapel of coats and jackets should be done as shown below. Shorten the stitch length as you stitch in the "seam well;" this keeps the gorge line perfectly flat at the collar and lapel edge.

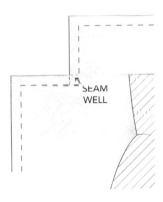

SEAM
WELL

Buttons should not cover the topstitching line when a garment is buttoned. Add extra width to the center front of the pattern, or narrow the topstitching line if you anticipate a problem.

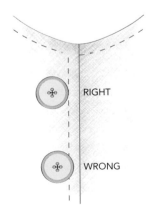

RIGHT

WRONG

Garment edges and seams can be stitched with one or more rows of topstitching using matching, contrasting or more than one color of thread for topstitching. Some topstitching styles are given below.

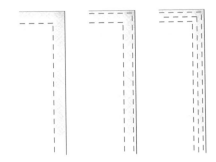

You will find that multiple rows of topstitching add body to the garment edge. Keep this in mind when considering hem finishes for sleeves, pants legs and overblouses.

For a padded look to the finished edge, place a layer of polyester fleece between the hem and the garment fabric before topstitching. This look can be achieved along collar, cuff and neckline edges if the seam allowance is trimmed just slightly short of the topstitching line. Trim the edges blunt rather than grading them. The seam allowance provides the padding for the garment's edge.

Decorative stitches can be used for topstitching. Experiment with your machine to see what you can come up with. Try a straight-stitch and zigzag combination like the one shown below.

STITCHING PROBLEMS

Occasionally you will run into stitching problems. These can be caused by a malfunctioning machine, a dirty, non-oiled machine, an incorrect thread and needle combination, or the "gremlin" under the table. A repair shop can fix your machine; you can clean and oil it, and also change the thread or needle size, but you can't do anything about the "gremlin." If you try all the following suggested remedies when you have stitching problems, and they still continue, blame it on the "gremlin" and put your sewing away until tomorrow.

Breaking Thread

Old, dried-out thread breaks more readily than new, fresh thread.

A machine needle with too small a hole causes threads to break.

High needle temperature also causes broken threads. Slow down the speed of your stitching. Synthetic fabrics generate more heat than do natural fiber fabrics.

Threads made with short, rather than long fibers tend to "shave" at the needle, eventually causing breakage. Purchase long-fiber, polyester thread.

Rethread your machine. An improperly threaded machine causes broken thread.

Thread catching in the notch on the spool's edge also causes breakage. Placing the spool on the machine with the thread notch on the bottom helps eliminate this problem.

Skipped Stitches

Skipped stitches are very frustrating and are caused by many things.

- A ballpoint needle used on a coarsely knitted or woven fabric causes an excessive deviation of the needle from the hook. The needle will slip along the fabric thread trying to find a gap to go through, which results in faulty loop formation. Change to a finer ballpoint or a regular point needle.

Sometimes increasing the pressure of the presser foot will eliminate this problem. Adjust your machine accordingly. If it isn't possible to adjust the pressure on your machine, press your index finger against the toes of the pressure foot while you sew; this gives you the needed extra pressure. Just make sure your finger doesn't slip off and get caught by the needle!

- Fabrics such as lingerie tricot and chiffon that tend to draw down into the needle hole can cause skipped stitches. The needle pushes slippery fabrics down into this wide opening and the bobbin timing is thrown off. The result is a skipped stitch. Prevent this by using the straight-stitch throat plate that has only a small, round hole. (Now don't forget and start zigzagging or you'll break the needle!) Holding the fabric taut while stitching or increasing the pressure on the presser foot to hold the fabric more firmly also helps.

If neither of the above are possible on your machine, tape a piece of Magic Scotch tape over the opening. The needle now creates its own small hole. Caution: Do not cover the teeth or feed dogs, as you will hamper the proper feeding of the fabric.

- Bent needles, coated needles or ones with damaged points can also cause skipped stitches. Fabric finish can build up on the needle, causing skipped stitches. Eliminate this by always preshrinking washable fabric in the washing machine with detergent; then put it through the dryer cycle. Some other residue may be on the needle. Did you stitch through tape? Clean the needle with rubbing alcohol or change to a new needle.

Dull needles can cause skipped stitches. So do needles put in backwards! (A sewing machine mechanic told me that 95 percent of the sewing machine problems could be cured by using the correct needle and inserting it correctly.)

- If the thread is too thick or too thin for the needle size, it will interfere with the proper loop formation. Change to a different size needle.

Use a yellow-band needle, or let your regular machine needle drop down an 1/8" in the needle clamp to add extra length. This longer needle allows the top thread to get down to the bobbin hook better so that it doesn't skip a stitch.

Uneven Stitching

Uneven stitching is caused by machine difficulties or by using the wrong size needle for the fabric. Thin ballpoint needles when used on coarse fabric will be pushed to the side, as they seek a gap between the fabric threads. Use a heavier needle that can force its way better, or change to a sharp-point needle.

Puckered Seams

Seams can pucker after washing if you use a thread that is made of a different fiber than the fashion fabric.

Thread tension that is too tight can also cause puckered seams. Synthetic thread should be sewn with a loose, but balanced tension because it has some built-in "give."

Shifting fabric layers can also result in puckered seams. Pin or baste more securely.

Puckering can be reduced by holding the fabric taut while stitching. Hold the fabric in front of and behind the presser foot, but allow it to feed naturally—don't pull the fabric, just guide it through the machine. This stitching technique will solve 90 percent of your puckering problems and eliminates skipped stitches on slippery fabrics.

STITCHING TIPS

Press open side seams only after the garment has been fitted. Sometimes creases are hard to remove if you have to let out a seam.

Add strength to corners of pockets and the ends of fly zippers with a bar tack. Use a narrow zigzag with a short stitch length. Test on a scrap of fabric until you get the desired look.

Mark seam widths with small clips in the fabric edge. This helps you to start the seam at the correct width.

When topstitching, "help" your machine around corners and points by taking a stitch through the edge of the garment with a hand needle and thread. Use the

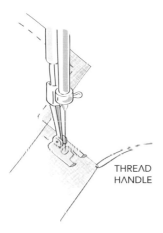

THREAD HANDLE

thread ends as a "handle" to help ease the fabric around the needle. Without this handle, the presser foot has no traction and will stitch in place or make shorter stitches, thereby ruining the look of the topstitching.

Always stop sewing with the "take-up" hook at the highest point. If you don't, you may unthread your needle when you start sewing again. Also, if the bobbin has not completed its cycle, it may cause the thread to jam.

Use the edge of the wide zigzag foot as a seam guide as much as possible. Many special knit patterns call for a 1/4" seam. Stitch perfect 1/4"-wide seams by keeping the edge of the presser foot along the edge of the fabric.

Use the right and left needle position to vary seam width, allowing you to keep the edge of the presser foot along the edge of the fabric as a guide. The needle in the right position will make a 1/8" seam and in the left position a 3/8" seam.

Few machines have the stitch-length regulator marked in stitches per inch. They are usually marked in numbers 1 to 4. This is the metric system of measurement and is the stitch length in millimeters. For example, a setting of 2 means a stitch length of 2 millimeters. Determine the number of stitches per inch by stitching on a scrap of paper, measuring off 1" and then counting the stitches in that inch. Adjust your stitch-length regulator until you get the desired stitch length.

When hemming blue jeans, frequently the needle skips stitches as it crosses side seams because the presser foot is not level as it rides over the bulky seams. Solve the problem by placing several layers of cardboard under the left edge of the presser foot, thus leveling it. Also, stitch

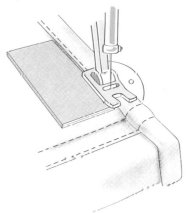

slowly, as the needle may be thrown off center by the excessive bulk; the needle angles slightly as it goes through the multiple layers, hits the throat plate and breaks.

Many times when topstitching, you run into trouble when crossing bulky seams, such as ones found at necklines. The machine begins to skip stitches, or stitches become shorter because the presser foot doesn't function properly when it has to ride up over ridges of fabric. This problem can be solved by leveling the presser foot with a folded piece of fabric or piece of lightweight cardboard. Place this "helper" under the back end of the presser foot to level the presser foot and help the fabric feed properly.

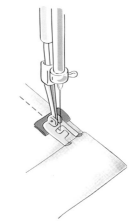

Practice sewing continuously. That is, sew all darts, facings, sleeve underarm seams, etc., in one continuous strip, connected by a few stitches. Sew as many seams as possible, then cut the pieces apart and have a pressing session. Remember though, you should never cross a seam that has not been pressed. (Operators in the factory always sew this way—to save time—and thread.)

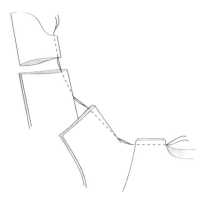

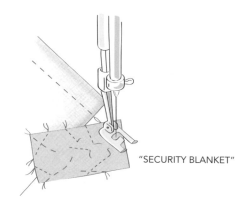

"SECURITY BLANKET"

Use a "security blanket" when ending seams. This is a scrap of firm fabric that measures about 1" by 3". Stitch across the blanket at the end of each seam. Snip the connecting stitches to release the garment. Cut the security blanket away from the next garment piece after you have started the new seam.

A security blanket speeds your sewing along because:

- You don't have to raise and lower the presser foot.

- You don't have to hold the thread ends to keep the machine from jamming.

- It eliminates cutting off long thread ends making for neater sewing.

- You can check the stitch setting before you begin sewing.

- You discover damaged needles on scrap fabric rather than on expensive fashion fabric.

- Your needle never comes unthreaded.

- It helps you get started at the edge of the fabric.

- It saves thread.

Do not stitch over pins; pull them out of the seam line just before you get to them. Hitting or just nicking a pin can damage the needle point, and then cause fabric damage. If you hit a pin when sewing at high speeds, it is possible to break the needle and have a piece fly up in your face.

Friction or "drag" and skipped stitches develop when sewing resistant fabric such as plastic-backed upholstery fabric, plastic raincoats or shower curtains. Spray needle and throat plate area with a shot of silicone spray. (Not WD-40 as it has an oil base and will ruin the fabric!)

Vinyl fabrics can be difficult to stitch. Spray the machine bed with a silicon spray so that it becomes slick to the vinyl fabric. "Sandwich" the vinyl between layers of waxed paper if you don't have any silicone lubricant.

HAND STITCHING

Fine sewing still requires some hand stitching. You must know the basic hand stitches and this section gives that information. First of all, let's discuss needles and thread.

BASIC SUPPLIES

Hand Needles

Choose a needle that is compatible with your fabric and the job at hand. Use a long, thin needle when working on sheers, and a heavier needle for coarser fabrics. A short needle is good when doing small detail work such as hand-pricking a zipper. Long needles are better for basting.

Needles come in various numbered sizes, from 1 to 24. The small number denotes a coarse needle while the large number denotes a fine needle. The most common sizes used for dressmaking are 6 to 10.

Thread

Most hand sewing is done with the same thread you use on the machine. A single thread is generally used, but a double thread can be used when you need extra strength, such as for buttons or hand-sewn zippers.

Always thread your needle with the thread-end that is cut from the spool to help prevent tangling. Cut the thread on a slant; this makes it easier to thread.

Thread sometimes gets tangled or knots up during hand sewing. Prevent this problem by cutting and threading the needle as directed above, running the thread through some beeswax or Thread Heaven, and using a relatively short thread length—18" to 20".

Thread will sometimes build up a twist when doing certain hand stitches. Eliminate this problem by occasionally dangling the threaded needle and allowing the thread to unwind before proceeding.

Use contrasting thread for basting so it will be easier to see and remove. Remove all basting done with regular thread before giving the garment the final press; otherwise, it may leave a mark. Silk thread is a good choice for basting. You can press over this thread and not leave a mark.

HAND-SEWING STITCHES

The following stitches are the ones you will use most frequently in your sewing.

Basting

Basting can be even, uneven or diagonal. Use even basting for holding seams together, uneven basting for marking the center front, holding up hems, and for holding the fashion fabric and underlining or interfacing fabrics together. Diagonal basting is used to hold interfacing to the garment before it is permanently stitched in place.

BASTING STITCHES

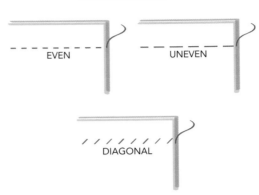

EVEN UNEVEN

DIAGONAL

Slip Basting

Slip basting is used when matching plaid or striped fabric seams and for making fitting adjustments on the right side of the garment.

Turn under the seam allowance on one garment piece and lap it onto the seam line of the other garment piece. Baste as shown, slipping the needle between the seam fold and bringing it out to catch a thread of the other layer of fabric.

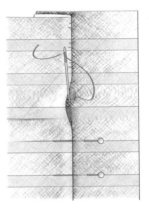

Backstitch

The backstitch is the strongest hand stitch. It is used to repair broken seams in hard-to-reach areas and for attaching patch pockets from the wrong side.

Make the stitches 1/16" to 1/8" long. Always insert the needle in the end of the last stitch and bring it out of the fabric one stitch ahead.

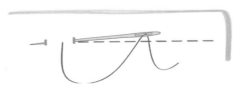

Hand Prick Stitch

Used for hand finishing zippers, it is a variation of the backstitch.

The needle takes just a small bite into the fabric so that only a small stitch shows on the right side.

Whipstitch

The whipstitch is used to hold two finished edges together, such as on welt pockets and bound buttonholes.

Insert the needle in the fabric at a right angle to the edge so the stitches are slanted.

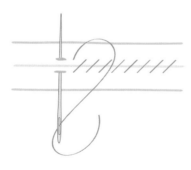

Fellstitch

This hand stitch is used to attach the raw edges of under collars to the garment and upper collar.

The stitches should be about 3/16" long, and 1/8" apart. They are at right angles to the fabric edge.

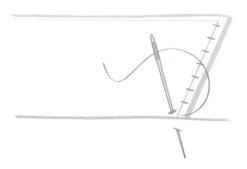

Slipstitch

Use this stitch to hold hems and linings in place.

The needle runs along the fabric fold, and then comes out to catch just a thread of the other piece of fabric. Stitches should be 1/8" to 1/4" apart.

Stabstitch

A stabstitch is used to hold shoulder pads to the armscye seam allowance. It is also used to secure the lower end of the zipper when applying an exposed zipper.

Insert the needle straight through the fabric from both directions so that the thread is perpendicular to the fabric layers.

Blindstitch

This stitch is used for hems and holding facings in place. It should not be seen on either side of the garment. This is the hem that should be used on knits, Ultrasuede and Ultraleather.

Catch just a thread or two of each fabric layer. Do not pull the threads tight, otherwise the hem will show on the right side.

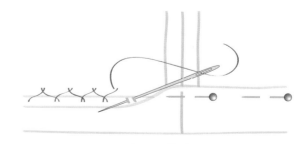

Catchstitch

The catchstitch is used over raw edges to hold the interfacing in place, or for woven fabric hems.

Stitch from left to right for a right-handed person and from right to left for a left-handed person. In either case, the needle is always inserted in the fabric opposite to the stitching direction, as shown.

French Tack

French tacks are used to attach two layers of fabric that require some space between them. Linings are attached to coat hems with French tacks, and tie belts can also be held in place with a French tack.

Using a double thread, attach a few stitches back and forth between the fabric layers, as shown. The length of the stitch determines the length of the tack. Finally, blanket-stitch over the strands of thread.

Arrowheads

Arrowheads are used to accent the ends of pockets, buttonholes and at the top of slits or pleats in shirts or skirts. They add a professional finishing touch.

Use a single thread of buttonhole twist or topstitching thread. Mark the outline of the arrowhead with fine stitches or chalk. Make a few small stitches in the corner of the arrowhead to secure the thread end and construct the arrowhead using the following instuctions.

An arrowhead shape can be cut out of Ultrasuede fabric or real leather and topstitched in place for a hi-style look.

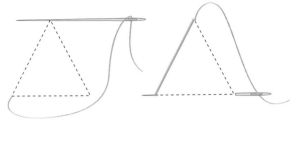

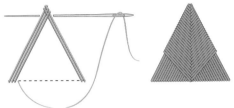

Chain-Stitch Carriers

Chain-stitch carriers are used to hold belts in position, or they can be used to hold two layers of fabric together that require a long linking thread, or for a thread eye to use with a metal hook.

Thread the needle with a double thread, knot it and run it through beeswax. Secure the thread to the wrong side of the garment with several small backstitches. Insert the needle in the fabric and pull it through to the right side.

Make a small stitch on the right side and bring up a large loop of thread.

Hold the loop open with the thumb and forefinger of the right hand. Hold the thread end taut with the fingers of the other hand.

Form another loop with the second finger of the right hand, as shown.

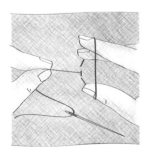
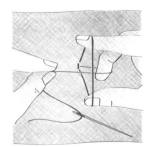

Release the first loop, allowing it to close down on the double thread. Open up the new loop with the thumb and forefinger and repeat the process until the chain is the desired length.

Finish the chain by inserting the needle through the last loop and pulling it tight. Stitch through to the wrong side of the fabric at the desired spot, and secure the chain on the wrong side with a few small backstitches.

PROPER PRESSING

Pressing as you sew is one of the most important concepts of the sewing process. All seams must be pressed either open or to one side, before they are crossed with another seam. Careful pressing of all garment edges before they are turned to the right side is absolutely necessary for a perfect edge. We can't stress proper pressing techniques enough. They are very important to a professionally finished garment.

Having the proper pressing tools is half the battle. Knowing when and how to use them is the other half. Check through the list of recommended tools to see what your sewing room needs. Each one serves a definite purpose, and speeds garment construction along to a perfect finish.

PRESSING TOOLS

As you will see, there are many pressing tools available today. Buying them all at once would take a fair investment. However, if you purchase them over a period of time, or put them on your wishlist for birthdays and Christmas, you will soon have what you need, without a big dent in the budget. It is possible to substitute homemade tools for some of the ready-made ones. This saves money, and some of the homemade tools work better than the purchased ones.

Iron

The iron is obviously the most important pressing tool. We recommend the kind that has a surge of steam, as well as the regular steam or dry option. Get one with a large water capacity, and follow the manufacturer's instructions about the proper water, and recommended method of cleaning the iron. Treat your iron kindly, and it will give you years of good service.

Ironing Board

An adjustable ironing board is a great help in the sewing area. Lower it to table height, and place it right next to the sewing machine, so you don't have to get up every time you need to use the iron. You will be surprised at how much time this saves, and what a convenience it is!

Use the type of ironing board cover you prefer. Just make sure it is kept clean. Change or launder it as necessary.

Make your ironing board tighter by using spring clamps to hold the cover taut. These are available at most hardware stores and are well worth the few dollars they cost. They can be re-used whenever you change covers.

A well-padded ironing board is a must to eliminate seam allowances from pressing through to the right side and to avoid losing the shape that is being built into the garment. Cut up an old wool blanket, (wool has excellent resilience), and pad the ironing board with four or five layers of wool. Cover with a heavy cotton duck cover. Mylar ironing board covers reflect heat and may cause scorching.

Iron Safe or Iron Shoe

An Iron Safe or Iron Shoe is an attachment for the iron that has a Teflon coating on the pressing surface. Made of a thin material, it fits over the sole plate of the iron. The surface is perforated so that the steam can get through.

It functions like a pressing cloth and helps control the heat of the iron so that you'll never have to worry about scorching a fabric, or leaving a shiny, iron mark. Fusible interfacings or web don't stick to it, and it helps the iron to glide over fabrics more easily.

It is a great sewing aid that is readily available. Once on the iron, it can be left on all the time.

Pressing Cloth

There are a variety of pressing cloths available. Some are made of see-through fabric, while others are made of heavier material. Always test the iron and press cloth on a sample piece of fabric before pressing the garment. This is especially important when pressing Ultrasuede fabric, as you may permanently glaze the fabric with a too-hot iron or a too-thin pressing cloth.

You can either buy one or use a square of fabric you have in your sewing room. Many people like old sheeting or muslin. Use whatever works best for you; just remember to launder your pressing cloths often.

Handy Wipes also work for pressing cloths. They are a good size, and hold moisture well. It is easy to keep a package with your sewing supplies.

Rajah Press Cloth

Make **permanent** pleats in 50/50 polyester/cotton-blend slacks or skirts with this 12" x 30" special press cloth. It even takes out ironed-in creases! The heat and steam of the iron releases chemicals that set sharp creases in trousers, uniforms and any fabric with a 50 percent polyester fiber content. It's safe for all fabrics. The cloth can be used up to 1000 times.

Paper Strips

Another useful pressing aid to prevent seam impressions from showing through to the right side of the garment is paper strips. Heavy brown paper can be purchased in pad form, but this is quite expensive when you consider how much it costs to cut up brown kraft paper or a brown paper bag. Small and large envelopes can also serve the same purpose, and they are easier to handle than paper strips.

Hem Marker

Metal hem guides can be used to help you press up even hems. They have various hem widths marked on them. A heavy piece of poster board can be used for the same purpose. Measure and mark your own hem widths.

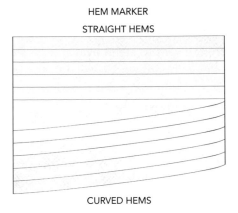

HEM MARKER

STRAIGHT HEMS

CURVED HEMS

Point Presser

A point presser is a wooden tool used to help press open seam allowances, especially in hard-to-reach areas, such as collars and lapel points.

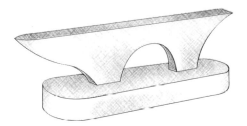

A pencil, rolled in several layers of fabric, or the handle of a wooden cooking spoon, can serve as a substitute point presser for hard-to-reach areas.

Tailor's Board

This device is an all-purpose pressing board that combines the point and flat surface of the point presser with various curves and extensions for hard-to-reach places.

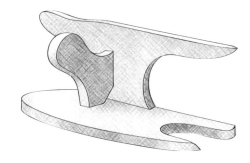

Sleeve Board

A sleeve board is used for pressing open sleeve seams. There are various styles available. A stationary, one-sided, sleeve board works well, but the folding kind that has two different-sized pressing surfaces is very handy but not as sturdy.

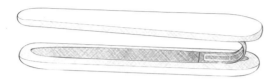

A seam roll can be used in place of a sleeve board, if necessary.

Seam Roll

Ready-made seam rolls are about 13" long. They are useful for pressing open short seams as the rolled surface prevents the seam allowance from making an impression on the right side. A longer seam roll is more efficient for pressing long seams.

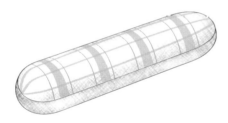

An alternative is to buy a length of half-round banister railing at the lumberyard and cover it with a piece of flannel.

A heavy cardboard tube from a fabric store can also be used to make your own long seam roll. The kind of tube used for rolls of corduroy or suede cloth works best. Cut the tube to a handy length or leave it long to press pant leg seams all at one time. The best thing about this seam roll is that it's free!

When pressing seams on slacks, insert the tube in the pant leg and press the seam. No seam impression is made on the garment because the seam is pressed over a curved surface and only the seam is pressed—not the seam edges. Don't bother to cover the cardboard roll. If it becomes too soggy from the steam, throw it away and ask for another roll at the fabric store.

Tailor's Ham

A tailor's ham is used for pressing curved seams, darts and curved areas of the garment. Pressing over a rounded surface helps build in garment shape.

Tailor's hams are covered with two fabrics. One side is covered with wool and the other side is covered with cotton. Use the wool side up when you are working with wools or softly napped fabrics and the cotton side when working with most other fabrics.

Tailor's Mitt

This pressing aid is used for hard-to-get areas that need steam shaping. The mitt is covered with two different fabrics, just like the ham. It also has a pocket on one side so that it can be slipped over the sleeve board. It is used this way to steam sleeve-caps. It also will bend over a seam roll allowing you to press seams without leaving seam-edge impressions.

Clapper or Pounding-Block

A clapper and a pounding-block are the same thing. They are just different names for the same tool. This tool is used to help flatten seam and garment edges.

Many times an iron may leave a pressing mark where a combination of steam and the clapper will not. It is usually the best way to flatten out seam areas of bulky or resilient fabrics.

Steam the area to be pressed, then quickly strike the area with the clapper, holding it in place for a short time until the heat and moisture have dissipated.

An ordinary child's wooden block can be used in place of a clapper. Use an unpainted one that fits your hand easily.

Needle Board

A needle board is used for pressing velvet or velvet-like fabrics. It prevents the pile from being crushed by the iron.

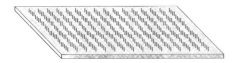

Commercial needle boards are small and expensive. The Industrial Velvet Needle Board is 14" x 19". Used in designer workrooms, it looks like the "pokey" side of Velcro. It eliminates flattening of velvet, corduroy and other pile fabrics.

Brush and Tape

A good clothes brush is nice to have for the final touch-up. It is also handy for keeping your fabric lint-free during the construction process.

Three-inch-wide masking tape is also useful for removing lint from the fabric. In fact, it is a good thing to have in your suitcase when you travel. It keeps you lint-free the easy way.

Cool Fingers

This unique 2"-long finger protector is knit out of heat-resistant yarn. Slip it onto your finger to keep it from getting burned by a hot iron. It's a "must" when pressing narrow strips and when using a hot glue gun!

PRESSING TECHNIQUES

The proper pressing technique is just as important as using the proper pressing tool. It is possible to over-press as well as to under-press. Use the guidelines below to help you get that smooth look.

- Coordinate the iron temperature setting with the fiber content of the fabric. An iron that is too cool won't do the job, and an iron that is too hot can scorch or melt your fabric. If you are in doubt about the proper iron setting, test the heat on a scrap of fabric before you press the garment.

- Always use an up and down motion, rather than a back and forth motion when pressing. Press, don't iron! This keeps the fabric from stretching and reduces the possibility of making new wrinkles.

- Steam-press seams in the closed position before you do anything else to them. This sets the stitches and makes for a smooth seam line. Handle darts this way, too.

- Always press each seam before it is crossed by another seam. It is impossible to have a well-pressed garment if you leave everything until the end.

- Finger-press seams just ahead of the steam iron, this helps to open them all the way. Be careful not to get the iron so close to your fingers that they burn.

- Press open seams along all facing edges before you turn the facing to the right side. This can be done with the help of a point presser.

If a point presser is not available, try this technique.

With the facing side up, open up the seam allowance with the tip of the iron, and press. Carefully work all around the facing.

Fold both seam allowances over to the facing side, as shown, and press again. This makes the turning and finishing process much easier.

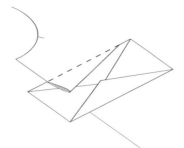

- Roll seams to the underside when pressing all faced edges. A garment with a turn-back lapel should have the seam rolled to the facing side below the roll line, and rolled to the garment side above the roll line. This keeps the facings from showing on any visible part of the garment.

- Press curved seams over a curved form, such as a tailor's ham, in order to preserve their shape.

- Use a moist press cloth when you need more moisture than your steam iron can produce.

- Prevent seam, hem or dart impressions from showing on the right side by placing an envelope or strip of heavy paper between the two layers of fabric when pressing. Use the same technique whenever you press pleats, so that the underside of the pleat isn't impressed on the right side. The envelope-paper technique is also good when pressing the mitered corner of sleeves and back vents.

- Use a clapper or pounding-block to set creases. This technique works particularly well on polyester knits or other resilient fabrics. Place a towel-covered wooden block or cutting board under the section to be pounded so that you have a firm surface on which to work.

- Most pressing is done from the wrong side. This prevents press marks and keeps hem, dart and seam allowances from showing through. If you do need to press on the right side, let the steam do the work for you. Hold the iron above the fabric rather than actually touching the fabric. This is usually all you need; however, if you feel more pressing is required, protect the right side of the fabric with a press cloth, before touching it with an iron.

SCISSORS

The origin of scissors as we know them today may have been with the 16th century Venetians. In Medieval days, scissors were kept in a sheath and hung from the waist. Scissors with folding handles date from the Renaissance. They were carried in elaborate sewing cases or "etui" which also held a toothpick, earspoon, pencil plus often a paper knife or sheet of ivory on which to write notes. (Etui is a favorite word used in crossword puzzles.) In the mid-18th century, the Persians invented scissors in the form of a bird with the beaks serving as blades. The Dutch long ago laid claim to being the originators of stork scissors.

Early steel scissors had ornamental handles which were made separately and soldered onto the shank. They were very expensive. The common people had to use iron scissors. Scissors after the middle of the 19th century had the handles made in one piece. In the 18th century scissors were kept in metal sheaths to prevent their sharp points from tearing pockets and workbags and also to protect their delicate points.

Dutch scissors c. 1730. These have elaborate silver handles soldered onto steel blades.

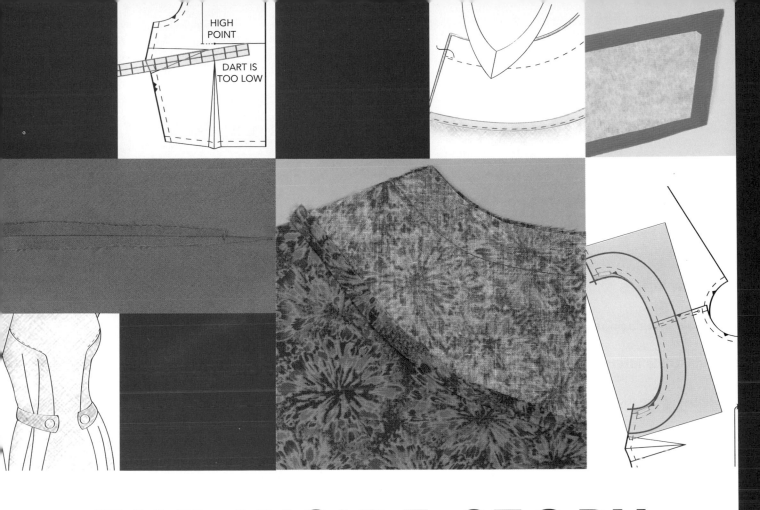

THE INSIDE STORY

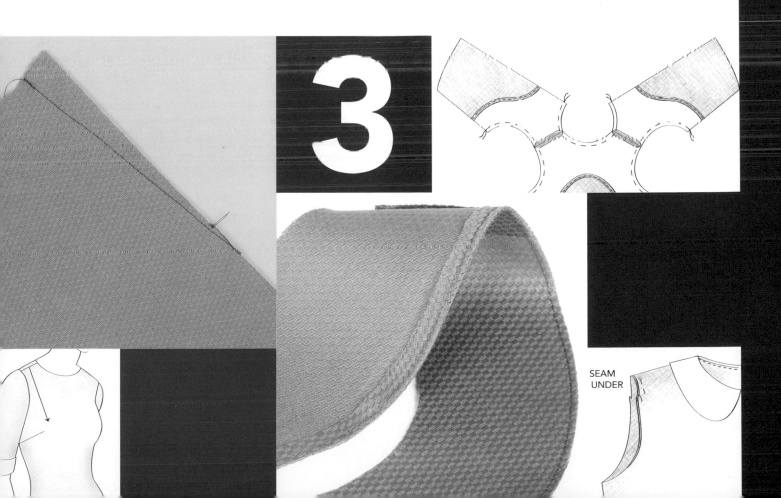

3

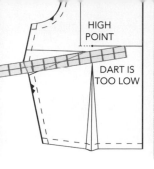

Chapter 3: The Inside Story

INTERFACING fabric is an important part of most garment construction. It gives the support and firmness so necessary in well-made clothes.

Some of the areas usually interfaced are collars, cuffs, button and buttonhole areas, facings, pockets and flaps, waistbands, sleeves and hem edges, and belts and straps.

INTERFACINGS

There are many different interfacings available in fabric stores today. You need some knowledge of each in order to choose the one most suitable to the garment you are making. Make a habit of reading hangtags, bolt ends and other consumer information provided by the interfacing companies. This gives you the necessary information for making the right choice.

FUSIBLE INTERFACINGS

Fusible interfacings have been eagerly adopted by the home sewer because they are quick and easy to use. When first introduced they were called iron-on interfacings. Several years later the term was changed to fusible, as too many sewers literally ironed it on and it came off after several washings.

Some of the advantages of fusible interfacings are listed below.

- Fusible interfacings are fused to the fashion fabric so that the two layers can be handled as one.

- Seam allowances can be removed from the interfacing before fusing, in order to reduce thickness and bulk in the finished seam.

- Small detail pieces, such as pocket flaps or welts, are easier to work with if the interfacing can be fused in position.

Fusible interfacings are available in woven or nonwoven fabrics, with or without stretch, and in light, medium and heavy weights. Keep these characteristics in mind when selecting an interfacing to go with your fashion fabric.

NONFUSIBLE INTERFACINGS

There are many nonfusible interfacings available to the home sewer that can be used for fabric from light to heavy weight. These can be used for most interfacing applications. However, they won't give as flat a finish at seam lines and garment edges as fusible interfacings do, as they are included in the seam.

CHOOSING THE RIGHT INTERFACING

Keep your fashion fabric in mind when choosing an interfacing. Your choice should be governed by the desired finished look. The old rule of a lightweight interfacing for a lightweight fabric and a heavyweight interfacing for a heavyweight fabric just doesn't work. Details on garments made from lightweight fabrics sometimes need the firmness and support of a medium-weight or heavyweight interfacing. Many heavyweight fabrics need just a lightweight interfacing; a heavy interfacing might create too much stiffness and/or bulk.

A good procedure to use when selecting an interfacing is to drape the fashion fabric over various interfacings to see which combination is going to give the desired "hand" or appearance. Sometimes you will find it necessary to use two different interfacing fabrics on one garment in order to get the right look in different areas. For example, you might need a firm, medium-weight interfacing for cuffs and pocket details, but a more supple, lightweight interfacing for the roll collar.

Interfacings with an all-bias or crosswise stretch are ideal for knit garments. They add the needed support but still retain the "give" of the knit. Be sure to cut the interfacing pieces so that the stretch goes around the body. This gives the most wearing comfort.

Nonstretch woven interfacings can also be used for knits. However, it is best that they be cut on the bias when covering large areas of the garment so that the interfacing gives with the knit.

Fusible interfacings can be used for nearly all interfacing requirements. Nonfusible interfacings can be used anywhere too, but they sometimes require some handwork. They are not quite as easy to handle as a fusible interfacing that is bonded to the fashion fabric.

Some delicate, lightweight synthetic fabrics cannot stand the heat needed to apply a fusible interfacing so a nonfusible one should be used instead.

Tailored garments can be made with either a fusible or nonfusible hair canvas. The fusible hair canvas works best with synthetic fabrics. It is quick to use and eliminates the need for hand-padding stitches. Nonfusible hair canvas is a better choice for natural fiber fabrics because they mold and shape nicely and can really take advantage of hand pad stitching.

Interfacings are made in various colors. The most common is white, but you will see some cream, gray and black interfacings. Use the darker colors only on dark or heavy fabrics where the color will not show through.

Machine-buttonhole areas should always be supported by some type of interfacing. If you use lining or under-lining fabric that is color-matched to the fashion fabric, you avoid a line of white showing along the edge of the buttonhole. If you have to use white interfacing, once you cut the buttonholes, camouflage the white line with a matching colored pencil or pen. (Honestly, that's the technique used in the industry.)

APPLYING INTERFACING

Read the manufacturer's instructions for the recommended application methods for your chosen interfacing. Proper application is the key to a good-looking garment. The following points apply to both fusible and nonfusible interfacings. Special help specifically for fusible or nonfusible interfacings will be given afterward.

- Some interfacings tend to shrink, wovens more so than nonwovens. Unless the hangtag or bolt end states differently, it is advisable to preshrink all interfacing fabrics. Nonfusibles can usually be preshrunk in the washing machine and dried in the dryer. A rule to follow is to use the same method to preshrink the interfacing that you will use to clean the finished garment.

- Even fusible interfacing should be preshrunk to be on the safe side; however, **not** in the washer and dryer as that will cause the fusing material to come off. Place the fusible interfacing, neatly folded, in the kitchen sink. Cover with hot tap water and allow interfacing to soak for 10 minutes. Gently hand-press out most of the water, don't wring, as you don't want to wring in wrinkles. Spread out flat and allow piece to dry naturally.

- Cut all interfacing pieces accurately. Cut on the same grain line as the garment piece when using a woven interfacing. Exceptions are bias cuts for knit garments and collars. Stretch interfacings should be cut with the stretch going around the body.

- Apply interfacing to the wrong side of the garment piece that will be visible on the finished garment. For example: interface the upper pieces of collars, cuffs and pocket flaps; apply interfacing to the visible side of waistbands, front bands and plackets; apply the interfacing to the wrong side of the facing when the garment has a turn-back lapel. This prevents "shadowing through" of the seam allowances and is especially important on lightweight or sheer fabrics.

- Trim away the interfacing at corners and points, as illustrated, before applying to the fashion fabric. This eliminates bulk in these areas and allows them to turn smoothly.

Applying Fusible Interfacing

Fusible interfacings have application requirements other than those listed above because of their special finish. Since the interfacing is held to the garment by a bonding process, it is possible to remove seam allowances from all interfacing pieces before they are fused to the fashion fabric. This reduces thickness at seams and garment edges. Corners and points of the interfacing should also be trimmed as previously shown, for the same reason.

Fusibles are easy to work with if you just keep in mind the following points.

- Follow the manufacturer's instructions exactly when bonding the interfacing to the fashion fabric. If an imperfect bond is made, the interfacing will blister and pull away from the fabric in the first washing or cleaning. It is very difficult, if not impossible, to re-bond the interfacing after this happens.

- Make sure you get the proper bonding instructions when you purchase the interfacing. Each interfacing seems to require a slightly different technique, and what works with one doesn't necessarily work with another.

Use the instruction sheet to store leftover fusible interfacing. Fold the sheet in half, stitch the sides. Insert the interfacing remnants. Now you know which interfacing it is and the specific instructions for its use. Or, store both in a resealable plastic bag.

- The factors necessary for a successful bond are: proper iron temperature, steam, if needed, and adequate pressing time. An iron that is not heated to the proper temperature will not completely melt the fusing material, and you will end up with an imperfect bond. Too hot an iron will scorch your fabric. Some fusibles call for a dry iron, while others need steam. If you suspect that your steam iron isn't putting out enough moisture, place a damp press cloth underneath the iron during the fusing process. A certain number of seconds of heat, steam and pressure is necessary for a perfect bond. Follow the recommended pressing time to the second. Remember, it must be done right the first time, so be patient and count the seconds on a clock.

- Fuse-baste large pieces of interfacing to the garment before starting the fusing process. This is done by positioning the interfacing over the garment piece and then touching the tip of the iron to the interfacing at various key points to hold the interfacing in place. This prevents the interfacing from slipping while fusing smaller sections.

- Occasionally small pieces of fusing material will stick to the ironing-board cover. This can be prevented by covering the ironing board with a piece of sheeting or an old pillowcase. Or place a No-Stick Sheet that is fiberglass impregnated with Teflon on top of the ironing board to keep "crumbs" from adhering to your cover. Keep this handy so that you can use it whenever you fuse interfacing.

Let's hope you never need to use this bit of information. But—if you ever fuse interfacing to the face side of the fabric instead of the wrong side where it belongs, all is not lost. Avoid an utter disaster by re-steaming the interfacing. While it is warm, peel off as much of the interfacing as possible. Use denatured alcohol (available at paint stores) to remove the remaining residue.

- Fusible interfacing should completely cover the garment piece to which it is being applied. Failure to do this will leave a visible line on the right side of the garment, where the interfacing ends.

WRONG   RIGHT

Interface **all** garment pieces when making a blazer from cotton velveteen. Noninterfaced velveteen blazers can look like old dish cloths after being worn a few times. The interfacing also prevents seam allowances from shadowing through to the right side.

Summer jackets are left unlined to reduce the weight and extra warmth of the lining. Expensive unstructured and unlined ready-to-wear linen and raw silk jackets eliminate the facing by cutting **four** fronts. Fusibly interface the entire "inside front." Clean-finish all the exposed seam allowances with a serger or Seams Great. Slip-stitch side seams together. The "inside front" covers any inside pocket construction and eliminates facings that gap out because there is no lining to hold them flat.

The "inside front" replaces the facing. Since the facing should always be slightly larger in the lapel area (see Front Facing in Chapter 7), remember to cut the "inside front" 1/8" wider from the collar notch to the cut edge and 1/8" longer from the top cut edge to the roll line mark to give the designer ease needed for the lapel to roll properly.

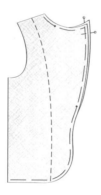

Applying Nonfusible Interfacing

Nonfusible interfacings are held in the proper position by including the interfacing in the seam line or by trimming away the entire seam allowance and catching the interfacing to the fashion fabric by hand. The first method is used for most interfacing applications, while the second method is used on a tailored garment.

Trim nonfusible interfacing seam allowances so that just 1/8" is left. Pin the interfacing to the fashion fabric and catch the interfacing in the seam.

Trim nonfusible interfacing as close to the seam line as possible when grading and turning an enclosed seam. This reduces bulk in the seam area.

FUSIBLE WEB

Another product that is related to fusible interfacing is a fusible web such as Stitch Witchery or Steam-A-Seam 2. This consists of a thin web of fusing material. It is available as narrow, prepackaged strips or in wider widths by the yard. It is used to bond two layers of fabric together, and it can be used to put up hems (a quick way to do that) and to hold appliqués or patches in place while stitching. It is also handy for many craft projects. Because the fused web adds some firmness to fabrics, it can be used across the top of pockets and at the hem and sleeve edges to add a bit of crispness. Remember to carefully follow the fusing instructions that come with each brand of web so that you get a perfect bond.

Also available is a fusible web spray. Simply spray the fusible web on the fabric using 606 Spray and Fix and iron it to the second fabric. They're now permanently held together. This works for craft projects, too.

DARTS

One of the secrets of a well-fitting garment is perfect darts. Since they build the garment's shape, they should be of the proper size, accurately positioned and stitched so that they can function as designed. Darts that are too long or too short, too high or too low, can ruin the look and fit of an otherwise perfect garment.

A perfect dart has the following characteristics:

- It is directed toward the fullest part of the figure.

- It ends 1/2" to 1" short of the fullest part of the figure.

- It is the correct width.

- It has a smooth point that doesn't bubble or pucker.

You have probably seen darts that don't display the above characteristics. The most common fault seems to be darts that are not positioned properly. However, before we start solving problems, let's review the various types of darts found on patterns.

TYPES OF DARTS

Different types of darts are used in pattern design. Some are just functional, while others add design interest, as well as shape. Plain, functional darts should be as inconspicuous as possible. Darts that combine design and shape should be accentuated, by stitching or fabric treatment, so they add interest to the finished garment.

Straight Darts

The horizontal bust dart and vertical waistline darts are good examples of straight darts. They are generally just functional darts, giving shape to the garment. However, they can have one of three different shapes, as illustrated below.

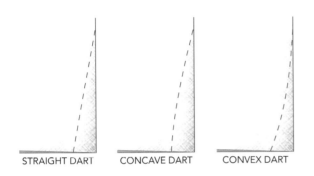

STRAIGHT DART   CONCAVE DART   CONVEX DART

Straight darts are used mostly at the bustline, elbow, below the waist, at the neck or shoulder, and above the waist on the back of the garment.

Concave darts are usually used above the waist in the midriff area. They can have a small or large outward curve. The more curve, the closer the fit.

Convex darts are perhaps the least used shape. They are found wherever the body curves outward, such as over a round tummy. They can also be used at the bust, if the figure is extremely full. Convex darts are used at the hip when a dart replaces the side seam.

Note: *Have you ever wondered how to tell the difference between convex and concave? An easy way is to relate the word "concave" to the word "cave." Caves go in, so concave curves also go in.*

The dart shape marked on your pattern can be changed if you want a different type of fit. Body-hugging clothes use more curved darts than straight darts. Just match the dart curve to the body curve, and stitch away.

Curved Darts

The curved darts that we refer to in this section are different from straight darts with curved stitching lines. A curved dart is actually drawn along a curved line, and it is used as a style line in some women's fashions.

Curved darts should be carefully marked, matched and pinned before they are stitched so that the dart doesn't ripple.

Double-Pointed Darts

Some darts have points at each end. They are used in the waist area of one-piece dresses, and coats and jackets. They usually have curved sides, which can be curved more for a closer fit.

Open Darts

Most darts have a fold down the middle. Some will be open, or part of a seam.

Extra-wide darts, especially curved darts, usually have an open middle. Sewing these darts is like sewing two seams together. The open middle reduces the bulk in the dart area and makes a smooth curve.

Darts can also become part of an intricate design, which requires a seam rather than a fold.

French Darts

The French dart is not really a dart type; rather, it is the way the dart is positioned. It angles from somewhere on the side seam up to the bust.

The French dart can start at the hip or closer to the waist. It can be either straight or curved.

One thing should be kept in mind when working with long French darts. They are not suitable for fabrics

CURVED DART

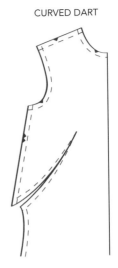

OPEN DART

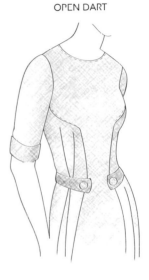

FRENCH DART

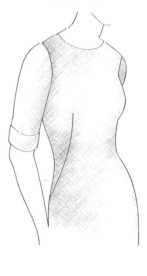

that have to be matched. The fabric pattern will be off the length of the dart.

DART PLACEMENT

The proper placement of darts is the key factor in their fit. When taking bust measurements, always wear the same foundation garment as you will when wearing the completed garment. Make sure the shoulder straps are properly adjusted. A high bustline is more youthful than a low bustline.

Rules to Remember

- The first and most important rule to remember is that darts should always point toward the fullest part of the figure. This means the high point of the bust, tummy, derriere, shoulder area or elbow.

- Secondly, darts should end 1/2" to 1" short of the fullest part of the figure. Darts that are sewn too close to the full point will "peak" and darts sewn beyond the full point will be very unattractive.

- The third rule is that the dart width must accommodate the fullness of the figure. Obviously, an A-cup bust needs less dart width than a D-cup bust.

Proper Position

As previously stated, darts should be directed toward the fullest part of the figure. Let's use the bust dart as an example.

Too High: This dart is directed above the high point of the bust, so it releases the fabric fullness above the

bust. This causes wrinkles above the bust, and perhaps tightness below. This is a very common fitting fault.

Too Low: Directed below the high point of the bust, this dart releases the fullness below the place that it is needed.

Just Right: This dart is directed toward the high point of the bust, releasing the fabric fullness where it should be. Garments should be fitted this way.

Since patterns are not custom-designed, it is up to you to check the dart placement on each pattern before you cut your fabric. Dart position is not always the same on every pattern, so you cannot make a general rule about how much you have to raise or lower the dart. Check each pattern!

Locate your high point by measuring from the middle of the shoulder seam, down to the high-point of the bust. Mark that measurement on the pattern.

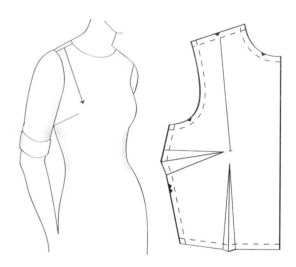

Measure the distance between the high points of the bust with a tape measure. Divide by two, and measure that amount from the pattern's center front, at the level of the previous mark. Place a dot to mark the high point location.

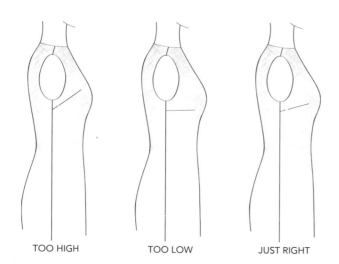

TOO HIGH   TOO LOW   JUST RIGHT

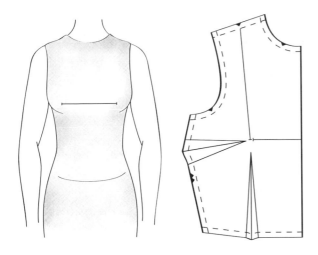

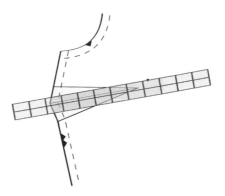

Check to see if the dart is properly positioned by placing a ruler along the dart's centerline, as shown. The edge of the ruler should go right through the high point mark. Raise or lower the dart if it is not correctly positioned.

Redraw the other dart lines by positioning the ruler parallel to the lines, keeping the distance between the old and new lines the same as measured above.

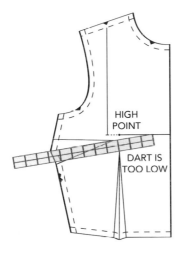

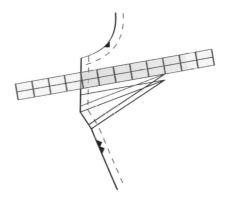

How to Alter Position

There are two ways to change the bust dart location. One works best if very little change is needed. The other method should be used if a major change is required.

Redrawing Method: Use this method when you are moving the dart just a small amount, 1/2" or less. A see-through plastic ruler is a great help here.

Position the ruler parallel to the dart fold line, so that the edge intersects with the high point mark. Draw a new fold line. Measure the distance between the old and new fold line.

Cut and Fold Method: Use this method when you have to make a large change. It will retain the proper shape at the end of the dart so that you have a smooth sideline after the dart has been stitched.

To raise the dart, cut the pattern below the dart and up around the point, making sure the vertical cut is parallel to the center front. Use a ruler to mark the cutting lines so they are straight.

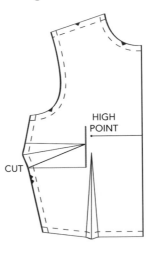

Fold the pattern until the dart is directed toward the high point mark. The fold should be at right angles to the center front, and the vertical cut edges should meet evenly. Tape the fold in place. Fill in the gap below with an extra piece of paper and redraw the side of the pattern.

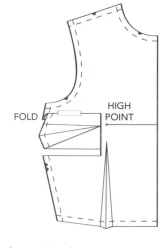

Lower the dart by going through the same process except, make the first cut above the dart.

Change the position of vertical darts by redrawing each side parallel to the original one. Use the cut-and-fold method for curved darts.

Proper Length

Darts should not be sewn all the way to the fullest part of the figure. The fabric should be released slightly short of the fullest part so that the dart doesn't "peak." Underarm darts should end 1" short of the high point, while waistline darts should end 1/2" to 1" short of the high point, whichever gives the best appearance for a particular figure and fabric combination.

Short darts should be lengthened, and long darts shortened, so that the fabric fullness is released where it does the most good.

How to Alter Length

Adjust the length of the dart only **after** it has been properly positioned.

Shorten the dart by marking the correct length on the dart's centerline and redrawing each side, as shown.

Lengthen the dart by extending the dart's centerline and locating the new length on it. Redraw each side.

SHORTEN

LENGTHEN

Proper Width

The dart width should relate to the cup size of the bust, or the fullness of the other parts of the figure. Figures with full curves need wider darts than figures with straighter curves. Patterns are designed for a standard body shape, and you will have to alter dart widths if you deviate from this standard.

Darts that are too wide cause wrinkles in the bodice, and the garment looks too big, even though it fits elsewhere.

Darts that are too narrow cause the garment to bind over the bust, making you think you might need a larger size, making it too big elsewhere.

How to Alter Width

Dart width alterations are best done in muslin. Once you see just how wide your bust dart should be, you can easily compare it to darts on all patterns and make the necessary alteration.

Small Bust: Construct and try on the muslin. Pin tucks across the chest and down over the bustline, as shown, until you get the proper fit.

Transfer the alteration to the pattern by slashing and overlapping. Reduce the width of the dart the same amount as the width of the horizontal fold.

Large Bust: Construct and try on the muslin. Slash the pattern, as shown, and fill in the gaps with strips of muslin. Adjust the gaps until you get a comfortable fit.

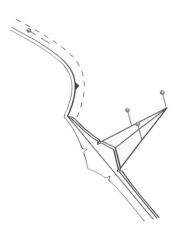

Transfer the alteration to the pattern, increasing the dart width by the width of the horizontal slash.

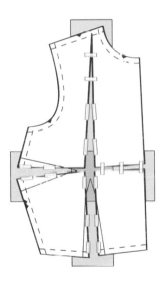

DART CONSTRUCTION

Darts that bulge, pucker or come to points are very unattractive. Stitching perfect darts is simple with a little understanding.

Marking

First of all, the dart must be accurately marked using the pattern as a guide. It is best to mark the dart right after the garment piece is cut, before it has been allowed to shift. Misplacement can happen quite easily if the pattern piece is picked up and moved.

Mark the ends of the dart with small clips. Mark the

point of the dart by inserting a pin through both layers of fabric at the dart point.

Lightly mark the fabric with pencil or chalk where the pin goes through. Then insert pins along the sides of the dart, and mark.

Stitching

Pin the dart, right sides together, sticking pins through each construction mark. Check to make sure the pins are accurately placed on each side of the dart. Pin from the wide to the pointed end of the dart.

Always start stitching at the widest point of the dart. Backstitch at the beginning of the stitching, and gradually taper to a point at the end of the dart. The last three or four stitches should be precisely on the fold. Continue stitching a few stitches off the edge of the fabric.

GRADUAL TAPER
CORRECT

Raise the presser foot and needle, and pull the fabric toward you about 3/4". Lower the presser foot and needle and take a few stitches in the fold of the dart, with the stitch length regulator set at 0. This secures the thread ends, and you can clip them close without having to worry about their coming loose. This process beats tying knots in the end of all your darts.

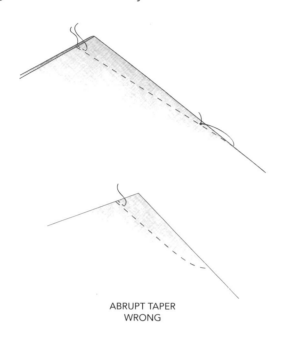

ABRUPT TAPER
WRONG

Note: *Darts that are stitched with an abrupt point will "peak" when worn.*

Continuous-Thread Dart

Darts in sheer fabrics should be made with a continuous thread so that the knot and thread ends can be eliminated at the point of the dart. Darts stitched on the right side of the garment for decorative effect should also be stitched with a continuous thread. Follow the instructions below for the continuous-thread dart.

Unthread the machine needle. Pull a long thread out of the bobbin and insert it through the eye of the machine needle, in the opposite direction in which it is usually done. Tie the bobbin thread to the spool thread, then pull the bobbin thread up through the thread guides. Wind enough bobbin thread onto the spool to stitch the dart. Start stitching the dart at

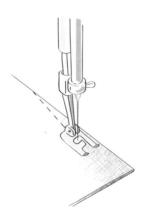

the pointed end. This is the only time you should start stitching at the tip end. Make sure the needle goes into the fabric exactly on the fold. Stitch the dart to the wide end, backstitch and cut the threads. Rethread the machine for each dart.

Pressing

Horizontal darts are pressed downward, and vertical darts are pressed toward the center of the body. Open darts are pressed open. Work from the wrong side and use a good steam iron. Place an envelope between the dart and fabric so an impression won't show through on the right side (see Pressing Techniques in chapter 2).

Darts in bulky fabrics should be slashed open, trimmed if necessary, and pressed open. Handle wide darts the same way, slashing to within 1/2" of the point. "Squash" the point flat, and press.

Darts in sheer fabrics look best if they are stitched twice and trimmed to 1/4". Press the dart in the correct direction and then overcast the raw edges by hand.

SEWING TIPS

Clip double-pointed darts as shown, so that the curve is released and they will lie flat.

Double-pointed darts can be topstitched for a designer look. It is a good technique for bulky or resilient fabrics.

Trim away fusible interfacing, within dart lines, before fusing it to the fashion fabric. Use the cut edges of the interfacing for a stitching guide. This process reduces bulk in the dart area.

Bust darts can be eliminated from a pattern by making a fold across the pattern that is the width of the dart. (You may want to do this when using a stretchy knit with darts in the pattern.)

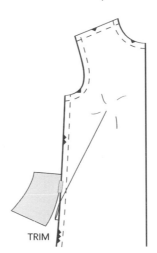

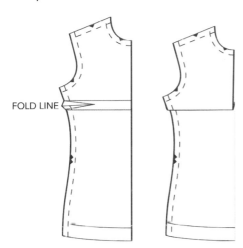

FOLD LINE

Back shoulder darts can be eased in, rather than stitched in, when using knit fabrics. This reduces bulk at the shoulder seam.

The shape at the seam end of a dart has a direct relationship to the length and width of the dart. If you make any length or width adjustments, you must also change the end shape.

Draw in the new dart lines and tape an extra piece of paper to the pattern at the end of the dart.

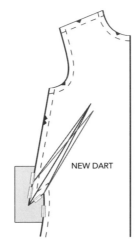

NEW DART

Fold the dart along the new stitching lines and press the fold down or toward the center of the body, just as it would be done in the finished garment. Trim along the edge of the pattern while the dart is still folded. This gives you the correct end shape.

TRIM

If you are underlining a garment with darts, stitch down the center of the dart through both the fashion fabric and the underlining. This holds the fabric layers together along the fold, resulting in accurately stitched darts.

FACINGS

Facings are an important part of the sewing process. You should know how to handle them so that all your faced edges are smooth and flat, without any of the facing "peeking" to the right side. Many ideas for professional touches are given in this section, as well as basic construction information.

FACING ADAPTATIONS

A facing is a piece of fabric cut in the same shape as the garment piece to which it is being sewn. Sometimes the facing is the same width as the garment piece, as in cuff or pocket flap facings; sometimes it is just a narrow strip, as in neckline or armhole facings. Let's see just how you should go about making your own facing.

Lay a piece of pattern or tissue paper over the garment edge to be faced. Trace around the edges, next draw in a lower facing line, so that the facing is about 3" wide. Use this traced-off pattern to cut the facing.

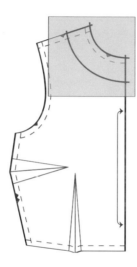

Some faced edges include one or more darts; i.e., the back of the neck, or the waistline of a skirt or pants. The dart should not be included in the facing, in order to reduce bulk.

Fold out the dart and trace along the garment edges. Draw a lower facing line making the facing approximately 3" wide.

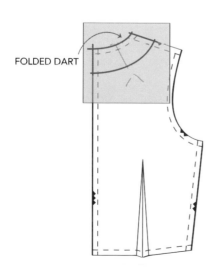

FOLDED DART

Sometimes it is advantageous to combine two facing pieces into one. This saves fabric, reduces bulk in the seam area and simplifies the construction process. Some facings that can be cut all in one are the back and front armhole facings, back and front neckline facings, armhole and neckline facings, and garment front and front facing.

Armhole Facings

Eliminating the seam at the shoulder of the armhole facing reduces bulk in that area. Construction time is speeded up because you are working with one rather than two pieces of fabric.

Combine the two facing patterns by overlapping the shoulder seams until the seam lines meet; tape or pin them in place. Use the grain line on the front facing piece when cutting the fashion fabric. Mark the shoulder seam with a small clip.

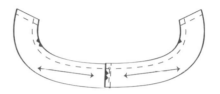

Thickness can be reduced in the underarm area by offsetting the underarm seam of the facing. This is a good technique to use for bulky fabrics. Make this alteration before you eliminate the shoulder seam.

Overlap the facing pattern until the underarm seams meet, and tape them in place.

Measure 1 1/4" toward the back, and draw a line parallel to the underarm seam line. Cut the new facing apart along this line.

Add a 5/8" seam allowance to each cut edge. (Don't rely on your memory for this addition.)

Finally, eliminate the shoulder seam, as previously described, and you will have a neatly faced armhole.

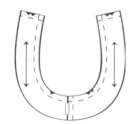

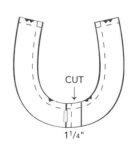

CUT

1 1/4"

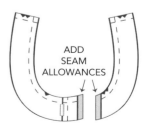

ADD SEAM ALLOWANCES

If you ever decide to change a set-in sleeve armhole to a sleeveless armhole, you will have to make your own facing. Use the following directions.

First of all, raise the underarm point by taping an extra piece of paper to the front and back pattern pieces, then draw a new underarm line 1/2" above the given line.

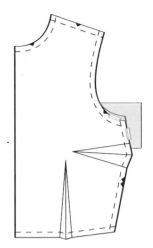

Narrow the underarm 1/2" also; this prevents "gaposis." Always try on the garment before finishing the armhole to see if you need to make further adjustments.

Overlap the front and back pattern pieces until the shoulder seams meet. Pin in place. Lay a large piece of pattern or tissue paper over the armhole area and trace the outside edges. Draw another line making the facing 3" wide. Make the facing's grain line parallel to the grain line on the front pattern piece.

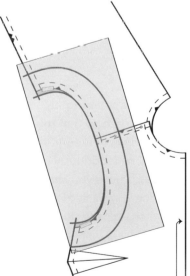

Neckline Facings

The back and front neckline facings can be combined so that the shoulder seam is eliminated. Just overlap the two pattern pieces until the seam lines meet, and pin in place. Cut the fashion fabric using this combined pattern, remembering to designate the shoulder seam with a small clip.

Neckline-Armhole Facings

Sleeveless, scoop-necked garments usually require a facing at both edges. Since separate facings tend to leave ridges that show through to the right side, combine the neckline and armhole facings for a smoother finish.

Lay a large piece of pattern or tissue paper over the front pattern piece. Trace around the edges as shown, marking the center front as a fold. Draw in a lower facing line that curves up over the bust. This curve is necessary to allow the facing to lie smoothly over the bust area. Cut the new facing pattern.

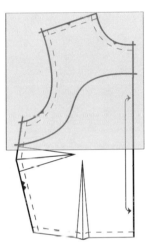

Duplicate the procedure for the back facing, curving it in the shoulder blade area, and marking the grain line the same as the pattern back. Cut out the back facing pattern.

Use these two new patterns to cut the fashion fabric. Application methods for this facing are given at the end of this section.

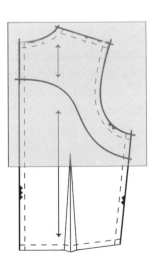

Garment Front and Front Facings

The garment front and front facing can be cut all in one when the front edge is a straight line. This gives one less seam, and it is a good way to reduce thickness at the garment's front edge when working with a bulky fabric.

Overlap the front and front facing pattern pieces until the front seam lines meet. Tape or pin in place. Use this modified front pattern to cut the fashion fabric. The front edge will now be a fold rather than a seamed edge.

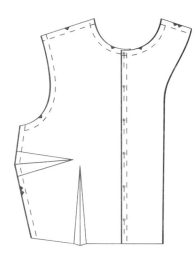

FACING APPLICATIONS

Interfacing should be applied to the wrong side of the **garment** rather than to the facing to prevent seam allowances from "shadowing through" to the right side. Fusible interfacing usually leaves a line where it ends, and you don't want that to show on the right side of your finished garment. However, if you are using a fusible interfacing at a neckline or armhole edge, apply the interfacing to the facing piece.

Unstructured garments that have turn-back lapels should also have the interfacing applied to the facing rather than the garment piece. This gives a firm look to the visible part of the lapel and prevents the seam allowance from shadowing through.

Edge Finishes

The free edge of the facing should be finished in some manner. You should use the method that gives the flattest finish for your particular fashion fabric so that facing ridges won't show through to the right side. The finished edge of a facing is then called "clean finished."

Edge Stitch: Fold over a 1/4" seam allowance and edge-stitch. If you have difficulty turning this narrow seam allowance, stitch 1/4" from the facing edge. Then turn the seam allowance back along this stitching line and edge-stitch. Use whatever method works best for you. This turned-and-stitched technique works well with most lightweight woven fabrics. It is too bulky for knits.

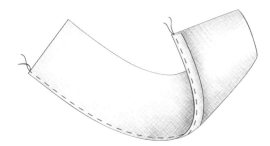

Pink or Overcast: Stitch 3/8" from the facing edge and trim the edge with pinking shears, or overcast the raw edge with a zigzag stitch or serger. Use this method for knits or woven fabrics that don't fray easily.

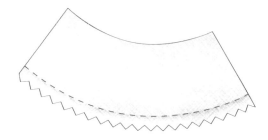

Faced Facing: Face the facing with a lightweight fabric. This gives a beautiful inside finish and is a good way to handle fabrics that fray. See Facing Tips in this chapter.

Hong Kong Finish: Use a Hong Kong finish for heavy fabrics. See Seam finishes in Chapter 2.

Facing Placement

Facings should always be slightly smaller than the comparable garment piece so that the facing rolls to the underside and doesn't show around the finished edge. This can be achieved by laboriously trimming 1/8" away from all facing edges before you stitch them to the garment. However, since you must trim the garment seam allowances after stitching, why do it twice? Make the facing smaller by the way it is pinned to the garment.

Position the facing against the garment piece, right sides together, so that the facing extends beyond the garment edges 1/8". Pin in place and stitch with the given seam allowance, measuring in from the garment rather than the facing edge. This offset makes the finished facing slightly smaller than the garment. Caution: Do not make facings smaller on silk blouse-weight fabrics. The facing is made smaller to compensate for the thickness of the fabric, which is not necessary on thin fabrics.

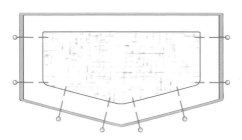

Stitch all facings carefully so that they have a smooth finish. Shorten the stitch length around all corners and sharp curves, remembering to take a diagonal stitch across each corner to give turning room. While stitching curves, keep the machine constantly moving to stitch a smooth line. Make sure all seam widths are exact. Use a seam guide or mark the seam widths with a small clip at the beginning and end.

Finishing

The secret to a smooth facing line is in the trimming and turning procedure. First of all, trim the interfacing close to the stitching line if you have used a nonfusible type.

Press all seams in the flat position to set the stitches.

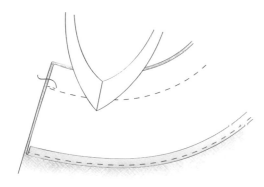

Grade the seam allowances. Average-weight fabrics should be trimmed to about 1/4". For thin fabrics the seam can be trimmed slightly closer, for heavy fabrics the seam should be trimmed slightly wider. Seam allowances

that lie just under the visible part of the garment should be left the longest. The seam can be graded in one quick operation by holding the scissors at an acute angle and cutting both seam allowances at once. This creates a beveled seam edge.

Clip the curved areas using just the tips of your shears. Clip just to the stay stitching or stitching line, making sure you don't cut any threads. The clips should be perpendicular to the seam line and evenly spaced. Deeply curved sections require closely spaced clips, while more shallow curves need fewer clips. (A good rule of thumb is that the clipped curve can now be held "opened" in a straight line.)

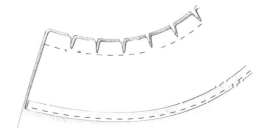

Occasionally turn the facing to the finished position, while clipping curved areas, to see if you are making enough clips. An uneven edge indicates the need for more closely spaced clips.

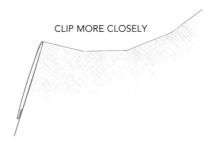

CLIP MORE CLOSELY

Pinking shears can be used to trim curved seam allowances, if desired. They trim and clip in one operation.

Press open the seam allowances to facilitate the turning process. A point presser helps you get in those hard-to-reach areas, or you can use the technique described below.

With the facing up, use the tip of the iron to press open the seam allowances.

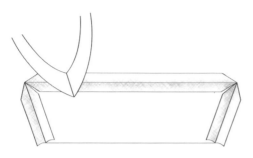

After they are all pressed open, press both seam allowances over to the facing side. This gives a firm turning edge.

Understitch the facing edge. This keeps the facing in place and also gives a firm turning edge. Turn the facing to the finished position and press, rolling the seam to the underside. Make sure all corners are sharp and curves are smooth.

Some facings need to be tacked in place so that they won't flip out to the right side. This applies mostly to armhole, neckline and waistline facings. Never completely stitch down the entire outer edge of a facing unless the garment has been lined or underlined; otherwise it will show on the right side giving that "loving hands at home" look. There are three methods you can use. Choose the one that works best for your particular garment.

Machine Stitch: Pin the facing in position and stitch in the ditch on the right side of the garment. Shorten your stitch length so the stitches will bury in the seam line. This technique can be used with most wovens and knits.

Fusible Web: Hold the facing in place with a small piece of fusible web placed between the garment seam allowance and the facing. Never fuse the whole facing to the garment. This usually shows on the right side.

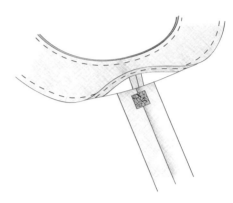

Hand Stitch: With the facing and garment seams aligned, catch the facing edge to the garment's seam allowance only, as shown.

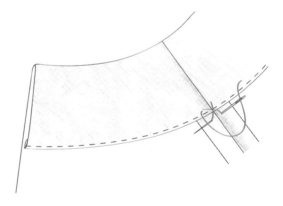

FACING TECHNIQUES

The following facing techniques can be used on many garments. They give a smooth, professional finish to the faced edge.

Offset Sleeveless Armhole Facing

The offset sleeveless armhole facing is a good technique for thick fabrics. It moves the facing edge 3/8" back away from the garment's edge at the top of the armscye, so there is less bulk at the finished edge.

Prepare the garment and facing by stitching the shoulder and underarm seams, pressing them open, and then clean finishing the facing edges.

Pin the facing to the armscye so that the facing extends 3/8" beyond the garment edge at the top of the armhole, and 1/8" around the rest of the armscye. Stitch the facing in place taking the given seam allowance. Measure the seam width from the edge of the facing at the top of the armhole, and from the edge of the garment around the lower part.

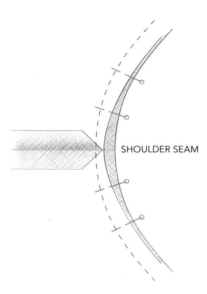

SHOULDER SEAM

Press, grade and clip the seam allowance. Press open the seam allowance at the top of the armscye, and understitch the facing seam. Turn the facing to the finished position, rolling the seam 3/8" to the underside at the top of the armscye, and just slightly to the underside around the rest of the armscye. Tack the facing into position.

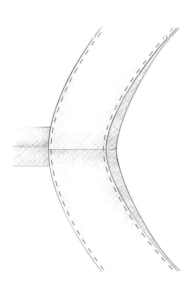

Bias-Finished Sleeveless Armhole

Many ready-to-wear garments use a folded bias strip, rather than a shaped facing, for sleeveless armhole finishes. You will see this technique used on many de-signer clothes. It is easy to do and can be used for both knits and wovens.

Knit fabrics can use a strip cut across the stretch of the fabric rather than a bias cut. You can use a self-fabric strip if the knit is not too bulky. Thick knits should have the armhole strip cut from a lighter weight knit that is color-matched to the garment fabric.

Stitch and press open the shoulder and underarm seam of the garment. Trim the armscye seam allowance to 1/4". Measure the circumference of the armscye. Cut the trim strip 11/2" wide and 1/2" longer than the armscye measurement. (This allows for 1/4" seam allowances.)

Join the strip ends into a circle with a 1/4" seam, right sides together. Press the seam open. Fold the strip in half, lengthwise, with the wrong sides together. Press the folded edge.

Pin the cut edges of the strip to the right side of the prepared armhole, placing the seam of the strip at the underarm seam. Stitch together with a 1/4" seam.

Clip the seam allowance and turn the facing strip to the inside. Press the edge, rolling the seam to the underside, and hold in place by edge stitching around the armhole. This stitching holds the facing strip in position.

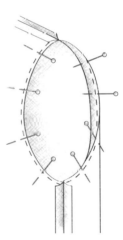

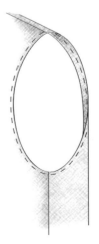

Combined Neckline-Armhole Facing

There are various methods of applying the combined neckline-armhole facing. Not all the methods given in pattern instructions give the professional finish you want. The three methods included below solve that problem. Each one is suitable for a different situation, so make sure you read the instructions before you start to work.

Pull-Through Method: This facing technique is used for garments that have a center back or center front opening and a finished shoulder width of at least 4". This width is necessary to allow you to pull the back section of the garment through the shoulder area without making the garment look like it has been through the wringer. This technique can also be used for fully lined vests. Handle the lining pieces as though they were the facing. Do not use this method for full-length dresses or jumpers, as pulling that much fabric through the shoulder could damage the finished look of the fabric. Prepare the garment by stitching and pressing open the shoulder seams. Stitch and press open the facing shoulder seams and clean-finish the lower edges.

Position the facing against the garment, right sides together, extending the facing 1/8" out beyond the garment edge at the neck and armscye. Pin in place and stitch with the given seam width. Press, grade and clip the seams.

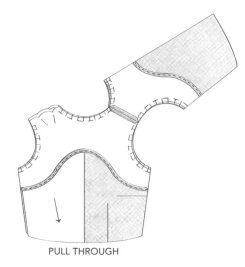

PULL THROUGH

Finish the underarm seam by stitching the garment and facing in one operation. Make sure the underarm seams exactly match, and the seam allowances are pressed up into the facing when stitching.

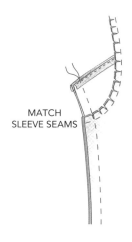

MATCH
SLEEVE SEAMS

This technique can also be used for a garment with a collar. Pin and stitch the collar to the garment's neckline before the facing is pinned in place. Continue as directed above.

Sleeveless Scoop-Necked Facings: Sleeveless, scoop-necked garments that pull over the head require a different facing technique. Prepare the garment and facing by stitching and pressing open the underarm seams. Clean-finish the facing edges.

Pin the facing to the garment, right sides together, extending the facing 1/8" beyond the garment's edge. Stitch the neck and armscye edges with the given seam width. Careful—be sure that both shoulders are the same width. Backstitch at each shoulder seam. It is im-

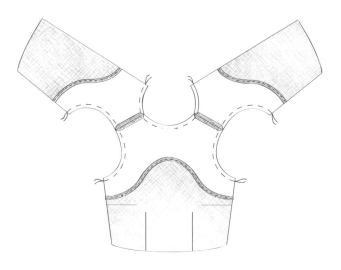

Turn the facing to the finished position by pulling the back garment sections through the shoulder. Press the garment edges, rolling the seam to the underside.

portant that the backstitching be done at the shoulder **seam line** rather than the shoulder edge because the shoulder seam allowance will be trimmed. Press, grade and clip the seam allowances, and turn the facings to the finished position.

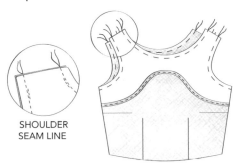

SHOULDER
SEAM LINE

Working on the inside, press the neck and armscye edges, rolling the seam to the facing side. Understitch these edges as far as you can go. Trim 3/8" from each shoulder seam.

TRIM

Pin the front and back shoulder, right sides together, leaving the facings free. Reach in from the back (between the facing and garment back) and pull the shoulder seams out between the back and the back facing. The front shoulder unit is now sandwiched between the back shoulder and the back facing.

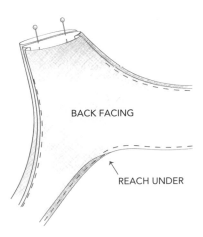

BACK FACING

REACH UNDER

Finger-press the seams and pin them so they match exactly. Stitch the shoulder seams around in a circle, taking a 1/4" seam.

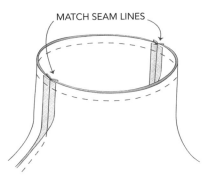

MATCH SEAM LINES

Pull the garment to the right side and press the shoulder area from the wrong side. You now have a nice, smooth finish with no lumpy shoulder seams that have been whipped together.

Shoulders narrower than 1 1/2" need a slightly different technique since they are very difficult to stitch in the circle.

Position the shoulders and prepare for stitching as described above, but stitch straight across all four layers of fabric.

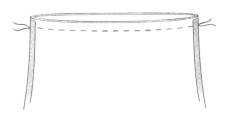

Make sure the shoulders are precisely the same width; otherwise you will have a "jog" at the seam when finished. Turn the garment to the finished position and press the shoulder area from the wrong side.

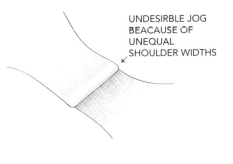

UNDESIRBLE JOG
BEACAUSE OF
UNEQUAL
SHOULDER WIDTHS

Sleeveless Garment With Collar: This is an excellent finish when a full or drop lining is used in a garment with a collar. If a lining is not wanted, use the combined neckline-armhole facing, as described previously.

Prepare the garment and lining (facing) by stitching and pressing open the shoulder seams. **Important**—be sure to backstitch where the seams cross, rather than at the edge of the fabric. Prepare and attach the collar and zipper according to the pattern instructions. Stitch and press the underarm seam of both the garment and lining (facing). The garment is now finished except for the armscye.

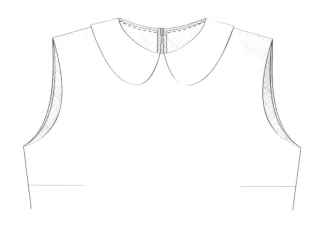

Trim armscye 3/8". Trim the lining (facing) armscye 1/2".

Arrange the garment and facing in the finished position, wrong sides together. Turn under a 1/4" seam allowance at the top of the shoulder and pin in place.

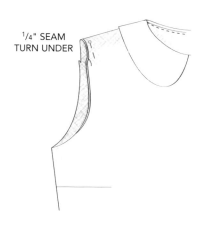

1/4" SEAM
TURN UNDER

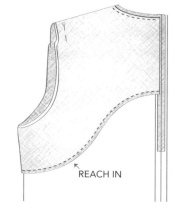

REACH IN

Reach in from the back between the garment and lining (facing), grab the pinned seam allowance at the shoulder, and pull to the wrong side. Don't let the pin fall out while doing this, or you may twist the pieces incorrectly.

|Begin stitching at the shoulder, taking a 1/4" seam, making sure the cut edges of the garment and lining (facing) are kept even. Continue stitching around the armscye, lining up the underarm seams. This looks like a mess while you are doing it, but take heart—it will all turn out in the end.

Clip the curved areas, understitch if desired, and press the armscye edges for a neat finish.

FACING TIPS

Faced Facings

The technique of "facing the facing" gives a custom inside finish to your garments. It is a good way to handle fabrics that fray easily.

Cut the facing pieces from the fashion fabric, and then cut another set of facing pieces from a color-matched, lightweight fabric such as batiste or organza.

For an armhole facing, join both the fashion fabric and facing fabric into a circle. Trim and press open the seams. Pin the two facings right sides together, and stitch the outer edge with a 1/4" seam. Press, grade and clip the seam allowance.

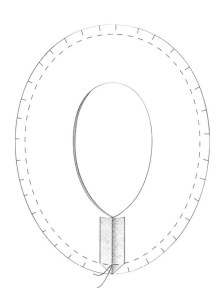

Turn the facing right side out. Press again, and edge-stitch.

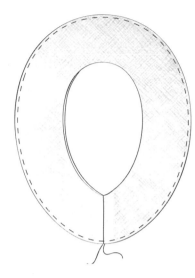

Now apply this "faced facing" to the garment's edge in the normal manner. Other facings, such as neckline and sleeve facings can be handled using this technique.

Facing Sheers

Garments made of sheer fabrics present some problems when it comes to facings. They always show through to the right side, which isn't very attractive. You can handle this problem in several ways.

Underline the garment so that the facings won't show through, or use a drop-lining to eliminate the facings entirely. However, these methods aren't practical if you want to retain the sheer look.

The neckline and armhole edges that require facings can be finished with matching or contrasting bias binding.

If you have to use a facing, use the "faced-facing" technique. This looks the best. If your sheer fabric is printed, use a solid-color fabric to face the facing so the print doesn't show through to the right side. For a perfect zipper finish, use the technique shown in Chapter 6 for center slot zippers or lapped zippers.

Waistline Facings

Waistline facings can be used on skirts and pants instead of a waistband finish. If one always wears over-blouses, or has a short waist, the faced waistline is usually more comfortable to wear, and it also eliminates the problem of rolling waistbands.

Cut the waistline facing pieces as described in the first part of this section.

A full lining (drop lining) can also take the place of waistline facings for a skirt. Apply the lining as for the facing, hand-stitching around the zipper opening as explained in Chapter 6, Zippers. Understitch or topstitch the waist edge to hold the lining in place.

Facing Thick Fabrics

A lightweight fabric should be used for facings when your fashion fabric is thick. This reduces bulk in the seam areas and along the facing edges. Color-match the facing fabric to the fashion fabric.

Back Facings on Ready-To-Wear

Many ready-to-wear garments have an extra wide back facing extending down 12" or more from the neckline. This is done to give the garment "hanger appeal," but wide facings are a bother when the garment is worn. They always seem to flip to the outside.

Solve this problem by trimming the facing to 2 1/2" and using one of the clean-finish methods to finish the cut edge.

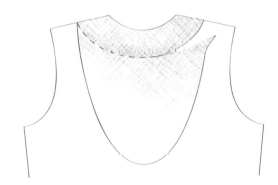

Short of Fabric

Facings can be cut on the cross-grain rather than the length-wise grain if it will save fabric needed for something else.

From the earliest of days, some form of pins and needles has been used. Until the 18th century, they were so precious a possession that the loss of a needle was a disaster to an entire household. In medieval days, some needles had a kink placed halfway between the point and eye to prevent the needle from dropping out of the material and becoming lost. Pins and needles could be bought only at provincial fairs and markets or from traveling peddlers whose visits were infrequent. The fairs were attended by the wealthy and common people alike. But today we sometimes don't even bother to pick up a dropped pin or needle—let the vacuum cleaner do it!

The first pins may have been split from the spine of bird feathers, as the Latin root word *pinna* means feather. Certainly, spikes, thorns and fish bones were used as early pins. The Egyptians used small fish bones to secure the eyes of the dead. A type of lace called "bone lace" was so named because the pins used to make it were made of fish and chicken bones.

Pins were once made by filing fine wire to a point and twisting a finer wire around the opposite end to form the head. These heads often fell off, and the rough ends would snag the material. A new type of pin was sought, and the French and Germans developed the art of wire-drawing, which was the basis of the modern pin. In 1797 pins with solid heads were being manufactured and came into general use.

In the 14th century pins were very expensive; they were considered appropriate gifts for a man to give to his sweetheart. "I'll give you a paper of pins, cause that's the way that love begins," is the first line of a folk song that was written around the 15th century. In France their sale was restricted by rules of the needlemakers' trade guilds. No pinmaker could have more than one shop for the sale of pins, except on New Year's Eve day, when all merchants were allowed to sell pins. It was the custom for a merchant to give a gift of pins or the money with which to buy them upon the completion of a sale: hence, the word "pinmoney."

To protect the local industry, in 1483 Richard III prohibited the importation of pins, and Englishmen had to use the inferior iron wire pins that were made domestically. Henry VIII's wife, Catherine Howard, was allowed to introduce the fine brass pins that were then made in France. During Elizabeth's reign, a well-filled pin cushion was a necessity, as many garments were literally pinned together when worn.

In the Stone Age, sharp awls were used to puncture holes in skins, which were then "sewn" together with sinews. This "sewing" was used for many kinds of packages that had to be covered with an outer layer of cloth or skin for purposes of storage and transportation. When woven cloth was invented, a fine, thin needle with an eye could be used, and sinews were replaced by spun thread.

Supposedly the Chinese invented the steel needle to sew their fine silk fabrics. The steel needle was carried by traders to Damascus, which was a famous steel center. From there, the Moors brought needles to Spain. References in history call a steel needle a "Spanish Needle." Catherine of Aragon must have brought these steel needles with her when she came to England to marry Henry VIII, as she was noted for her fine needlework.

Commemorative pincushions, c. 1817. Made of cardboard, covered with printed silk, these were given as souvenirs at the death of Caroline (George III's granddaughter) in 1817. Around the pincushion are mourning pins made from iron and coated with black enamel. The heads are bits of coiled wire.

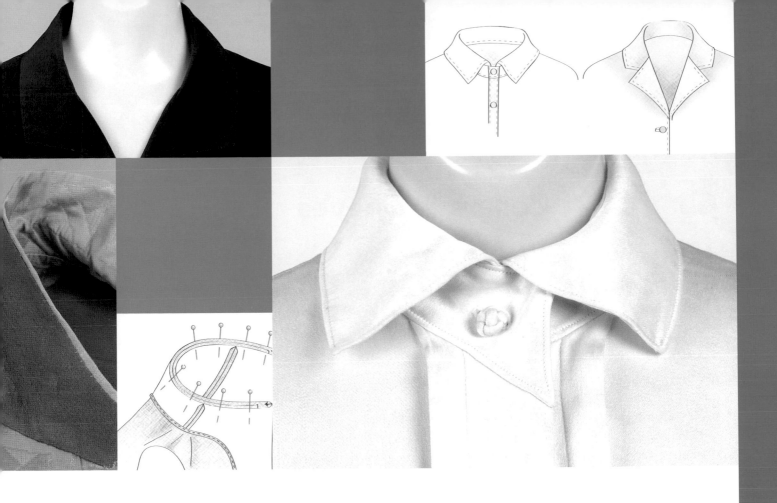

COLLARS & SLEEVES

4

Chapter 4: Collars & Sleeves

PERFECT COLLARS AND SLEEVES

don't just happen. They are the result of careful work at each stage of construction and a complete understanding of how they work. Professional-quality garment construction always shows up in the finished collar.

COLLARS

A well-made collar has the following characteristics: Each side of the collar is identical in size and shape; the collar fits smoothly around the back of the neck, hiding the neckline seam; the collar points lie flat against the garment; the under-collar doesn't show; and the collar either hugs the neck or stands away, as designed. If your finished collars don't always fit this description, then you can benefit from the techniques given in this section.

ANATOMY OF A COLLAR

Before we go much further, it might be a good idea if we clarify the various collar terms that will be used.

Stand: The section of collar that stands up around the neck. Not all collars have a stand and not all stands are of the same width. Some are cut as part of the collar and some are cut separately.

Fall: The collar section that folds over the stand. It must be wider than the stand in order to cover the neckline seam.

Roll Line: The line on which the fall rolls over the stand.

Outside Edge: The finished edge of the collar.

Neck Edge: The edge of the collar that is sewn to the garment's neck edge.

BASIC COLLAR STYLES

Even though you see many different collars on garments and patterns, there are just three basic collar styles. The various looks are achieved by size and shape changes and small details. If you learn how to properly construct the three basic styles, you can give any collar a custom fit and finish.

The three basic collar styles are: the flat collar, the partial roll, and the full-roll collar. Each one is used for a specific fashion look, and fits the body differently.

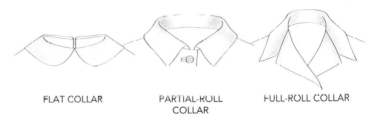

FLAT COLLAR   PARTIAL-ROLL COLLAR   FULL-ROLL COLLAR

Flat Collar

The flat collar or Puritan collar has a very deep curve at the neck edge. In fact, it will almost match the neckline curve of the garment. It lies flat against the body with just a slight roll up the neck. It can be cut in many shapes and sizes.

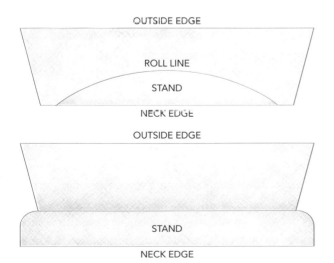

Since the flat collar has no stand, it is always applied with a full neck facing so that the neckline seam allowance can be pressed down into the garment. If the collar and neckline seam allowances are allowed to go up inside the collar (the technique of finishing without a facing), the seam allowances will interfere with the smooth roll at the neck edge.

The facing can be either a full fitted facing or a strip of bias-cut fabric. Since the full width of a flat collar lies against the garment, you can secure the lower edge of a bias-cut facing by machine and not have to worry about the stitches showing.

Partial-Roll Collar

The partial-roll collar has a slight curve to the neck edge. It rolls higher up the neck than a flat collar, but the stand is always shorter than the fall. The size of the collar and shape of the outside edge can be varied to give different looks.

A partial-roll collar can be applied with or without facing. The facing is used when the stand is not high enough to allow for turned-up neckline seam allowances.

Full-Roll Collar

The full-roll collar comes in two styles: the straight full-roll collar, which can have the stand cut as one with the collar or as a separate piece, and the convertible full-roll collar, which will fit more snugly around the neck than the straight collar.

The neck edge of the full-roll collar is either straight or convex. Straight full-roll collars are the kind used on shirts and blouses. The convertible full-roll collar has a convex neck edge and is the style used on tailored suits and jackets with turn-back lapels.

Note: *Because of the shape, it is easy to mistake the neck edge for the outer edge on a convertible full-roll collar. Keep this in mind as you apply the collar to the garment.*

Full-roll collars, either straight or convertible, can be applied without facings because the stand is high

enough to allow the neckline seam allowances to be turned up into the collar.

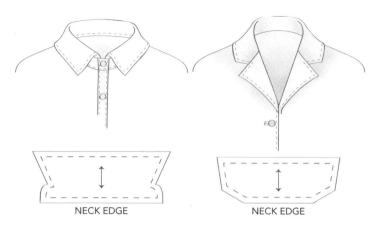

NECK EDGE   NECK EDGE

The stand-up or mandarin collar and the turtleneck collar are modifications of a full-roll collar; the fall has been completely removed and only the stand remains. Shawl collars can be made from either a full- or partial-roll collar.

UPPER AND UNDER COLLARS

Each collar consists of an upper and under collar. The upper collar is the piece that shows on the finished garment and the under collar acts as a facing.

The under collar should always be smaller than the upper collar for two reasons. First, it helps the collar roll smoothly and stay in its proper position; second, it prevents the under collar from showing around the edges of the finished collar.

Patterns featuring some type of flat or partial-roll collar usually give just one pattern piece that is used for both the upper and under collar. The under collar is made slightly smaller during the stitching process.

Patterns featuring a full-roll collar usually have separate pattern pieces for the upper and under collar. If you compare the two pieces you will see that the under collar is indeed smaller. This size difference provides the nice roll that is so important to this collar style.

The amount of size difference between the upper and under collar is governed by the thickness of the garment fabric. Thick fabrics require a greater difference than thin fabrics. Patterns are designed with average fabrics in mind, so you may have to increase the width of the upper collar by 1/4" to 3/8", depending on the fabric thickness. Make this change at the outer edge of the upper collar. Do not trim the outer edge of the under collar; this will affect the stand/fall relationship and can result in the neckline seam showing around the back of the neck.

The under-collar pattern for a convertible full-roll collar is cut on the bias, unless a double knit fabric is used. Under collars cut from double knit fabric should be cut across the stretch; the center back seam can be eliminated. Bias-cut under collars are seamed at the center back so that the grain runs the same way on each end of the collar. This ensures that the ends of the collar are identical in shape after they have been stitched.

COLLAR CONSTRUCTION

As stated above, proper construction techniques are the key to perfect collars. Each step should be carefully done, following the instructions given below.

Interfacing

Interfacing adds the shape and body so necessary to a perfect collar. Choose the style and weight of interfacing that complements your fashion fabric. Fusible interfacings are a good choice for collars because they allow you to trim away the seam allowances, thus reducing bulk. Nonwoven interfacings can also be used, if desired.

Collar interfacing should be applied to the wrong side of the upper collar, except for collars on tailored coats and jackets. This is contrary to many interfacing instructions, but it makes for a nicer collar finish because the interfacing prevents the seam allowances from "shadowing through" on the right side of the finished collar. This is especially important on lightweight fabrics.

The convertible full-roll collar, used on tailored jackets and coats, should have the interfacing applied to the under collar in order to give more support to the stand. Sometimes an extra piece of interfacing is applied to the stand area only, for greater firmness. If the under collar is going to be applied by hand, and a fusible interfacing is being used, trim away the seam allowance plus an extra 1/8" before fusing the interfacing in place. This ensures that the interfacing will not be visible around the edge of the collar after it has been stitched in place.

The grain line or direction of stretch on the collar interfacing affects the way the collar rolls. Woven interfacings should be cut with the collar on the lengthwise grain for a sharp crease along the roll line, and on the bias for a softer roll. Nonwoven interfacings should be cut with

the stretch running the length of the collar for a soft roll line, and on the lengthwise grain for a sharper crease. Collar interfacing for knit fabrics should be cut across the stretch or on the bias, in order to preserve the stretch of the fabric and give a soft roll.

To use an Ultrasuede under collar in Chapter 8 for construction.

Collars that have separate stands should have the outer stand piece interfaced. For even more support, interface both the inside and outside stand piece.

Fusible Interfacing Application: Cut the interfacing using the collar pattern. Trim away all seam allowances and the corners, as illustrated. Fuse in place, carefully following the instructions for your particular brand of interfacing.

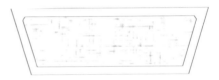

Fuse an extra patch of interfacing to the collar points. This helps keep them neat and flat.

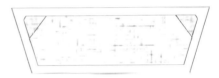

Nonfusible Interfacing Application: Cut the interfacing using the collar pattern. Trim only the corners, and machine-stitch the interfacing to the collar seam allowance. Stitch just 1/8" outside the given seam line. Trim the interfacing close to the machine stitching.

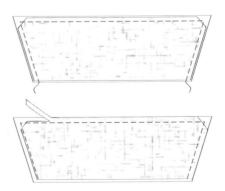

Stitching

Pin the upper and under collar pieces together, right side to right side.

Collars that have the upper and under collar cut from the same pattern should be pinned with the under collar extending out beyond the upper collar by about 1/8". This makes the under collar smaller after the stitching has been completed.

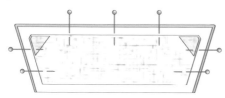

Collars with a separate upper and under collar should be pinned so that the edges are even. Ease the upper collar to fit, since it was cut slightly larger.

Stitch on the upper collar side, and hold the collar pieces taut while stitching so that the upper collar doesn't pucker.

Shorten the stitch length and take one or two diagonal stitches across the collar points. This diagonal stitching provides turning room and helps make fine collar points. The length of the diagonal is governed by the fabric thickness. Thick fabrics need more turning room than thin fabrics. The short stitch length at the points strengthens that area and allows you to trim the seam closely without having it fray away when you turn the points. Use a short stitch length on collar curves and on other detailed shapes.

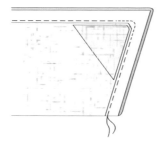

Trimming

Trim the collar seam allowance to approximately 1/4". Grade seam allowances so that the upper collar seam

allowance is longest. This can be easily accomplished by holding the scissors at an acute angle so that a beveled cut is made.

Trim the points, as shown, so that they miter neatly when turned. Do not trim loosely woven fabrics too close to the stitching or the seam allowance will fray away before you get the point turned.

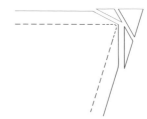

Trim curves with pinking shears. This eliminates the need for notching and clipping.

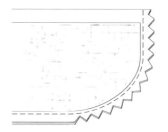

Pressing

Steam-press the collar flat after trimming the seams but before turning it to the right side to set the stitching and give a more professional look to the collar when finished. Now, press the collar seams open, using either a point presser or the following method.

With the under collar up, press open the seam allowances, as shown.

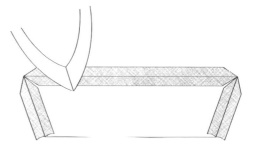

Now press both seam allowances over to the under-collar side. This helps to set the edge.

Understitch the long collar edge if you are not going to topstitch the finished collar. This gives a hard edge on which to turn.

Finishing

Turn the collar to the right side; finger-press the edges, rolling the seam to the under-collar side. Use a point-turner or threaded needle to coax the points out fully. Do not use scissors; the points can very easily make a hole in the fabric.

Steam-press the collar edges so the seam rolls to the under-collar side. This makes sure the under collar doesn't peek through to the right side. Bulky or resilient fabrics, such as wool and polyesters, will get a flatter edge if a "clapper" is used.

When working with a partial-roll or one-piece full-roll collar, roll them over your hand into their finished position then place some pins along the roll line. The under collar will extend a little below the neck edge of the upper collar. Trim the under collar until it is even with the upper collar. This shortens the under collar so it will stay properly positioned. It also helps to build in the collar roll.

Collar With Separate Stand

The upper part of this type of collar is constructed according to the above instructions. Apply the separate stand as directed below.

Sandwich the upper-collar portion between the two stand pieces; the interfaced, outside stand piece should be against the under collar. Match up construction marks, making sure equal amounts of stand extend beyond both sides of the collar. Stitch as indicated, remembering to shorten the stitch length as you go around the curve of the stand.

Trim the seam allowances, pinking the curves; turn to the right side and press. The seam on each end of the stand should not be rolled to the underside; keep it on the edge.

TOPSTITCHING

Topstitching is an attractive detail used on many collars. It can be done with a matching or contrasting color, using either regular or buttonhole thread.

Various looks can be given to a collar just by using different topstitching patterns. See topstitching in Chapter 2.

Collars are topstitched either before they are applied to the garment or after, depending on the type of collar used for the garment.

- Flat and partial-roll collars that have full or front facings are topstitched before they are applied to the garment's neck edge.

- Partial-roll and full-roll collars without front facings, using either the wrap or double-stitched method of application, are topstitched after the collar has been applied.

- The convertible full-roll collar, even though it has a front facing, is also topstitched after the collar has been applied.

APPLICATION TECHNIQUES

There are quite a few methods of applying a collar to the garment's neck edge. The method you use is determined by the type of collar and whether a front facing is given.

Prepare the garment for the collar by stitching and pressing the shoulder seams. Stay-stitch the garment's neck edge and clip to the stitching at regular intervals so that the neckline can straighten out to match the neck edge of the collar.

Collars With Facings

Collars with neckline facings are attached to the garment using the "sandwich" method; the collar is sandwiched between the garment and facing. This technique can be used for both of the collar styles shown below.

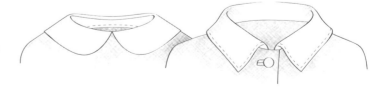

Flat collars can use a full, fitted neckline facing, while partial and full-roll collars should have just the front faced. Directions are given for both finishes.

Fully Faced Collars: Stitch and press the facing shoulder seam and clean-finish the free edge of the facing. A bias strip, instead of a full, fitted facing is sometimes used around necklines that have center-back zippers. The construction technique is the same as for the full facing.

Pin the collar to the neck edge, making sure the distance between the collar edge and the front edge of the garment is the same on both sides. Position the facing over the collar so all the neckline edges are even. The collar will be sandwiched in between the garment and facing. Check again to make sure the collar edges are of equal distance from the front edge of the garment.

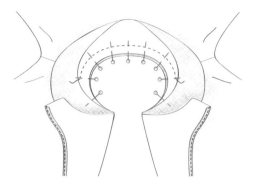

Fold the facing back over the collar so that it is sandwiched in between the garment and the facing. Pin in place. Check to make sure the same amount of fabric extends beyond the collar edge on each side of the collar. Adjust the facing folds if necessary. Stitch each side of the collar from front to back.

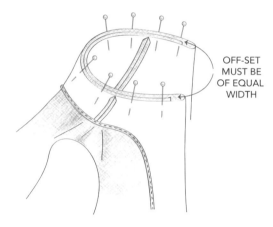

OFF-SET MUST BE OF EQUAL WIDTH

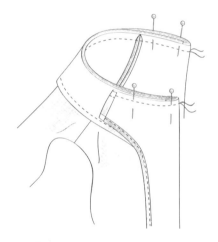

Stitch the collar to the garment, starting at each front edge, joining the stitching at the center back. Collars should **always** be stitched in this manner so that drag doesn't accumulate around the neckline and distort the way the collar lies in the seam.

Front-Faced Collars: Garments with a partial-roll or full-roll collar sometimes have just the front of the neckline faced. The seam allowances at the back of the neck are turned up into the collar and the open seam at the back of the neck is closed by hand. The free edge of the facing should be clean-finished before applying the collar.

Pin and stitch the under collar only to the neck edge, starting and ending about 1" in front of each shoulder seam.

Collars with separate or cut-on stands should be positioned so that their edges are **precisely** on the front edge of the garment. The facing should fold back tightly over the collar edges.

Make sure the facing is pulled snugly around the collar edges when stitching; otherwise you will get a "stair-step" finish.

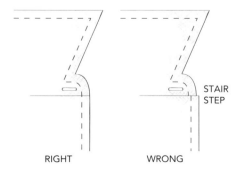

STAIR STEP

RIGHT   WRONG

Trim the neckline seam allowances; turn the facing to the inside and press the seam allowances up into the collar, around the back of the neck.

Clip the upper collar to the seam line, at the shoulder seams. Turn under the seam allowance and close the remaining open seam by hand or machine.

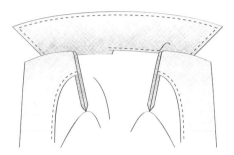

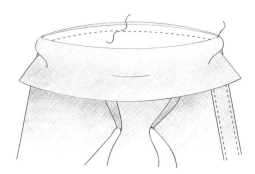

Mark the location of the shoulder seams on the neck edge of the upper collar with small clips.

A man's knit shirt will use a slightly different finishing technique. Press both collar and back neckline seam allowance down into the garment and hold in place with a line of topstitching 1/8" from the neckline seam. Trim away excess seam allowance.

Collars Without Facings

Many shirts and casual jackets have stitched-on front bands and no neckline facings. The accompanying collar style always has a stand, either cut-on or separate. There are two techniques that can be used to apply these types of collars.

The "wrap" method works best for collars with cut-on stands. The double-stitched method is more suitable for collars with separate stands.

Either of these collar methods makes a finish that allows the wrong side of the fabric to show when the shirt or jacket is unbuttoned at the neckline. Fabrics with very obvious wrong sides will not be as attractive as fabrics with identical right and wrong sides. Keep this in mind when selecting your fabric and pattern.

Prepare the garment by stitching and pressing the shoulder seams. Apply the front band and finish the other side of the garment front as directed in the pattern.

Wrap Method: Pin and stitch the under collar only to the neck edge, right sides together. The seam at the front edge of the collar should be precisely at the front edge of garments and the seam allowance should be pressed open. Stitch from front to back on both sides of the collar.

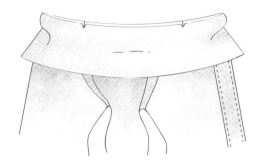

Now wrap the upper collar snugly around the front edge of the garment so that the right side of the upper collar is against the wrong side of the shirt. Pin in place as far as the shoulder seam, if possible, matching the clips with the seam. Check inside to make sure nothing is folded over or caught where it shouldn't be.

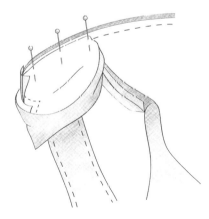

Stitch each side of the collar as far as you can go, making sure you keep the front edge wrapped snugly and the collar seam pressed open in order to avoid a "stair-step" finish. Always stitch both sides from front to back, sewing just below the first stitching line so that it will be covered when the collar is finished. Trim the seam allowance.

Clip the upper collar to the seam line at the point where the stitching ends. Turn under the remainder of the seam allowance and close the seam by hand.

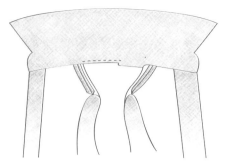

Double-Stitched Method: This application can be used with any partial-roll or full-roll collar. However, it is almost a "must" for collars with separate stands or the popular stand-up type of shirt band. You need a certain amount of maneuvering room to use the wrap method, and many stands and shirt bands are not wide enough to provide it.

The collar is constructed according to previous instructions with the following exception.

Press under and trim the neck-edge seam allowance of the outside stand or under collar before you stitch the two layers of stand or collar together.

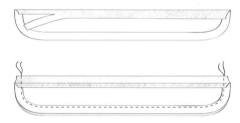

Pin the inside stand piece or the upper collar to the wrong side of the neck edge. Position the collar so that it is a scant 1/16" from the front edges. Start stitching on each side of the collar 1/8" less wide than the given seam width. Trim the seam allowance and press it up into the collar stand.

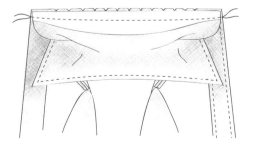

Fold the collar over and pin in the finished position around the neck, making sure the stitching line is covered on the right side. At each front edge, push the seam allowance up into the collar 1/8". Make sure the edge of the garment "fills" the collar all the way out to the edge. Pin in place. Topstitch the lower edge of the collar, stitching from front to back on each side.

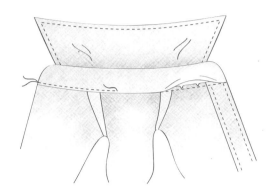

Note: *If you don't want topstitching around the collar, you can apply it in reverse and do the second stitching procedure by hand on the inside neck edge. Just pin and stitch the outer band or under collar to the right side of the neck edge to begin with.*

COLLAR TIPS

Occasionally you will find a nice ready-made garment that has the problem of "under-collar peek-a-boo." This happens quite often on shawl-collared coats. Eliminate the problem by taking the needed-size tuck along the fold of the under collar and slipstitching it in place by hand. This narrows the undercollar enought so that the upper collar will cover it.

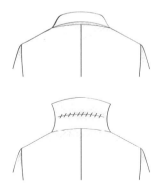

Collar and lapel points, on garments with turned-back lapels, are cut larger than the matching collar or garment piece. This helps these points lie flat against the body after they have been stitched and turned. A good way to control this extra size is to fold the point along the diagonal, right sides together; weave a needle along the fold, as shown. This pin takes up and controls the ease while you stitch the collar point to its facing.

Collars with a separate stand can be changed to a collar with a cut-on stand by overlapping the collar and stand pattern piece until the seam lines match. Tape or pin in place and use this modified pattern to cut the collar.

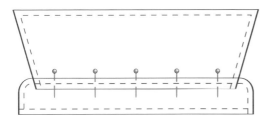

CUTTING ROUND AND V-NECKLINES

Care must be taken when cutting round and V-necklines so that the round neck will look round and the V-neck will look like a V when the garment is finished. It is very easy to give a little point to round necks and make V necks look round if you don't follow the correct cutting procedure.

Always cut V necks with a slight outward curve rather than just a straight line. V-necks tend to pull away from the center front when worn and the curved line now retains the proper shape of the V. Low V-necks should be cut with an exaggerated V at the point; otherwise they will spread apart when worn and become a bit revealing.

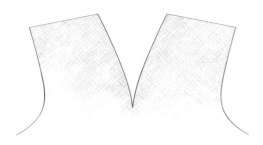

When cutting a deep V, square off the shoulder line about 1/4" at the neck edge only. This makes the garment hug the body rather than fall away from it. Another way to make the V-neck hug the body better is to cut the shoulder 1/4" wider at the neck edge and 1/4" narrower at the shoulder. The shoulder length remains the same, but the garment will fit better.

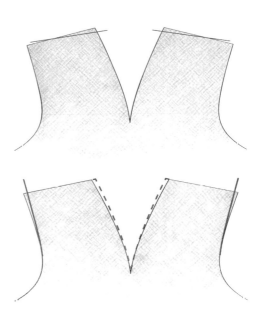

Cut V-neck facings 1/8" smaller at the center fold so that the facing is 1/4" narrower than the garment. Ease the V-neck to fit the facing and you will get a V-neck that stays snug against your body rather than one that gaps.

Always square off the pattern for $1/2''$ at the center front or center back when cutting round or scoop necklines. This eliminates the little dip you so often see on self-cut necklines.

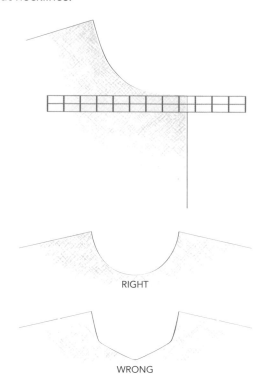

RIGHT

WRONG

Low-cut round necklines should have the shoulder squared off also. This helps keep the garment against the body rather than gapping away from your bustline.

A length of narrow elastic cut to fit comfortably around the rib cage can be attached to low-necked gowns to keep them in place. Sew a hook and eye at the ends of the elastic and attach the center of the elastic to the center-front seam of the neckline facing. Hook the elastic before you zip up the garment and dance and party in comfort.

SLEEVES

Different sleeve styles make up a large part of the fashion picture. The variety of sleeve shapes is large, and the various details that can be used to change the basic look seem endless. Sleeves are an important part of any garment, and your construction techniques should be flawless so that the custom look you want is reflected in the sleeves.

A perfectly made sleeve is a credit to your sewing ability, whether you use a simple short sleeve or a tailored sleeve, complete with placket, cuff and button. Once you have mastered the basic sleeve techniques, you can then improvise and add designer sleeve details to your wardrobe of custom clothes.

The information contained in this section is to help you sew the sleeve into the garment correctly. Construction details for traditional sleeve vent and cuff styles are also given. This information will help you make perfectly finished sleeves on every garment.

BASIC SLEEVE STYLES

There are three basic sleeve styles in the fashion world: the set-in sleeve, the raglan sleeve and the kimono sleeve. Each basic style has variations, which can change the look quite a bit. Set-in sleeves can have fullness added to the sleeve cap for a puffed finish. The raglan sleeve can be made from one piece of fabric, with or without a shoulder dart, or from two pieces of fabric with a seam down the middle of the sleeve. A gusset can be added to a kimono sleeve, or the width at the underarm can be extended to make a dolman sleeve. There are some other variations of these sleeves, but the basics remain the same.

Raglan and kimono-style sleeves are quite easy to construct. Most sewing problems appear with the set-in sleeve. Before we start solving construction problems, let's look at some set-in sleeve patterns and compare their shapes and functions.

Set-In Sleeves

There are two basic sleeve-cap shapes for a set-in sleeve. Each one was designed for a specific purpose, and these should be understood so that you can use each shape where it functions best.

The first shape is the tailored, set-in sleeve. It has enough height in the sleeve cap so that it fits in the armscye without any wrinkles. The shape below the sleeve cap will vary with the sleeve style.

The second set-in sleeve shape is called the shirt-sleeve. It has a very shallow cap that allows for greater freedom of movement. The sleeve is usually cut wider than the tailored set-in sleeve. Vertical folds will appear on this sleeve when it is worn.

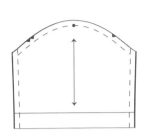 

The shirtsleeve should be used only for casual dress, sport and knit T–shirts. While it provides plenty of room for body movement, it doesn't give the slim, tailored fit that is desirable in most other garments. The tailored set-in sleeve gives a more fitted look, though it loses some of the wearing ease in the process.

All this is academic if you use and follow only printed patterns, since they will have the sleeve shape needed for that particular style. However, if you begin to do some style changes or designing on your own, you should know just how the two set-in sleeves will affect the look and feel of the finished garment.

SLEEVE PROBLEMS

The most common sleeve construction problems exist with set-in sleeves. Most of these problems occur in the sleeve cap. Either too much ease is allowed, or the ease is not distributed evenly when sewing the sleeve into the armscye. Other problems result from sleeves that are too narrow for the arm, incorrect armscye size and sleeves that don't hang properly. Solutions to all these problems are given below.

Sleeve-Cap Ease

Sleeve-cap problems result when the pattern includes too much ease or the chosen fashion fabric is not supple enough to handle the allowed ease. Real and fake leathers, hard-finished, firmly woven fabrics such as denim or permanent press fabrics, and most knits are fabrics that fit in this category.

Real and fake leathers, such as synthetic Ultrasuede, Ultraleather and vinyl need very little sleeve-cap ease because of their nonsupple nature. It is necessary to reduce the sleeve-cap ease to only **one inch** of ease to eliminate "no-no" puckers at the sleeve cap. Neither Ultraleather nor Ultrasuede will ease, so the ease **must** be taken out of the pattern.

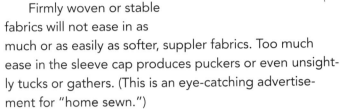

Firmly woven or stable fabrics will not ease in as much or as easily as softer, suppler fabrics. Too much ease in the sleeve cap produces puckers or even unsightly tucks or gathers. (This is an eye-catching advertisement for "home sewn.")

Knits have ease problems for two reasons. First, they are usually made of synthetic fibers, which are not as supple as natural fibers; second, they have quite a dense construction, which makes them difficult to compress or ease in. Knits also need less cap ease because the fabric itself has built-in ease. The amount of ease given in most patterns, unless they are designed for knits only, is usually too much.

The recommended amount of sleeve-cap ease for various fabrics is:

- 1 1/2" ease for supple fabrics.

- 1" ease for knits, firm-woven fabrics, permanent press, and real or fake leathers.

Many jacket patterns have 2" of ease, which is difficult to control and often ends up with a "puckered sleeve" look. Remember, you may change the pattern. (You paid for it—so do what you wish!)

Check the sleeve-cap ease on your paper pattern before cutting the fashion fabric. If you make a habit of this, you will soon develop a feel for the amount of ease each type of fabric can handle, and you won't run into problems when setting the sleeve into the armscye. Making ease alterations on the paper pattern is much easier and more accurate than trying to make them on an already cutout sleeve.

Determine the pattern ease allowance by overlapping the front and back pattern pieces until the shoulder seams line up; pin in place. "Walk" a tape measure around the armscye seam line, from underarm seam to underarm seam. This is easy to do if you place the tape measure on edge. Make a note of this measurement.

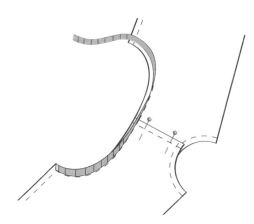

Now measure the sleeve **seam line** from underarm seam to underarm seam, with the tape measure on edge. The difference between the two measurements is the allowed sleeve-cap ease.

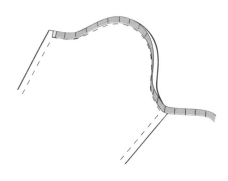

Also measure the garment's armscye from notch to notch.

Cut the sleeve apart where the armscye and underarm seam meet. Make two to four slashes in the sleeve cap as shown, use one slash for each 1/4" of ease you need to remove.

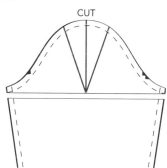

CUT

Overlap each slash up to 1/4" at **the seam line** and pin. Re-check the sleeve measurement and adjust the overlaps until you have the amount of ease you want. Tape the slashes in place; tape the sleeve back together. When the sleeve cap is taped back onto the sleeve pattern, the cap will overlap about 3/8" to 1/2" at the center, as the pattern must lie flat. This slight reduction of sleeve-cap height is good for stiff fabrics, otherwise the sleeve will have a puffed look. Use the altered pattern to cut the fashion fabric.

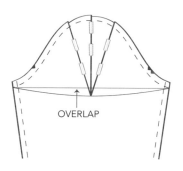

OVERLAP

Note: *Sleeve-lining pattern pieces should be altered the same as the garment sleeve pattern.*

When there is too much ease in the sleeve cap, the usual solution is to cut down the top of the sleeve cap. However, if too much is removed at the cap, the height of the cap is changed so much that you will end up with a shirt sleeve rather than a tailored sleeve.

Setting-In Sleeves

Sometimes sleeve-cap problems aren't really the result of too much ease; they are caused by the inability to handle the ease correctly. If the ease isn't evenly distributed around the cap, then puckers or tucks will result, and the sleeve will not hang correctly.

The easiest method to use for setting the sleeve into the armscye is to easestitch around the sleeve cap between the notches. Stitch just outside the given seam line. This stitching usually eases up the sleeve cap the right amount. However, some fabric will ease more than others. If you find the sleeve cap has become too small, "break" a few threads at regular intervals. If the cap is too large, pull up on the bobbin thread at regular intervals until you get the right amount of ease.

When basting a sleeve into a jacket, try an English tailoring technique. Hold the jacket and sleeve over the fingers while basting. This is the way it will be worn and it is easier to adjust the ease over the **outside** curve rather than in an inside curve.

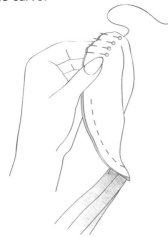

Stitch and press the sleeve underarm seam, and pin the sleeve into the armscye, matching up the construction marks. Hold the ease in position by placing pins every 1/2" to 3/4" around the sleeve-cap. Insert the pins right at the seam line. This is important for good ease control.

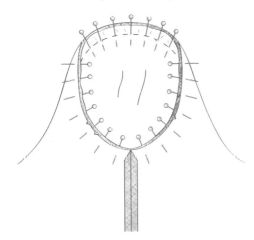

To control sleeve-cap ease on stiff or densely woven fabrics such as Ultrasuede, denim or corduroy, use a strip of 1/4"-wide Seams Great as an "ease strip." Measure the garment's arm-scye from notch to notch as shown.

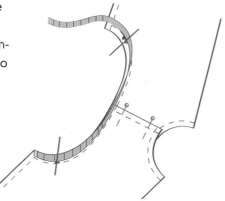

Cut Seams Great 1" longer than this measurement. (The extra 1" gives a 1/2" handle to hold onto at each end of the ease strip.) Stretch and stitch the ease strip to the sleeve cap just inside the seam allowance so the stitches won't show. Now the sleeve can be stitched into the garment without telltale puckers that ruin the smooth look that you want. The ease strip controls the ease in the dense fabric that cannot be easestitched. No need to trim away the ease strip as it helps fill in the sleeve-cap area.

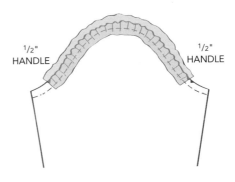

1/2"
HANDLE

1/2"
HANDLE

If you have a free-arm machine, place the sleeve over the free arm so that the sleeve is on the bottom and the garment is on the top. If your machine doesn't have a free arm, stitch with the sleeve on top and the garment on the bottom.

Start the stitching at one notch; go all around the sleeve, past the starting point, and end at the second notch. This gives you a double line of stitching in the underarm area for strength. Trim the seam allowance to 1/4" between the notches, and to 3/8" around the top of the sleeve.

Optional Method

There is another method of setting in sleeves that can be used for sleeves with a minimum amount of ease. The sleeve is sewn to the armscye **before** any of the underarm seams are stitched.

Easestitch the sleeve cap and pin the sleeve into the armscye, matching up construction marks. Start stitching at the notch and go around the sleeve to the other notch. Stitch and press the underarm seam of the garment and sleeve.

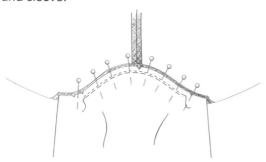

Complete the seam in the underarm area. Trim the seam allowance to 1/4" and zigzag or double-stitch it.

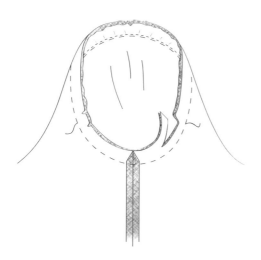

This method of stitching the underarm seam of the sleeve and garment is better than stitching the seam in one operation. It is less apt to pull out and gives a better fit because it follows the body contour.

Sleeve Width

Patterns are designed for an average-sized figure. If you have extra thin or heavy arms you may find that you have to alter the sleeve width. Sleeves that are too wide will sag and wrinkle, while sleeves that are too narrow will bind and pull. If you suspect any of the following sleeve problems, it is advisable to make it up in muslin

first to check the pattern fit. It is much easier to make alterations **before** the fashion fabric is cut.

Determine how much should be removed by pinning a lengthwise fold down the length of the sleeve. Allow enough ease for wearing comfort and to allow your hand to slip through the bottom of the sleeve.

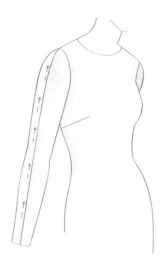

Make the same-size tuck along the lengthwise grain of the paper pattern. Use this new pattern to recut the sleeve. This alteration also reduces the sleeve-cap ease. Compare the altered sleeve with the armscye measurement to make sure you have enough ease. Too little ease will cause binding in the upper sleeve.

Determine how much extra width is needed in the sleeve by cutting the muslin sleeve open along the length, as illustrated. Allow the cut to spread as much as necessary and fill in the gap with a piece of fabric, pinned in place. Sometimes you will have to release the stitching at the sleeve cap and add extra fabric at the top of the sleeve as well.

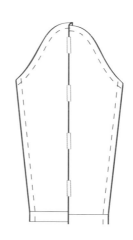
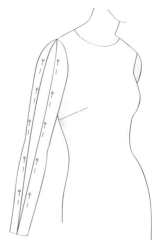

Slash the paper pattern down the center of the sleeve and out to each underarm point. Spread as needed and patch the slash with paper. Use this new pattern to cut the sleeves.

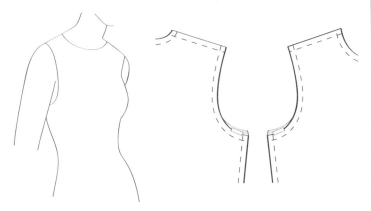

Armscye Size

A very important part of a well-fitting garment is the correct armscye size. Many people do not realize just how critical this is for a perfect fit. Perhaps you have heard that you should select your pattern size by the armscye fit rather than by the bust measurements. There is a great deal of truth to this statement, but when there is a great discrepancy between the armscye size and the bust measurement, it is probably better to buy the pattern by the bust size and adjust the armscye size. An armscye that is too small will give an uncomfortably tight fit. Armscyes that are too large will cause the sleeve to bind and restrict movement. Test for and correct this problem in muslin.

The sleeve should finish 1" below the armpit. A tight armscye will be higher than this and needs to be cut down. Alter the paper pattern the required amount. Remember that you are concerned with the fit at the **seam line**, not the cut edge of the garment. **Note:** *Tennis players or people engaged in similar sports sometimes need their serving arm's armscye cut lower in order to accommodate the extra muscle development in that arm.*

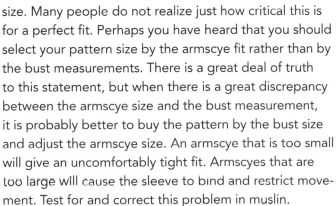

Large armscyes should have the underarm filled in with the needed amount. Add this to the paper pattern.

Sleeve Hang

Various problems will affect the hang of the sleeve. Many of them are solved if the sleeve is eased and re-stitched correctly. Some will be caused by posture or figure shape and require the repositioning of the sleeve in the armscye, or by the following pattern alteration.

Too Much Sleeve-Cap Height: This problem makes the sleeve wrinkle just below the shoulder. It is solved by pinching out the excess fabric in a fold across the top of the sleeve. Do the same reduction to the paper pattern, then recut and stitch the sleeve.

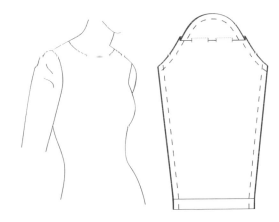

Too Little Sleeve-Cap Height: This problem causes the sleeve to pull and develop vertical wrinkles. Measure both armscye and sleeve seam line to see how much more ease is needed. Make the pattern adjustment by slashing the pattern apart in the upper portion of the sleeve cap, spreading it the amount needed to give the required ease, then filling in the gap with an extra piece

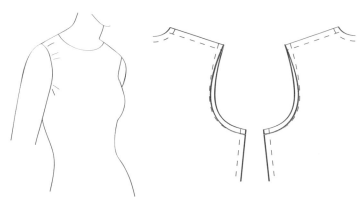

of paper. Now cut the sleeves from your fashion fabric with the altered pattern.

Improper Hang: Some figures need to have the sleeve repositioned in the armscye because of their posture or body build.

People with very erect postures, who tend to hold their arms toward the back will usually develop wrinkles at the back of the sleeve, as illustrated. This problem is solved by removing the sleeve from the armhole, rotating it toward the front and then restitching it.

People with round posture, who tend to hold their arms toward the front will usually develop wrinkles at the front of the sleeve, as illustrated. This problem is solved by removing the sleeve from the armhole, rotating it toward the back, and then restitching it.

ERECT POSTURE

ROUND POSTURE

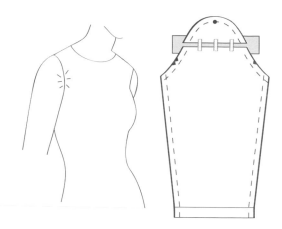

SLEEVES WITH A CUSTOM TOUCH

Sleeves that have the proper fit and are made with the correct sewing methods give your clothes a custom look. Listed below are some other techniques that will contribute to that look and also add a few designer touches not usually found on commercial patterns.

Lined Sleeve

A fully lined sleeve is a good technique to use with sheer or lightweight fabrics. It adds body to the sleeve and eliminates the need for a hem. Fully lined dresses can also use this method to line the sleeves.

The fabric that you use for the sleeve lining can be the fashion fabric or a color-matched lining fabric. The fashion fabric can be used only if it is a lightweight and of a solid color. Sheer prints will show through the sleeve layers and look unattractive.

Allow just a seam rather than a hem width at the bottom of the pattern. Cut two sleeves of fashion fabric and two sleeves of lining fabric. Trim 1/8" from the lower edge of each sleeve lining. This will allow the seam at the lower edge of the sleeve to roll to the inside after the sleeve has been constructed.

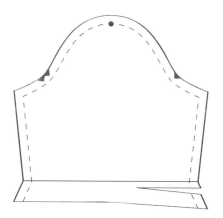

Stitch and press the underarm seam of each sleeve and sleeve lining. With right sides together, slip a sleeve lining down inside each sleeve and pin the edges together. Stitch around the sleeve edge with the given seam allowance and then trim the seam to 1/4".

Pull the two layers of sleeve apart and press the seam open.

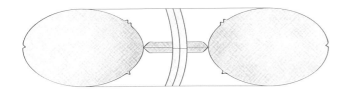

Tuck the lining up inside the sleeve, in the finished position, making sure the seam rolls to the inside. Press the edge of the sleeve with the point of the iron. Baste the upper edges of the sleeve together and you are ready to sew it into the armscye.

Making Short Sleeves

Patterns calling for long sleeves can easily be changed to short sleeves, if desired. First determine the short sleeve length by measuring from the shoulder to the level where you want the sleeve to end, or measure the length of a short sleeve on a finished garment.

Mark the sleeve length on the long sleeve pattern, measuring down from the seam line at the cap of the sleeve.

Next draw another line 1 1/2" below the first. This allows for a hem. Trace the sleeve onto another piece of paper, making sure that you indicate both lines. Trim away the excess paper along the lower line.

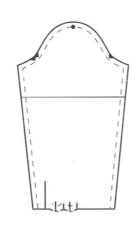

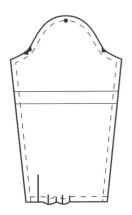

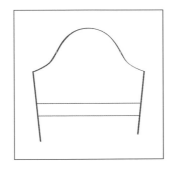

Fold the pattern up along the hemline. Trim the sides of the folded section so that they are even with the sides of the sleeve. Unfold the hemline and the finished pattern will look like the one shown. Use this new pattern to cut the sleeve from your fashion fabric.

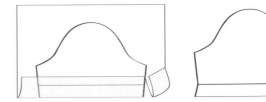

Trimming Sleeve Seams

Sleeve seam allowances should be trimmed once the sleeve has been sewn into the armscye. The amount trimmed will be determined by the fabric.

- Trim the underarm area between the notches to 1/4" for all fabrics then double-stitch, zigzag or serge the trimmed area.

- Trim the seam allowance around the top of the sleeve to 3/8" for woven fabrics and 1/4" for knits.

- Armscye seam allowance for sheer fabrics should be stitched twice, 1/8" apart, and trimmed close to the stitching line. Press the seam allowance toward the garment so it won't show through the sheer fabric.

Designer Details

If you look at designer fashions in department and specialty stores, you will notice that they feature some unusual details not found on other clothes. This extra touch is one of the things that sets designer fashions apart. Very few of these details are difficult to make; they are mostly imaginative.

Make it a habit to look at designer fashions when you are shopping to see what's new. You can easily copy most of these special details. This is a good way to have a fashionable but inexpensive wardrobe. Some sleeve details found on designer fashions are sketched on the next page along with suggested construction tips.

Short Sleeve With Fake Cuff and Tab: This design can be used for both men's and women's fashions. It looks great made up in interlock knits. Instructions for the fake cuff are given in Chapter 7, Tailoring Tactics. Just add your own tab and hold it in place with a button.

Sleeve With Patch Pocket and Flap: Apply this smart pocket detail to long or short sleeves of either knit or woven fabrics. Make your own pattern for the small patch pocket and flap.

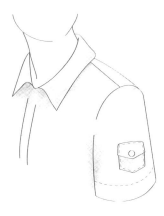

Notched and Buttoned Cuff: This cuff treatment is a good finish for a sport shirt. Increase the hem width to 3".

Fold the hem up, right sides together, and draw a notch at the center of the sleeve that is 3/4" deep and wide. Stitch along the notch lines; clip to the point of the V and trim the seam allowances. Turn the hem to the right side.

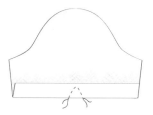

Stitch and press the sleeve's underarm seam. Turn the hem up into position and secure it with hand or machine stitching. Topstitch the hem edge, if desired, and hold the hem in position with two small buttons.

SLEEVE VENTS

There are many ways of finishing off the vents of long sleeves. Since each method gives a slightly different look; your choice should be influenced by the overall style of the garment. Instructions are given below for the three basic vent finishes that are used on sleeves with cuffs. These vents are constructed before the underarm seam is sewn.

Most sleeve patterns have vent markings on them. However, if you are making your own or adapting a sleeve pattern, the vent is located 2 1/2" away from the underarm seam on the back part of the sleeve. Vent lengths are 2 1/2" to 4" long.

THE PATCH VENT

This type of vent finish is probably the easiest to make and works well with knits because you don't have problems with fraying edges. It can be used with wovens also, but special care must be taken with the raw edges of the patch fabric. Directions for handling this problem are given at the end of this section.

Vent Construction

Cut two pieces of fashion fabric 1" longer than the vent length and 3" wide. Indicate the length of the vent down the center of the wrong side of the patch with a chalk or pencil line.

Position the patch on the sleeve at the vent location, right side to right side. Start stitching 1/4" to the side of the vent line, taper to the end of the line, take one straight stitch across the end and stitch along the other side ending 1/4" from the centerline.

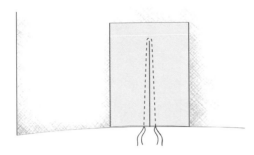

Slash to the point of the V. Turn the patch to the underside and press, rolling the seam to the wrong side of the sleeve. The patch is held in position by understitching, which is done at this point, or with topstitching or fusible web, which is done after the cuff has been applied.

This patch technique can be used with woven fabrics, but care must be taken with the cut edges of the patch. If the fabric is firmly woven and does not fray easily, then a zigzag along the cut edges is usually sufficient. However, if you are using a fabric that tends to fray, it is suggested that you face the patch with a lining type of fabric. Most lightweight, nonfusible interfacings can be used for this purpose.

Cut two patches from the fashion fabric and two patches from the lining fabric each 1/4" wider and longer than the measurements given above. These additional measurements allows for seams. Place the right side of a fashion fabric patch against the right side of a lining patch and stitch around three edges with a 1/4" seam. Trim corners; turn the patch right side out and press.

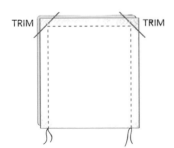

Construct the vent by placing the faced patch in position on the right side of the sleeve. Stitch and finish as directed above.

Apply the cuffs to the sleeves using one of the methods described in the following section.

THE CONTINUOUS-BOUND VENT

The continuous-bound vent is probably the most common vent finish found on shirts. The strip of fabric used to bind the vent edges should be cut on the lengthwise grain of the fabric.

Vent Construction

Cut two strips of fashion fabric twice the length of the vent and 1 1/2" wide. Press over a 1/4" seam allowance along one long side of each strip.

With a short stitch length, stay-stitch around the vent line starting 1/4" from the line at the sleeve edge, tapering down to the end. Take one stitch across the end and then stitch along the other side of the vent line, as illustrated. Slash the vent line down to the stitching at the point of the V.

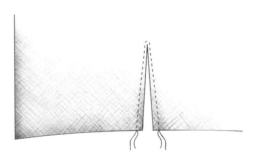

Place a vent strip against the slash, right sides together. The edges of the strip will be even with the edges of the slash except at the point of the V. Here, the strip will extend beyond the V about 1/4".

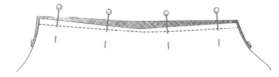

Working on the sleeve, stitch just outside the stay stitching line, creating a seam approximately 3/8" wide. Make sure that you catch just a thread or two of the sleeve fabric at the point of the V.

Fold under the pressed 1/4" seam and then fold the binding strip over the vent seam allowance until the edge just covers the seam. Stitch along the edge by machine or hand.

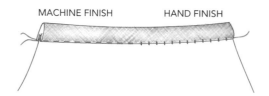

MACHINE FINISH   HAND FINISH

Pull the two sides of the bound vent out away from the wrong side of the sleeve. Stitch the top of the vent at an angle as illustrated. This helps to hold the vent in position after the cuff has been applied.

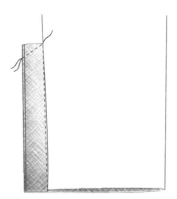

Note: *When applying a standard cuff to a continuous-bound vent, the upper part of the vent is folded under, against the sleeve, and the under part of the vent is pulled out away from the sleeve. If you are working with a French cuff, both vent sides will be folded under against the sleeve before the cuff is applied.*

THE TAILORED PLACKET VENT

The tailored placket is the type of sleeve vent found on men's and women's tailored shirts and jackets. This one is easy to do because it uses only one pattern piece for the placket rather than the two required by most patterns. Trace the Tailored Shirt Placket pattern at the end of this chapter and follow the instructions. It can be lengthened or shortened as needed, and it will work with any sleeve pattern.

It is suggested that you make a placket sample on some scrap fabric before you begin to work on your actual garment. This takes a few minutes but helps you decide if the length is correct. Once you see how easy this placket is to make, you will never again groan when faced with a tailored sleeve.

Placket Construction

Cut out two placket pieces and mark both fold lines with small clips. Transfer the stitching line "box" to the wrong side of each placket piece.

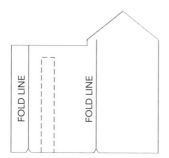

FOLD LINE   FOLD LINE

Baste under a 1/4" seam allowance on both long sides of the placket pieces and press. Turn down both sides of the placket point 1/4", clipping at the one side as needed, baste and press. You can miter the three points at the top of the placket piece by following the instructions shown for Basic Patch Pocket in Chapter 5.

This will reduce the bulk at the top of the placket, which is especially important with heavy fabrics.

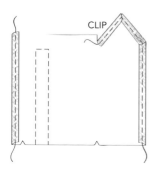

CLIP

Fold over both sides of the placket along the fold lines, wrong sides together, and press. The basted edges of the placket should just meet the sides of the stitching "box".

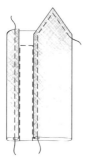

Place the right side of the placket pieces against the wrong side of the sleeve so that the stitching "box"

is centered over the sleeve vent line. The pointed side of the placket piece should be toward the front of the sleeve. Pin in place and stitch around the "box" with a short stitch length.

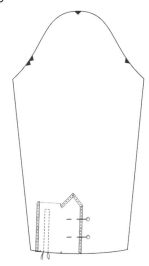

Slash down the center of the "box" to within 1/2" of the end, then cut into the corners as shown at right. Do not cut into the stitching.

Press each side of the placket toward the center, along the seam line. Turn the sleeve to the right side and pull the placket piece through to the right side. Press again so that the sleeve seam allowances are pressed **into** the placket.

Fold over the narrow side of the placket and pin so that the basted edge just covers the stitching line. Stitch close to the edge, ending at the top of the opening. Make sure that you don't catch any of the other side of the placket in this stitching.

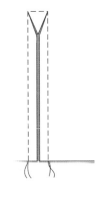

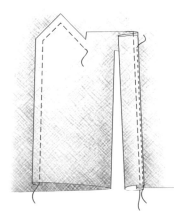

Pull the underneath part of the placket out to the side. Fold over the pointed section of the placket so that the basted edge just covers the seam line. Press and then stitch close to the folded edge, ending the stitching at the top of the opening. Pull the threads through to the wrong side and tie.

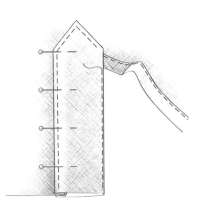

Now spread the sleeve out flat, right side up, and arrange the placket in the finished position. The basted edge should just cover the stitching line, and everything should be flat and smooth. Fold down the point of the placket and trim away some of the excess layers of fabric to reduce bulk. Pin or baste the placket in place.

Finish edge stitching the placket as illustrated. Pull the threads to the wrong side and tie them at the end of the stitching line at the top of the placket.

Press the placket Finish the sleeve by stitching the underarm seam and then applying the cuff.

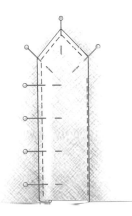

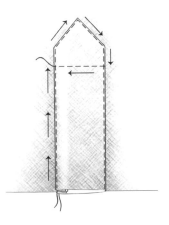

CUFFS

Perfect cuffs are a sure test of the expert seamstress. If you can construct and apply them so that the points or curves are exact, the facings don't "peek-a-boo" around the edges, bumps don't form at the sleeve-joining seam, and all edges are straight and crisp with even topstitching, then you are a success. This section should give you the help you need to make professional-looking cuffs.

TYPES OF CUFFS

There are two basic styles of the standard cuff, one that involves two pieces of fashion fabric and one that uses just one piece of fabric that folds back on itself. You may find that you prefer one type over the other. It is a simple matter to change pieces to the type you prefer.

The standard cuff is designed to be applied to a gathered, straight or pleated sleeve, with a vent opening. Because the lower sleeve edge is enclosed within the cuff, it can be rolled up the arm or turned back over a sweater or jacket sleeve without having visible raw edges.

Two-Piece Cuff

This type of cuff gives the finest finish, and it can have either square, angled or curved corners. The cuff consists of two identical pieces of fashion fabric, one of which is interfaced.

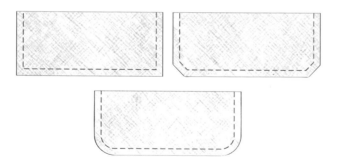

One-Piece Cuff

Made from one piece of fashion fabric, this cuff is folded back on itself. Interfacing is applied to just one half of the fabric piece. The corners will always be square on a one-piece cuff.

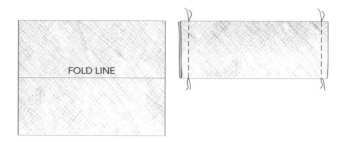

CUFF INTERFACING

Interfacing is applied to cuffs made from all types of fashion fabrics in order to add body and keep them looking crisp. Fusible interfacings, woven or nonwoven, are ideal for cuffs because the interfacing seam allowances can be trimmed away, eliminating bulk in the seam areas.

The interfacing should always be applied to the upper cuff piece so that it lies between the visible part of the cuff and the seam allowances. This prevents "shadowing through" of the seam allowances on lightweight fabrics.

One-piece cuffs should have interfacing applied to the upper half of the cuff piece only. The seam allowance of the interfacing should be trimmed away from each side and the interfacing should end just short of the fold line.

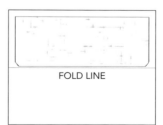

CUFF CONSTRUCTION

Pin the right sides of the cuff together and extend the facing piece out beyond the upper cuff about 1/8" at the outside edges of the cuff. This makes the facing smaller than the upper cuff and enables you to roll the seam to the facing side when pressing the finished cuff. Stitch the cuff on the interfaced side, using the edge of the interfacing as a guide.

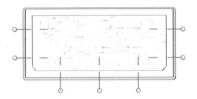

Always take at least one diagonal stitch across the points of square corners. This allows room for the fabric to turn smoothly in the corner and prevents "rabbit ears." One stitch of regular length is adequate for average-weight fabrics, while two stitches might be required for heavyweight woolens. Remember—the thicker the fabric, the more room is needed at the corner.

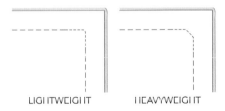

LIGHTWEIGHT   HEAVYWEIGHT

If you are working with fabric that tends to fray easily, you will find it helpful to shorten the stitch length as you go around corners and points. You will probably have to take two or three of the shorter stitches across the diagonal in order to give you the needed "turning room", but the shorter stitch length prevents fraying at the corners after the cuff has been trimmed and turned.

When going around curves a smooth stitching line is created by shortening the stitch length and keeping the machine moving slowly at all times.

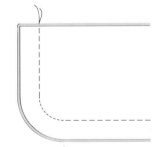

Once the cuff has been stitched, grade and trim the seam allowance. Turn the cuff to the right side and use a point turner or threaded needle to help you get the corners square. Thread a hand needle with a short, double thread. Insert the needle exactly at the cuff's corner and pull on the thread to bring the point all the way out. Remove the thread after the point is perfect. Press the cuff on the wrong side, rolling the seam so it doesn't show on the right side of the finished cuff.

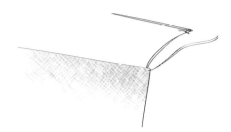

CUFF APPLICATION

The two methods of applying the standard cuff are the wrap method and the topstitched method. Try each method to see which one you prefer. The topstitched method must be used when working with very narrow cuffs, since it is impossible to wrap these and still have stitching room.

The following things should be kept in mind when applying cuffs: Make sure the sleeve ease is distributed evenly or pleated neatly into the cuff; don't let bumps form where the cuff ends join the sleeve; and make sure the topstitching is neat and even.

Wrap Cuff

Prepare the cuff as previously directed. The lower edge of the sleeve should be finished as indicated by the pattern, with a vent, pleats, gathers or left plain. Apply the cuff using the following instructions.

With the sleeve inside-out, pin the right side of the cuff to the right side of the prepared sleeve edge and stitch just the upper cuff layer to the sleeve edge with the given seam allowance. See illustration on the next page.

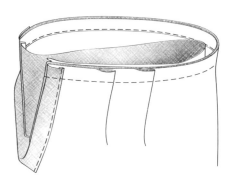

To ensure a neat finish at the vent edge, wrap the cuff facing back around the cuff. Now the right side of the cuff facing is to the wrong side of the sleeve, and the cuff's seam allowance is pressed open. Stitch for about 2" along the original seam line.

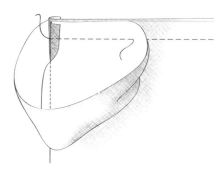

Trim and grade the seam allowance. Close the remaining part of the cuff's facing by hand, or, if you are going to finish the cuff with topstitching, close it during that process.

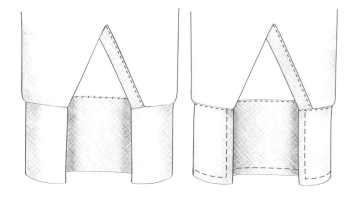

Note: *The seam allowance joining the cuff to the sleeve will be less bulky and visible on the right side if*

you make two rows of stitching about 1/8" apart when first joining the cuff to the sleeve. This is particularly important if you are working with a sleeve that has been gathered onto the cuff. The extra row of stitching helps control the thickness of the gathers. Trim the seam allowance close to the second stitching line.

Topstitched Cuff

Prepare the cuff as previously directed, except press down the seam allowance along the top edge of the interfaced cuff piece and trim it to 3/8" before stitching the two cuff pieces together. Stitch, grade and trim the seam allowance; turn and press the cuff, rolling the seam to the facing side.

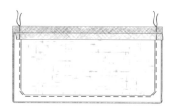

Note: *When possible, use the selvage as the finished edge on the **inside** of the cuff. Now there's no need to trim the inside seam allowance and turn it under, and you will reduce bulk. This is especially helpful when working with thick fabric such as denim or corduroy. (This technique also reduces bulk on a waistband.)*

With the prepared sleeve right side out, pin the cuff's facing to the sleeve edge, right side of facing to the wrong side of the sleeve. Extend each edge of the sleeve about 1/8" beyond the edge of the cuff to help eliminate bumps at the edge of the joining seam. The rest of the sleeve should just fit the top of the cuff. Adjust gathers or ease as necessary.

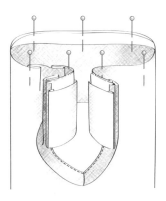

Stitch the cuff to the sleeve with the given seam allowance starting and ending the seam 1/8″ narrower than the given width. This allows space for the bulk of the trimmed seam on the finished cuff. Pull the folded edge of the upper cuff out of the way while stitching. Trim the seam allowance to 1/4″.

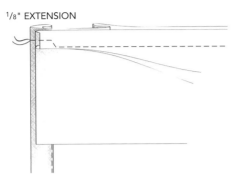

1/8″ EXTENSION

and behind the presser foot to eliminate puckers. A sewing machine with a free arm is excellent to use for this final stitching. Topstitch the edges of the cuff if desired.

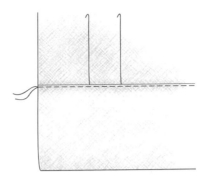

Turn the sleeve right side out and arrange the cuff in the finished position so that the folded edge just covers the stitching on the right side of the sleeve. The seam allowances at the ends of the cuff should be pushed down into the cuff and carefully pinned so that no bump forms and all the stitching is completely covered. Edge-stitch the upper cuff to the sleeve, holding the cuff taut in front of

Note: *For a cuff application that shows no topstitching, fold the seam allowance down on the facing part of the cuff instead of the upper cuff. Trim this folded seam allowance, then stitch the two cuff pieces together. Turn the sleeve inside out and apply the cuff to the sleeve with the right side of the upper cuff against the right side of the sleeve. Follow the above stitching instructions. Arrange the cuff in the finished position and slipstitch the facing edge of the cuff in place on the inside of the sleeve.*

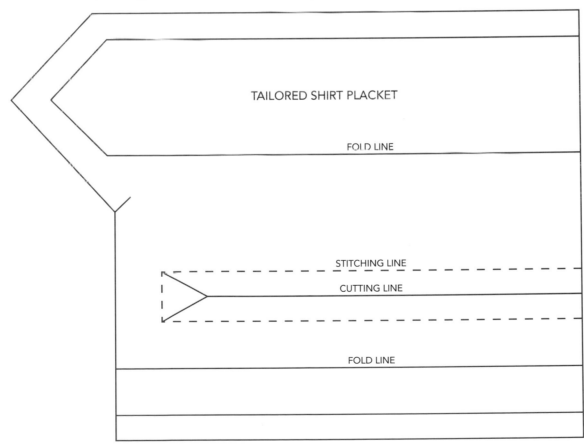

TAILORED SHIRT PLACKET

FOLD LINE

STITCHING LINE

CUTTING LINE

FOLD LINE

THIMBLES

In Central Europe in the Middle Ages, "thummels" or "thimels" were bell-shaped leather caps worn on the thumb—hence the word "thimble." Modern marine thummels are known today as "sailor's palms" and are necessary in sail making.

Bronze thimbles have been found in Greek and Roman ruins, some of which have open tops, a style still used by modern tailors. These open-top thimbles leave the fingertip free to pick up threads and pins—and they are perfect for the seamstress with long fingernails.

Ordinary thimbles were made of brass or steel, while ornamental thimbles were made of silver and gold and often were capped with semiprecious stones which were kept for fine needlework. Many thimbles were made of bone or ivory as well as delicate mother-of-pearl. Expensive China thimbles were favored in the

mid-19th century, as their smoothness prevented snagging fine threads and fabrics. In Siberia and Mongolia, brass thimbles were sewn on the borders of the garments as decorations.

In the 18th and 19th centuries, it was a common practice to give thimbles as betrothal or wedding gifts in small fitted cases in the shape of an egg or knife box. Many small thimbles have lasted through the ages; these were children's thimbles made in graduated sets. Children started sewing as early as 4 years of age.

Inlaid mother-of-pearl thimble case in the shape of a Georgian knife box. It also contains packets of needles c. 1850.

PICK A POCKET

5

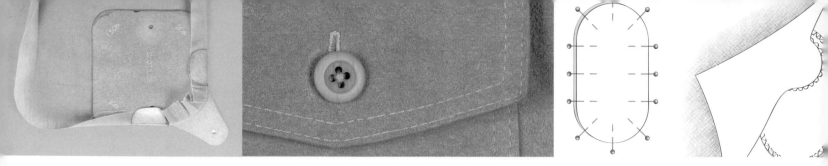

Chapter 5: Pick a Pocket

POCKETS make sewing fun. There are so many kinds that they seem to stimulate your creativity. A basic garment assumes many different looks by just using various pocket styles and/or placements.

Kids love pockets. You can please them with brightly colored appliqué or hole pockets, or put them in unusual places, such as on sleeves or the back of the lower leg. Ask for their suggestions. We're sure they can give you some interesting ones.

Tailored garments require more-traditional pockets and the challenge here is making them perfect. Our construction techniques will make these pockets easy, so you need no longer hesitate about making them.

PATCH POCKET

Some version of the patch pocket is the most common type of pocket found on garments. It is easy to do and can assume many looks, depending upon the design used. Instructions are given for a basic patch pocket plus some fun variations.

Basic Patch Pocket

The basic patch pocket consists of a pocket piece that has a round, square or angled bottom. The top edge can have a narrow or wide hem. The pocket is usually topstitched to the garment, but it can also be hand or invisibly stitched in place.

Patch pockets cut from fabrics with designs that need to be matched should be cut so they exactly match the garment fabric; or else they should be cut on the bias or opposite grain for effect. All-over printed fabrics should also be cut so the pocket matches the garment. This is a custom touch you see on many designer clothes.

For more information on cutting patch pockets from fabrics with designs such as all-over prints or plaids see Chapter 2.

Patch pockets are usually interfaced to add more body, and fusible interfacing is a good choice. Cut the interfacing from the pocket pattern and trim away all the seam allowances before fusing it in place. Also, trim the interfacing along the fold line at the top of the pocket.

The top edge of the patch pocket can be handled in two different ways. The topstitched edge gives a sporty look while the hemmed edge gives a more tailored look.

The topstitched finish requires a 3/4" hem allowance for woven fabrics, and a 1/2" hem allowance for knits. For woven fabrics clean-finish the edge of the hem. For both woven fabrics, and knits, press over the hem and finish with two rows of topstitching.

For a patch pocket with a hemmed edge, fold the hem back along the fold line, right sides together, pulling the hem edge 1/8" beyond the pocket edge. Stitch the given seam width. Trim the corner and seam allowance and turn the hem to the finished position.

Press the pocket hem from the wrong side, rolling the seam to the wrong side. Press over the rest of the pocket seam allowances.

Square or angled corners should be mitered for a neat finish. Rounded corners should be easestitched to help them turn smoothly.

Insert the desired curve of a Pocket Curve Template between fabric layers and press to result in two identical pocket curves.

Miter square or angled corners by pressing a diagonal fold across the corner, precisely where the seam lines meet. Trim the folded section to a scant 1/4" (**Fig. 1**). Press over the remaining seam allowances; the fold should now miter neatly in the corner (**Fig. 2**). Whipstitch the folds together with a few hand stitches. Trim the entire pocket seam allowance to 1/4".

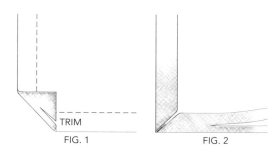

Miters can also be stitched rather than folded, if you prefer. This reduces thickness in the corner area and is the preferred method for thick or bulky fabrics. The following instructions are for a stitched miter.

Press over both seam allowances and mark the point where they meet with small clips (**Fig. 3**). Refold the corner on the diagonal, right sides together. Match up the clips and stitch from them to the point where the crease lines meet (**Fig. 4**). Trim the seam allowance, finger-press the seam open and turn the corner right side out.

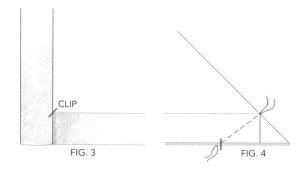

Easestitch rounded corners just slightly less than the given seam width. Trim the pocket seam allowance to 1/4" and notch the curves so they lie flat. Pinking shears are good for trimming this type of curve. Press over the seam allowance, rolling the stitching to the underside.

Press under the top corners of topstitched pockets, as shown. This keeps the raw edges from showing.

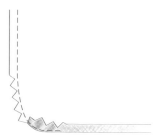

Stuffing a Kleenex between the pocket and garment while pinning or basting in place allows for needed "wearing" ease. This procedure is not necessary on children's or work clothes, but it does give a custom look to your better garments. Pin or glue-baste the pocket in place, using just enough pins to keep it from shifting while stitching. Some fabrics may need to be hand-basted in place.

Machine-stitch the pocket to the garment using the desired stitching pattern. Reinforce the pocket corners by stitching one of the following patterns. **Note:** *An extra piece of fabric placed behind the pocket corner on the wrong side of the garment adds reinforcement.*

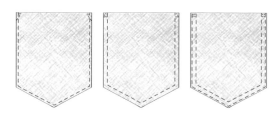

The pocket can be hand-stitched to the garment for a more tailored look. It is suggested that you first baste the pocket to the garment along the edge so you have a guideline to follow on the wrong side.

Always work from the wrong side when hand-stitching a patch pocket in place. This makes your stitches invisible. Catch just the pocket edge with small backstitches. Occasionally check the right side to make sure the stitches aren't showing.

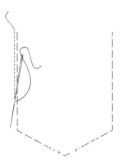

Instructions for invisibly stitching a patch pocket in place are given later in this chapter.

Lined Patch Pocket

Many patch pockets require a lining. This gives them a clean inside finish. Interface the wrong side of the upper pocket piece. Use a lightweight fabric for the pocket lining. Cut the pocket lining from the pocket pattern, using the following instructions.

Fold the pattern over along the hemline. Measure up 1/2" from the lower edge of the hem and draw a line. This cutting line is for the lining. Trace off the lining pattern onto a piece of tissue or pattern paper.

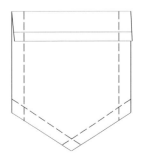

Stitch the lining and pocket along the top edge with a 1/4" seam, right sides together. Leave 1" unstitched in the center. Press open the seam allowance.

Pin the lining and pocket, extending the lining out beyond the pocket edge 1/8". (This makes the lining slightly smaller than the pocket when it is finished.) Stitch around the pocket. Grade the seam allowance, trimming the corner or notching the curves as needed. Turn the pocket to the right side through the opening in the seam.

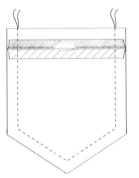

Press the pocket from the wrong side, rolling the seam to the underside. Close the open seam with a few hand stitches. You are now ready to topstitch a perfectly lined patch pocket to your garment.

Self-Lined Patch Pocket

The technique of self-lining a patch pocket can be used for medium and lightweight fabrics. It makes the lining process quick and easy because you don't have to cut and handle a separate lining fabric.

Fold down the hem at the top of the pocket pattern. Place the folded edge on a fabric fold and cut out a double pocket.

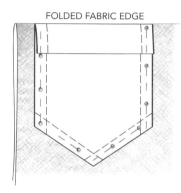

FOLDED FABRIC EDGE

Interface one half of the pocket piece, using fusible interfacing.

Fold the pocket piece in half, right sides together, and pin. Position one layer so that it extends 1/8" beyond the other layer. This will be the pocket lining. Stitch the layers as indicated, with the given seam width. Grade, trim and notch the seam allowance as necessary.

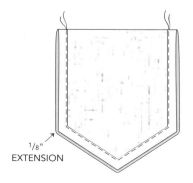

1/8"
EXTENSION

Cut a short slit in the lower part of the pocket lining. Cut woven fabric on the bias so that the cut edge won't fray. Turn the pocket to the right side through the slit.

With the lining side up, press the pocket, rolling the seam to the lining side. Whipstitch the slit closed, or patch it with a small piece of fusible interfacing. The pocket is now ready to be stitched to the garment.

The self-lined technique can also be used for novelty shaped pockets, such as the following illustrated shapes. Use your imagination to come up with unusual shapes. Combine the pocket with appliqué details for a special look. These pockets are fun to use on children's clothes. Cut the pocket from a double layer of fabric, and stitch the two layers, right sides together. Trim and clip the seam allowance as necessary. Cut the slit; turn the pocket to the right side and press. Stitch in place on the garment.

A big mitten is a cute shape to use on a child's jacket. Cut the pattern larger than the child's hand, allowing for seam allowances. Cut the lining piece from fleece for extra warmth. Construct the pocket as directed above and topstitch to the garment.

Patch Pocket With Self-Flap

This attractive pocket is seen on many designer clothes. It is basically a patch pocket, but it has an unusual self-flap. It can be topstitched or invisibly stitched to the garment. The pattern for the pocket is found on page 5-26.

Cut the pocket and flap facing from your fashion fabric. Use the upper part of the pattern for the facing. Interface the pocket piece up to the fold line with a fusible interfacing, remembering to trim away the seam allowances first. Also, interface the facing just to the fold line. In this pocket, the flap facing becomes the visible part of the flap. This is why the interfacing is divided between the two pieces.

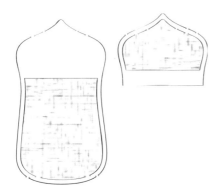

Stitch the facing to the pocket with a 1/2" seam. Extend the pocket 1/8" so that the seam will roll to the underside. Trim and clip the seam allowance as necessary. Turn the facing to the finished position. Press from the wrong side, rolling the seam so that it won't show on the finished flap.

Using a contrasting thread, machine-stitch a scant 1/8" outside the seam line, (within the pocket seam allowance), easestitching the curves. Trim the curves with pinking shears. Press over the seam allowance, rolling the stitching line just slightly to the underside. Make sure the curves turn smoothly. Trim the entire pocket seam allowance to 1/4".

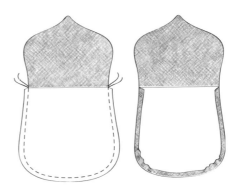

Use either the topstitched method or invisibly stitched method for stitching the pocket to the garment. The topstitched method looks sportier than the invisibly stitched method.

Topstitch around the flap portion of the pocket. Pin the pocket to the garment, position the Kleenex as previously described and topstitch in place. Backstitch at the ends of the stitching line for strength.

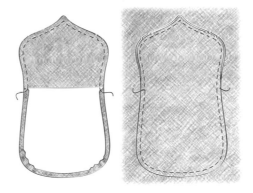

Press the flap down into position, using a press cloth to protect the right side of the fabric. A button can be added to the pocket if desired.

The invisibly stitched pocket may look difficult, but it is quite easy. It will really impress your friends and give them something to think about. The flap is usually not topstitched when you use the invisible stitching method.

Machine-baste the pocket to the garment using a zigzag stitch made with the longest stitch length and the narrowest stitch width. (Don't forget the Kleenex.) Stitch on the edge of the pocket so that one side of the zigzag just bites into the pocket edge.

Using a regular straight stitch, sew the pocket from the inside, starting at the fold line of the flap. You will have to separate the facing and seam allowance from the pocket to get started. Stitch along the first stitching line, on the inside of the seam allowance. Work around the entire pocket, ending at the opposite fold line. Backstitch each end of the stitching line for strength.

This pocket pattern can be enlarged for a companion pocket. Use the two pockets in combination on a jacket, the smaller one for the breast pocket and the larger one for the lower pocket.

The larger pocket needs to be made as a separate pocket and flap—it will gap open if made like the self-flap pocket. The pocket can be topstitched or invisibly stitched in place. Construct and apply the flap as instructed below.

Patch Pocket With Flap

Many patch pockets have flap coverings. They add a different look, and also make the pocket more secure if the flap is closed with a button or snap.

Always make the flap after the pocket has been stitched to the garment. This enables you to make the flap 1/4" wider than the finished pocket, which prevents the corners of the pocket from extending out beyond the edges of the flap.

The flap can be faced with a lining fabric or self-fabric. Choose whatever works best with your fashion fabric. Use fusible interfacing on the wrong side of the flap to add body, if necessary. Pin the flap and facing together, positioning the facing so it extends 1/8" beyond the flap edge. Stitch with the given seam width, trim and clip the seam allowance as necessary. Turn the flap to the right side and press, rolling the seam to the facing side. Topstitch if desired.

Position the flap so that the seam line is 1/2" above the pocket with the flap extending 1/8" on each side of the pocket. Stitch the flap, backstitching at both edges for strength. Trim the seam to a scant 1/4".

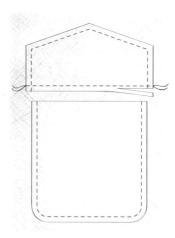

Fold the flap down and press, using a press cloth to protect the fabric. Topstitch 1/4" away from the fold. Do not backstitch at the seam ends. Pull the thread ends through to the wrong side and tie them with a square knot. This gives a much cleaner finish.

Patch Pocket With Fake Band

This patch pocket variation is suitable for both men's and women's fashions. It looks as though a separate band has been applied to the top of the pocket. Adjust the pocket pattern so that the hem is 2" wide. Interface the pocket as previously instructed.

Fold the hem over in the finished position and then fold it over again. Stitch 1/4" from the fold, catching the hem edge in the fold.

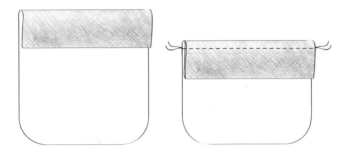

Unfold the hem and press from the wrong side. Topstitch across the pocket top if desired.

Press under the pocket seam allowances, mitering the corners or easestitching the curves. Trim and notch as necessary. Pin the pocket to the garment and topstitch in place. A pocket with round corners can be invisibly stitched in place.

Machine-baste the pocket to the garment using a zigzag stitch made with the longest stitch length and the narrowest stitch width. (Don't forget the Kleenex.) Stitch on the edge of the pocket so that one side of the zigzag just bites into the pocket edge.

Using a regular-length straight stitch, sew the pocket from the inside, starting at the top right-hand corner of the pocket. Stitch on the first stitching line, on the inside of the seam allowance. Work around the entire pocket, ending at the opposite corner. Backstitch each end of the stitching line for strength. Fold down the ends of the seam allowance at the pocket corner so that they won't show, and catch in place on the wrong side by hand.

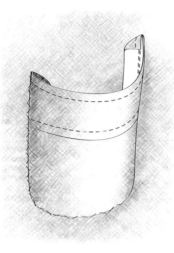

ZIPPER POCKET

Zipper pockets are quite useful as well as decorative. They are ideal for sports clothes and outerwear, but are also used on other types of clothing. A zipper pocket requires a 5" or 7" zipper. Heavy decorative zippers are especially suitable for pockets in outerwear. Regular zippers can also be used for pockets. Attach a ring or some sort of zipper pull to the slide, for convenience.

Two-Way Zipper Pocket

This pocket is ideal for outerwear because it provides both the security of a closed pocket and the ready access of a hand-warmer pocket. The pocket lining can be cut from a fleece fabric for extra warmth.

Cut the pieces shown for each pocket. Use matching or contrasting fabric, as desired. You will also need a 7" zipper for each pocket.

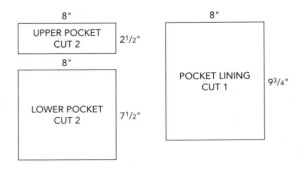

8"		8"
UPPER POCKET CUT 2 — 2 1/2"		POCKET LINING CUT 1 — 9 3/4"
8"		
LOWER POCKET CUT 2 — 7 1/2"		

Sandwich the zipper between the two upper pocket pieces, with the right sides together and the edges even with the zipper tape. There should be 3/8" of fabric extending beyond each end of the zipper teeth. Stitch this unit together with a 1/4" seam (**Fig. 1**). Separate the two fabric pieces and press so that the zipper extends below, as shown. Edge-stitch along the fabric fold (**Fig. 2**).

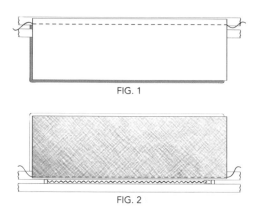

FIG. 1

FIG. 2

Repeat the above process with the two large fabric pieces so that the other side of the zipper is enclosed.

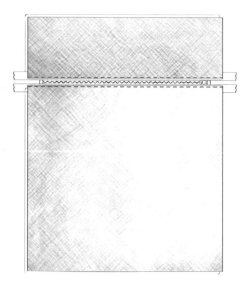

Pin the pocket lining against the zipper unit, right sides together. The lining should extend 1/8" beyond the zipper-unit edges. Using a zipper foot, stitch a 1/4" seam around the pocket.

Note: *Be careful as you stitch across the ends of the zipper. You need to stitch as closely as you can without*

hitting the zipper with your machine needle, which could break or damage your needle.

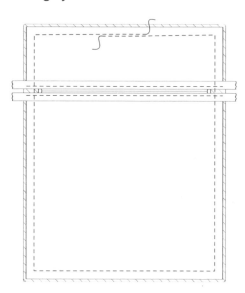

Trim the pocket corners and cut a slit in the lower portion of the pocket lining. Pull the pocket through to the right side and press. Close the slit with a few hand stitches or a small piece of fusible interfacing.

Pin or glue-baste the pocket to the garment in the proper position. Topstitch, as illustrated, leaving an opening on one side of the pocket that is wide enough for the hand. Backstitch or bar-tack both ends of the stitching for strength. The edge of the pocket opening can be topstitched before applying the pocket to the garment, if desired.

Patch Pocket With Exposed Zipper

Patch pockets with exposed zippers can be used on sport clothes. This technique is also useful for novelty pockets. Cut the desired pocket shape, making sure it is large enough to accommodate the chosen zipper. Interface the wrong side of the pocket with nonwoven fusible interfacing to help control any fraying.

Mark the zipper opening on the wrong side of the pocket piece. The opening should be 1/4" wide and 1/8" longer than the zipper. Using a short stitch, sew around the marked box (**Fig. 1**). Cut the box open, as shown, making sure you make a large wedge; clip all the way into each corner clipping to, but not through the stitch (**Fig. 2**).

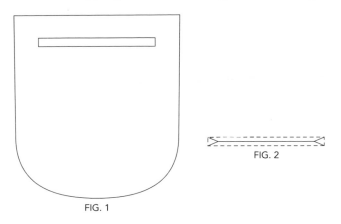

FIG. 1

FIG. 2

Working on the wrong side, press back the edges of the opening, rolling the fabric so that the stitches are on the wrong side. Baste around the seam allowance to hold it in place.

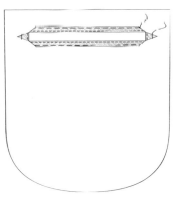

Position the zipper under the opening. Baste in place. Using a zipper foot, secure the zipper by edge stitching around the box on the right side of pocket. Make another row of stitching 1/4" from edge. This helps to control the zipper tapes, and makes the opening stronger.

Finish the pocket by pressing under the seam allowances as described in the basic patch pocket section. Pin the pocket to the garment and topstitch in place.

Covered Zipper Pocket

In this version of the zipper pocket, the zipper is covered and has a more tailored look. The construction is similar to a bound buttonhole, except a zipper is stitched under the opening. This pocket can be made as a patch pocket to be topstitched to the garment, or as a set-in pocket.

The pocket pattern should measure 7" by 8" for a 5" zipper pocket, and 9" by 8" for a 7" zipper pocket. Cut one pocket piece for the patch pocket, and two for the set-in pocket.

Cut two strips of fabric 1" longer than the zipper and 1" wide for each pocket. Press these strips lengthwise, down the middle, with the wrong sides together.

Patch Pocket: Mark the zipper position with a line that is 2" longer than the zipper. Indicate the exact length with two vertical lines, as shown. Draw these lines on the wrong side of the pocket, and transfer them through to the right side by machine basting.

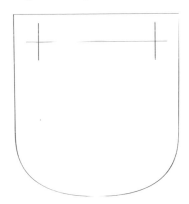

Working on the right side of the pocket piece, position one fabric strip so that the cut edges are even with the pocket mark and the ends extend 1/2" beyond the vertical lines. Stitch down the exact center of the strip, starting and ending exactly on the vertical lines. Position and stitch the other strip the same way.

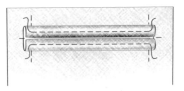

Turn the pocket to the wrong side and cut an opening as shown, making good-sized wedges in each corner. Make sure you cut just the garment fabric not the strips (or welts).

Turn both strips through the opening and adjust them so that they fill the opening. Whipstitch the opening closed and press from the wrong side. Remove the machine basting. You have just made a big bound buttonhole!

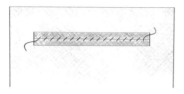

Center the zipper under the prepared opening, baste in place. Stitch in the ditch around the pocket opening to hold the zipper in place, or fold back the top and bottom sections of the pocket and stitch along the original seam lines. Use a zipper foot and a short stitch length for best results. Stitch slowly as you stitch across the ends of the zipper—or you may hit the zipper with the needle.

Finish the pocket by pressing under the seam allowance as described in the basic patch pocket instructions. Pin the pocket to the garment and topstitch in place.

Set-In Pocket: The set-in zipper pocket follows the same construction steps as above except the pocket opening is constructed in the garment fabric, rather than the pocket piece. After the zipper has been completed, the pocket piece is positioned behind the opening and stitched in place. This is an excellent pocket for a warm-up suit. You

can also make an extra-large pocket by cutting the pocket piece the same size as the lower half of the garment and catching the pocket edges into the side seam, center front and bottom edges of the garment.

If you don't want the pocket stitching to show, use two pocket pieces, placing one on the wrong side of the garment before you construct the opening. After the zipper has been stitched in place, pin the two pocket pieces together and edge-stitch around all four sides.

Beware of vertical side-front pockets on straight skirts. They look fine when standing but gap open when seated creating odd bulges where you don't want them. If the vertical pocket is an important design feature, leave the pocket basted closed and never use it. (If the pocket is not used, don't even attach the inside pockets, as they only add bulk to a slim skirt.)

To eliminate the bulk of a side zipper in a skirt or pair of slacks with pockets, sew the pockets into the skirt as directed but leave the **left** pocket open 7" on the inside edge as shown. Clean-finish this 7" opening on both pocket pieces. Make the waistband 4" or 5" longer than the pattern indicates so that it will extend to the inside edge of the left under pocket. Finallly, secure the waistband closed with several pant hooks.

POCKET STAY

A pocket stay keeps side-seam pockets from becoming "poppers" (pockets that bulge out when sitting down). It also keeps the pockets from flipping to the back. On skirts or slacks with pleats, the stay controls the fullness in the front where it should be, rather than drifting to the back where it should not be.

Estimate the width between the two pockets and add 2" for the seams. Cut a rectangle of lightweight woven lining fabric this width and 8" deep. The stay can be extended into the waistband. Clean-finish the horizontal edges and baste as shown to the two pockets. Try on the garment, checking to see that the stay is not too tight or too loose. Stitch the stay to the pockets. On slacks, two separate stays are stitched to the center-front seam allowance.

On slacks with a fly-front zipper, use two narrow stays that are stitched to zipper seam allowance.

Pocket stays can also be added to a ready-to-wear garment.

ONE-PIECE WELT POCKET

This welt pocket is easy to make and has many applications. It was originally designed for sweaters, but is equally good for sport shirts, pants, jackets and even dresses. A word of caution: Use a regular patch pocket on a sport shirt made of lightweight fabric. This welt pocket's construction would shadow through to the right side.

The welt and the pocket are made from one piece of fashion fabric, and it can be used with knits and medium-to lightweight woven fabrics. Use the welt pocket technique given later in this chapter for thick or bulky fabrics.

The measurements given in the diagram below are for the average-size shirt pocket. You can change the width of the pocket or welt by changing the distance between the vertical or horizontal lines. The back pocket on men's pants should be 5 1/2" wide to allow for the hand. We will refer to the diagram below as the pocket grid.

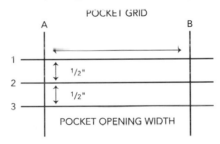

Cut a pocket piece 2" wider than the pocket opening and 10 1/2" long. This makes a pocket with a finished depth of about 4". Adjust the length of the pocket piece if you want a deeper or more shallow pocket.

Cut a piece of stay fabric for each pocket that is 2" longer and wider than the grid. Use a nonfusible, woven interfacing for the stay fabric. Trace the grid onto the pocket stay with a pencil or marking pen, being accurate with your lines.

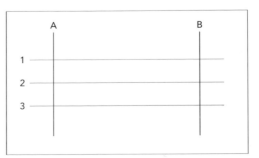

Position the pocket stay on the wrong side of the garment so that **line 2** is centered over the pocket location marks. If you are working with a horizontally striped fabric, make sure the pocket location mark is on or parallel to a stripe. Using a contrasting thread and a long stitch, machine-baste along the grid lines so that they are transferred to the right side of the garment. Stitch the vertical and horizontal lines from the same direction so that the grid will stay square. Change back to a matching thread and adjust your machine to the normal stitch length.

Again, working on the right side, fold over and press 1" of the free end of the pocket piece and bring the fold down to **line 3**. Pin in place. Turn the garment to the wrong side and stitch along **line 2** between **lines A** and **B**, backstitching at each end.

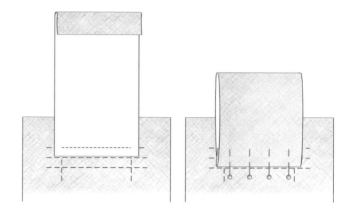

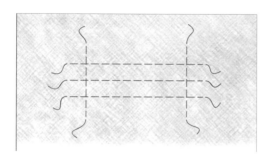

Working on the right side of the garment, pin the bottom edge of the pocket piece 1/8" above **line 2**. The piece should be centered over the horizontal grid lines, with the right sides of the fabric together.

Cut the pocket open between **lines 1** and **2**. Make a good-sized wedge at each corner. Be careful not cut through the pocket fabric. Hold it out of the way and cut just the garment and interfacing fabric. To avoid overcutting at the corners, place a pin at the corner so that you cut to but not through the corner.

On the other hand don't be a "chicken clipper." It is important that you clip right **to** the stitching—not a fraction of an inch back from it—so that the corners turn smoothly. Too many people are afraid to clip all the way, and they end up with a homemade look.

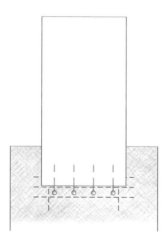

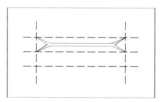

Pull the pocket through the opening to the inside, and arrange the welt so that it completely fills in the opening. Whipstitch the pocket closed with a few hand stitches or hold it closed with a strip of transparent tape.

Turn the garment to the wrong side and stitch along **line 1**. Begin and end the stitching line where **line 1** crosses **lines A** and **B**. Backstitch at each end for strength.

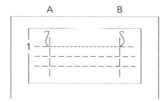

Fold back the side of the garment until you see the wedge on top of the pocket fabric. Stitch across the base of the wedge through all fabric layers. **Note:** *It is important to make this stitching line slightly convex to help square the pocket corners.* Continue stitching down the side of the pocket. Make another row of stitching beside the first one, using either a straight or zigzag stitch. Trim the seam allowance. Serge the edges or zigzag stitch to clean-finish them.

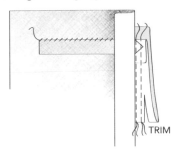

A pencil slot can be made on a man's sport shirt pocket by stitching another line of stitches 3/4" from the front edge of the pocket.

Finish the opposite side of the pocket in the above manner. Press the pocket from the wrong side, remove the basting and whip stitches, and trim away the stay fabric close to the stitching lines. Bar-tack the pocket ends for extra strength.

The pocket welt can be made from a contrasting fabric if desired. This looks very nice when you match the welt to the pants or skirt fabric. Cut a contrasting welt 2" wider than the pocket opening and 2 1/2" long for woven fabrics, or 2" long for knits or Ultrasuede fabric.

Trim 2" from one end of the pocket piece and stitch the woven fabric welt to the end of the piece with a 1/4" seam. Press the seam open (**Fig. 1**). Attach the knit or suede welt piece by overlapping the pocket edge 1/4"; zigzag in place (**Fig. 2**). Important: The fashion fabric must **always** be underneath the opening—**not** in the pocket or lining fabric.

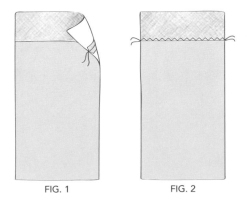

FIG. 1   FIG. 2

EXPANDABLE POCKET

This expandable pocket gives a designer look to sport clothes used for golf, tennis or hiking. Once you try it, you'll find many other uses for it also. The pocket is very attractive if you add machine-embroidered initials or a name to the front of the pocket. Edge-stitch it in a contrasting color or apply for fun an appliqué or sport motif, such as a golf tee or tennis racquet. The pattern for the pocket is found on page 5-27.

Cut a piece of fusible interfacing to fit within the inside fold lines of the pocket; fuse it in place on the wrong side.

Turn down the top of the pocket along the fold line, wrong sides together, and stitch a machine buttonhole, as indicated. Stitch across the bottom of the hem, if desired. Apply any appliqué or monogram.

Fold the lower corners of the pocket on the diagonal, right

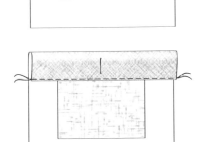

sides together, and stitch along the marked lines (**Fig. 3**). Use a short stitch length and take one stitch across the bottom point, as illustrated. Backstitch or tie the thread at each end. Trim the seam to a scant 1/4", cutting away excess fabric at the points; clip into the point of the "V" (**Fig. 4**).

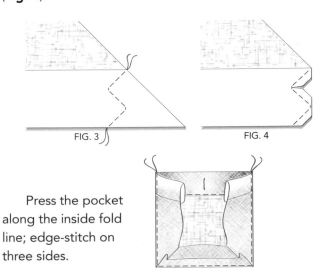

FIG. 3   FIG. 4

Press the pocket along the inside fold line; edge-stitch on three sides.

Turn under a 1/2" seam allowance around the outside edge of the pocket, and press.

Pin the pocket to the garment making sure that the back edges are directly under the front edges when the pocket is in the folded, closed position. Stitch the pocket to the garment.

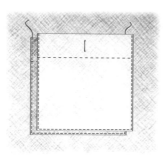

Fold the sides of the pocket together at the top edge and stitch a small triangle in the corner to keep the pocket top from gapping open. Sew a button to the garment underneath the buttonhole.

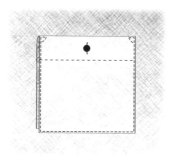

A flap can be added to this pocket if desired. Cut it so that the finished measurement is 1/4" wider than the finished width of the pocket. Stitch the flap in place as previously directed.

FACED-HOLE POCKET

The faced-hole pocket is decorative as well as functional. It is used mainly on children's clothes, but can also be applied to some adult sports clothes. Use a matching or contrasting fabric behind the pocket opening; top-stitch with a matching or contrasting color; or combine the pocket with a large appliqué. It is fun to think up new designs for this pocket (see some of the following design ideas). You are limited only by your imagination.

First, determine the size and shape of the pocket opening. Make it large enough for the hand to slip through easily. If you are combining the pocket with an appliqué, stitch the appliqué to the garment before you begin the pocket construction.

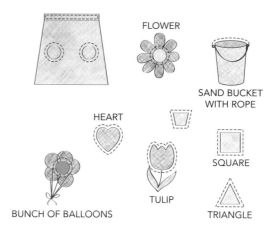

FLOWER

SAND BUCKET WITH ROPE

HEART

SQUARE

BUNCH OF BALLOONS

TULIP

TRIANGLE

Draw the pocket hole on a piece of paper and draw a pattern for the pocket piece around the hole, as illustrated. The pocket pattern should be 1" larger than the hole around the top and sides, and long enough to give the desired pocket depth plus 1/4" for a seam.

Cut an upper and under pocket piece from the pattern. The under pocket piece will be visible through the faced hole, so cut it from the fabric that you want to show.

Draw the hole design on the wrong side of the upper pocket and pin it in position on the right side of the garment. Stitch around the hole, using a short stitch length (**Fig. 1**). Cut out the hole, leaving a 1/4" seam allowance. Clip the seam as necessary (**Fig. 2**).

FIG. 1

FIG. 2

PICK A POCKET

Turn the upper pocket to the inside of the garment and press so that the seam is on the edge. Topstitch around the opening with one or more rows of stitching. You now have a neatly faced hole in your garment.

Working on the wrong side, pin the under pocket to the upper pocket only. Stitch around the outside of the two pocket pieces with a 1/4" seam. Make a second another row of stitching—regular or zigzag. Now how's that for a fun pocket?

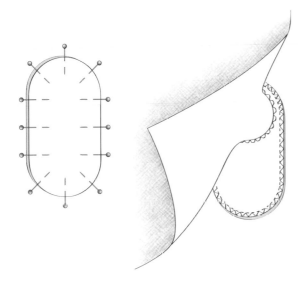

POCKET IN A SEAM

This pocket technique is used for small, concealed pockets in a waistband seam, flap pockets in a waistline or yoke seam, or men's or boy's pants pockets in either the back yoke or waistline seam. It can be large or small, topstitched for emphasis or left plain.

Instructions are given for the small waistline pocket. Directions for other versions can be found at the end of this section.

Mark the desired pocket width and placement on the pattern's seam line. Transfer these marks to your fashion fabric with small clip marks at the fabric's edge.

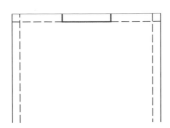

Cut one pocket piece 1" wider than the pocket opening, and twice the desired pocket depth plus two seam widths. This pocket piece is usually cut from the fashion fabric. If a flap is being used with the pocket, the pocket piece can be cut from the lining fabric.

Position the pocket piece over the opening marks, right sides together. Stitch the pocket opening making the seam 1/8" wider along the lower edge. Trim and clip the seam allowance.

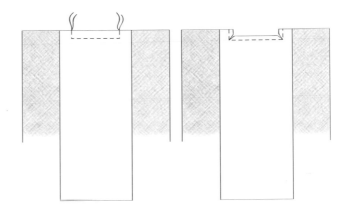

Turn the pocket to the wrong side of the garment and press the edges. Bring the bottom edge of the pocket piece up behind the opening, and pin.

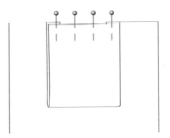

With the garment right side up, fold it back until you see the pocket's seam allowance. Stitch along the seam line, continuing down the side of the pocket. Double-stitch the seam, trim the seam allowance and repeat the process on the other side of the pocket. Press from the wrong side.

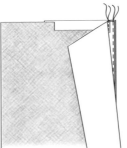

Pin the waistband in position and stitch in place, making sure you don't catch the edge of the pocket opening. Backstitch at both ends of the pocket opening for strength. The pocket opening is now barely visible below the waistband seam.

Flaps are added to this pocket when it is placed in a yoke seam. Construct the flaps according to previous instructions. Make the flaps 1/4" wider than the finished pocket opening.

Pin the flap over the opening after the entire pocket has been finished. Stitch in place just above the given seam line.

You are now ready to sew the yoke to the garment. Just make sure you don't catch the edge of the pocket in the yoke's seam.

Pockets that don't have flaps can be topstitched for emphasis. Topstitch the lower edge of the pocket, from corner to corner only, after the pocket piece has been turned to the wrong side and pressed (**Fig. 1**). Pull thread ends to the wrong side and tie. Complete the topstitching after the pocket has been completed, exactly meeting the existing line of topstitching (**Fig. 2**). Pull the thread ends to the wrong side and tie.

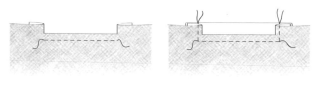

FIG. 1   FIG. 2

TAILORED PATCH POCKET

The tailored patch pocket is used on men's and women's tailored coats and jackets. It is lined and invisibly-stitched in place. This isn't as difficult as it sounds, and it is very impressive when perfectly finished.

Lined Tailored Patch Pocket

Many tailored garments are cut from patterned fabrics that must be matched. Be extremely careful when cutting out the patch pocket so that it exactly matches the pattern of the garment. Being "off" a little bit can ruin an otherwise perfect garment.

Interface the wrong side of the patch pocket. Use a fusible interfacing and trim away the hem and seam allowances of the interfacing before fusing in place. This preserves the pocket's shape, and keeps it from becoming baggy.

Leave the hem at the top edge of the pocket unstitched at the sides. Stitch the sides of the pocket a scant 1/8" from the seam line, within the seam allowance, easestitching around the corners. This is a guideline for the final stitching. **Note:** *Use a lighter color thread for the seam allowance stitching if you have a dark fashion fabric. This makes it easier to see when you work inside the pocket.*

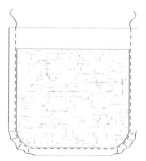

Press the pocket from the wrong side, rolling the seam allowance so that the stitching line is 1/8" from the folded edge. Notch the pocket corners as necessary to reduce bulk.

Cut the lining to match the finished size of the pocket and trim 1/8" from the three outside edges. Fold down 1" at the top edge of the lining and press. This slightly smaller lining supports the pocket and keeps it from becoming baggy.

Pin the lining to the garment right sides together, remembering to insert the Kleenex to give wearing ease. Now stitch it to the garment using a zigzag stitch. **Note:** *The lining is finished slightly smaller than the pocket to prevent the pocket from stretching out of shape.*

Position the pocket over the lining with the pocket edges extending 1/8" beyond the lining. Machine-baste the pocket in place, using a zigzag made from the longest stitch length and the narrowest stitch width. Start the stitching at the hem fold line and adjust the stitch so that the zigzag just bites into the edge of the pocket.

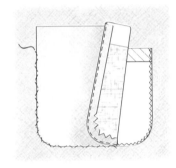

Adjust your machine to a regular straight stitch. Working **inside** the pocket, start at the hem's fold line and stitch on top of the first stitching line that you made around the seam allowance, backstitching at each end for strength. (When stitching around the bottom of the pocket, check to make sure unwanted fabric isn't caught in the stitching.)

Finish the top corner by wrapping the hem so that the hem's seam allowance is against the pocket's seam allowance. Stitch next to the existing seam line, making sure you don't catch any garment fabric. Turn the facing to the inside. If you don't topstitch, reinforce the pocket corners from the back with invisible hand-stitching.

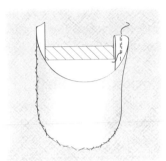

Slipstitch the lining to the pocket's hem. Topstitch around the pocket if desired. This pocket technique gives a neater, more finished looking pocket than one that is separately lined and then topstitched in place.

Unlined Tailored Patch Pocket

An unlined patch pocket, with rounded corners, can also be invisibly stitched in place. Prepare the pocket as described above except eliminate the pocket lining. Stitch the pocket to the garment with the long, narrow zigzag stitch. Start and end the stitching at the hem's fold line.

Working on the inside, stitch the pocket to the garment with a regular straight stitch; using the seam allowance stitching as a guideline. Start and end the stitching at the hem's fold line, backstitching for strength.

Finish the top corner by wrapping the hem so that the hem's seam allowance is against the pocket's seam allowance. Stitch next to the existing seam line, making sure you don't catch any garment fabric in the stitching. Turn the hem to the inside; topstitch the pocket's edge if desired, or secure the corners with several invisible stitches from the wrong side.

WELT POCKET

Welt pockets, with or without flaps, are used extensively on tailored garments. They should be carefully constructed so that companion pockets are identical in size and placement, and they exactly match or artistically contrast with the garment fabric. The welt pocket can have a single or double welt. Look at fine ready-to-wear to see how the two types are used.

Stabilize all pocket openings with a woven pocket stay placed in them. Use a piece of lining fabric or light-weight, nonfusible interfacing for the stay. This adds support to the pocket's opening and eliminates unattractive shadow-through of seam allowances.

As a rule of thumb, welt pockets in the back of pants are 4" long. In women's jackets they are 5" long and men's welt pockets are 6" long as their hands are larger.

Single-Welt Pocket With Flap

Transfer the pocket opening marks to the right side of the garment with hand or machine stitching, using a contrasting thread.

Cut two pocket pieces, 7 1/2" by 18" from the lining fabric or pocket drill (a heavy pocket fabric used to withstand the wear and tear of keys and coins). Use lining fabric for women's garments and pocket drill for men's garments. Cut two welt pieces 2 1/2" by 7 1/2" from the fashion fabric. Match the welt pieces to the garment if you are working with a patterned fabric.

Construct the flap as previously described and position it on the garment, right sides together, with the edge of the flap on the pocket's opening line. Stitch the flap with a 1/4" seam, backstitching at each end. Trim the seam allowance to 1/8".

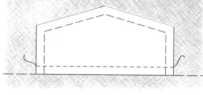

Prepare the pocket lining by stitching the welt piece to the top of the lining piece. Press the seam allowance down into the lining (**Fig. 1**). If using pocket drill, appliqué a 3"-wide strip of lining fabric to the bottom end of the pocket drill (**Fig. 2**). This lining strip will back the pocket opening and be more attractive than plain drill.

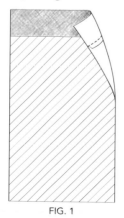

FIG. 1   FIG. 2

Center the welt piece over the flap. The welt edge should be at the flap's seam. Pin in place. Draw a line 1/2" below the flap's stitching line and machine-baste along this line through all layers. Be sure this measuring and stitching is accurate.

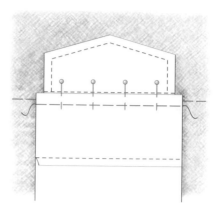

Press the pocket welt up along the basted line and pin.

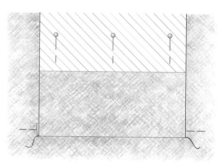

Working on the wrong side of the garment, stitch 1/4" below the flap's stitching line using a regular straight stitch. Start and end the stitching 1/16" short of the flap's stitching line. This makes the pocket opening slightly narrower than the flap and makes sure the opening is completely covered by the flap when the pocket is finished.

1 STITCH SHORT   1 STITCH SHORT

Remove the welt's basting stitches, unpin the lining and cut the pocket open, as indicated. Cut just the garment and interfacing fabric, making a good-sized wedge in each corner.

When stitching "boxes" that are to be cut open and turned—as for set-in pockets—start the stitching 1/2" **away** from the corner, **not** in a corner. This prevents a buildup of thread in the corner which will interfere with a perfect turn.

Pull the pocket lining through the slash and arrange the welt so that it completely fills the opening under the flap. Whipstitch the pocket closed and press from the wrong side.

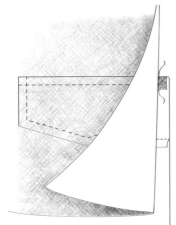

Working on the right side, fold back the garment until you see the wedge lying on top of the welt; machine-stitch across the base of the wedge catching it to the welt fabric. Remember to make this stitching curve slightly **inward** toward the pocket. This helps to square the pocket opening. Repeat this step on the other side of the pocket.

Pin the free end of the pocket lining into position behind the pocket. Turn the garment to the right side and fold down the top of the garment until the flap's seam is exposed. Stitch along the flap's seam line, catching the pocket lining.

Stitch down the sides of the pocket with a double row of stitching. Trim the seam allowance and press from the wrong side.

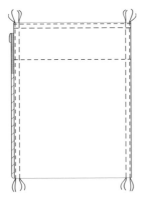

Double-Welt Pocket With Flap

Do not construct the pocket flaps for this type of pocket until the double-welt opening has been finished. Carefully measure the opening and then make the flaps 1/16" wider. The flaps are then squeezed into the opening, which prevents having open gaps at the pocket corners.

Each pocket needs two welt pieces. The top welt should be cut 1" wide and 2" longer than the pocket opening. The bottom welt should be cut 3" wide and 2" longer than the opening. Cut the pocket lining 7 1/2" by 18". Use lining fabric for women's garments and pocket drill for men's garments.

Cut two strips of 1/2"-wide fusible interfacing and apply them to each welt strip as shown.

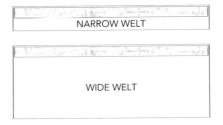

Press the narrow welt piece in half lengthwise, wrong sides together. Position it on the right side of the garment with the cut edges along the pocket opening line. Stitch in place down the **exact** center of the welt, backstitching at each end. Make sure the stitching starts and stops on the vertical lines marking the ends of the pocket.

Stitch the wide welt piece to the top of the pocket lining with a 1/2" seam. Press the seam down into the pocket lining.

If you are using pocket drill, it is important to appliqué a 3"-wide strip of lining to the lower edge so that when the pocket is opened, the lining rather than the pocket drill will show.

Working on the right side of the garment, center the lower welt over the pocket marks with the edge of the welt on the pocket opening line. Machine-baste exactly 1/2" below the top of the welt. Press the welt and lining up along this line and pin in place.

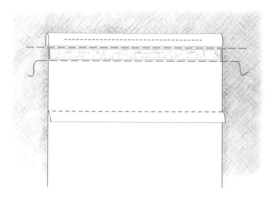

Turn the garment to the wrong side; stitch **exactly** 1/4" below the pocket opening line, starting and ending 1/16" short of the vertical lines. Backstitch each end. Be sure the stitching lines are parallel and exactly 1/2" apart.

Remove the welt basting and cut the pocket open as shown, making a good-sized wedge in each corner. Cut through **just** the garment fabric and interfacing. Don't cut through any pocket or welt pieces.

Turn the welt and pocket lining through to the inside. Adjust the welts so that they meet in the center of the opening. Whipstitch the welts closed and press from the wrong side.

Working on the right side, fold back the garment until the wedge is exposed. Stitch across the base of the wedge, catching it to the welt fabric. Make the stitching curve slightly toward the pocket. This helps square the pocket corners. Repeat the process on the other side of the pocket.

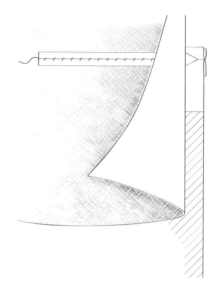

Remove the whipstitches across the pocket opening. Construct the flap so that it is 1/16" wider than the opening.

Mark the line where the top welt falls on the flap with a strip of drafting tape. (Use drafting tape as it's easy to remove and leaves no residue.) It tape should be positioned a welt width down from the seam line at the top of the flap. It is important to make sure the distance from the bottom of the tape and flap edge is equal on both sides.

Slip the flap into the opening so that at least 1/4" extends above the upper-welt seam. Pin and baste in place. Fold down the top of the garment until the welt seam is exposed. Stitch along the seam catching the flap in the process.

Bring the free end of the pocket lining up into position and pin. Stitch again along the welt seam, catching the pocket lining. Backstitch at each end for strength.

Finish the pocket by stitching the edges with a double row of stitching. **Note:** *Always stitch bottom corners with curved lines to avoid square corners that become "lint traps." Trim the seam allowance. Press the pocket from the wrong side.*

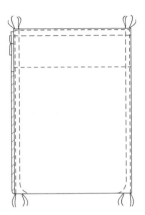

The width of the upper welt can be made smaller by cutting the welt piece 1/2" rather than 1" wide. This makes the finished welt 1/8" wide.

Double-Welt Pocket Without Flap

The double-welt pocket is sometimes made without flaps. Just follow the instructions above, except omit the flap. The corners of this pocket can be finished with an arrowhead if desired. Make the arrowhead by hand or cut one from leather or Ultrasuede fabric for a designer look. (Or, save yourself aggrivation and use the Double Welt Pocket Maker tool that makes perfect pockets so quick and easy.)

BUTTONHOLE POCKET

A buttonhole pocket can be made with the previous instructions, however, eliminate the flap and add a self-fabric facing behind the opening, as the lining should **never** be seen peeking out between the welts. Using this method, the top-welt seam allowances are turned up away from the pocket opening. In lightweight fabrics, the seam allowances add unwanted bulk and may shadow through the jacket fabric.

An alternate, all-in-one buttonhole pocket method is recommended by pattern companies for women's jackets. This method requires one large pocket welt of the fashion fabric. Following are instructions with several very important additional steps.

Buttonhole pockets are not difficult to sew; however, the stitching and measurements must be precise. Transfer the pocket position to the right side with soap or a disappearing marking pen. Pin a 2"-wide strip of firmly woven fabric on the wrong side as a pocket stay and to add support. With a contrasting-color thread, machine-baste the pocket line and the ends of the pocket. Measure again to be sure that the pocket is equidistant from the hem and from the front edge. (You don't want to have "drunken" pockets.)

With right sides together, center the pocket welt over the pocket line. Working on the wrong side, stitch 1/4" above and below the pocket line and across each end. Count the stitches across the ends so that they are of equal width.

Note: *Start the stitching line on one side of the "box," never in a corner. This prevents a build up of stitches in the corner that will interfere with a smooth turn.*

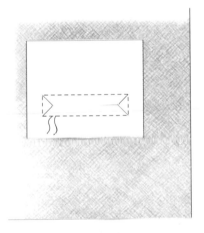

Cut the pocket opening along the centerline, making a good-sized wedge in each corner. Cut all the way to the corner stitching so the corner turns neatly. If the clipping stops short of the corner, the result is a rounded corner. Place a pin diagonally at the corner to avoid over-clipping and a disaster. (If this should happen, cover it up by making patch pockets instead of buttonhole pockets!)

Turn the welt through to the wrong side, wrapping the welt around each 1/4" seam allowance. This now forms two pocket welts. (To hold securely in place, position a strip of 1/4" Wash-A-Way Wonder Tape on the welt side.) Working on the wrong side, form a tiny box pleat at each end of the pocket. Make sure that each side of the pleat is the same width by hand-stitching across each pleat for a precise pocket corner. Important: Check that the welts are the same width for the entire length of the opening. Uneven welts are definitely a "loving hands at home" look.

Baste the welts closed to hold them in position when pressing. Press from the wrong side. On the right side, secure in place by stitching in the ditch. (Remember to shorten the stitches to 16 stitches per inch.)

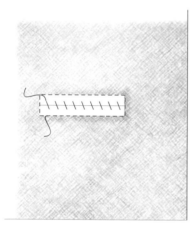

Stitch the pocket lining to the welt piece.

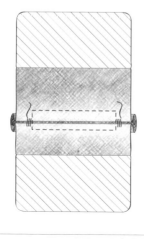

Turn the welt down into position. Finish the pocket by stitching the edges with a row of stitching. On the pocket lining, round the corners to eliminate lint traps.

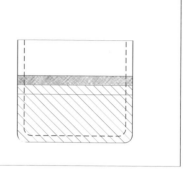

For a final designer touch, sew a snap on the inside of the lower welt and to the back of the pocket to hold the pocket in a straight line. Otherwise, the lower welt droops in jackets made of soft fabrics such as raw silk and velveteen. (Use a snap to hold welt breast pockets in a straight line as well.)

TAILORED BREAST POCKET

Used on tailored suit coats and sport jackets, this pocket is used for both men's and women's clothes and is always placed on the left side of the garment.

Cut the welt from the fashion fabric, matching it to the garment if the fabric is a plaid or a stripe. Cut the pocket lining 5 1/2" by 12" long. Interface the upper half of the welt piece with fusible interfacing. Construct the welt as given in the pattern instructions. It can be top-stitched if you wish. Transfer the pocket marks to the right side of the garment with machine basting, using a contrasting thread.

Position the welt on the right side of the garment, centering it between the pocket marks, as shown. The cut edge should be along the centerline. Pin and stitch with a 1/4" seam, backstitching at each end.

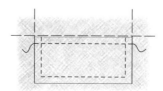

Center the pocket lining over the welt, right sides together, and pin in place.

Working on the **wrong** side of the garment, stitch 1/4" above the centerline then restitch on the first welt stitching line, being sure not to overstitch at the ends. Stitch the top line 1/16" short of the vertical lines on both ends. Make sure to backstitch at the ends of both stitching lines (**Fig. 1**). Cut the pocket open as indicated, cutting large wedges at each end. Cut through the garment and lining fabric (**Fig. 2**).

FIG. 1

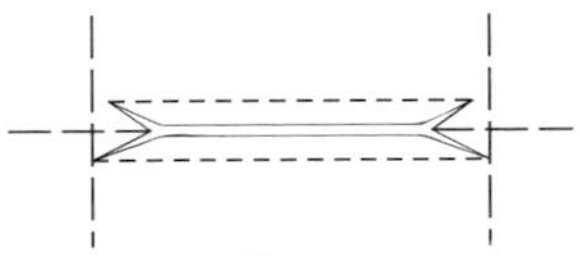

FIG. 2

Pull the lining through to the wrong side and press the opening. The welt should be pressed up into the finished position (**Fig. 3**). Fold down the top half of the lining and pin to the lower half. The bottom edges will not meet exactly; just pin them as they fall (**Fig. 4**).

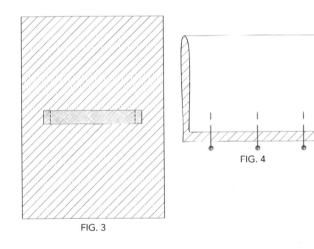

FIG. 3

FIG. 4

Working on the right side, fold back the garment until you see the wedge. Stitch across the base of the wedge, catching it to the pocket lining. Make the stitching line curve slightly toward the pocket. This helps to square the pocket ends. Backstitch for strength. Continue stitching down around the pocket lining and up the other side, making sure to stitch along the base of the other wedge. Stitch another row of stitching and trim the seam allowance.

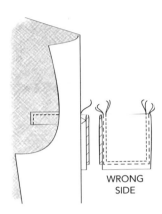

WRONG SIDE

Hand-stitch the edges of the welt to the garment from the wrong side.

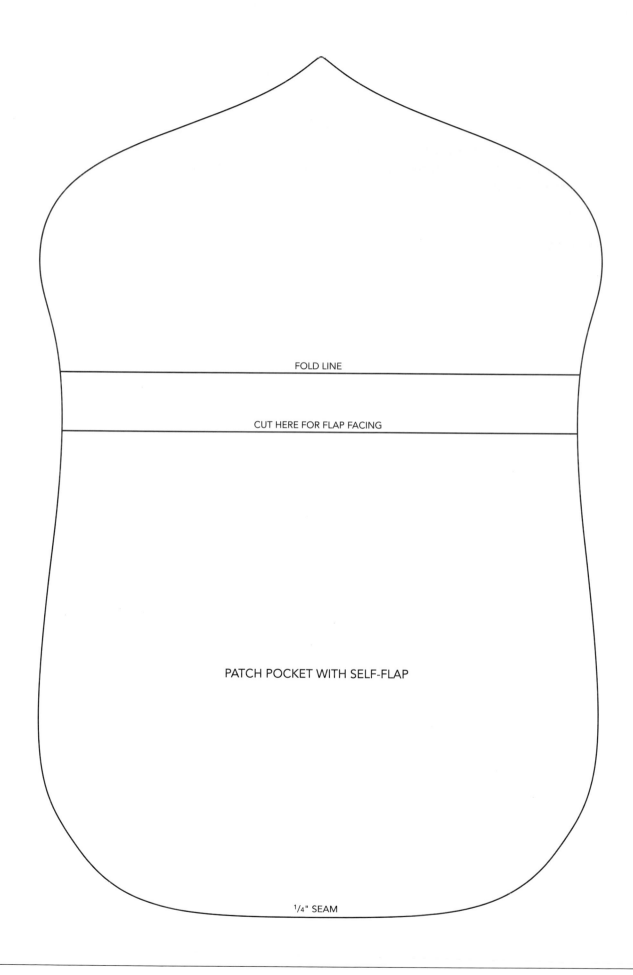

FOLD LINE

CUT HERE FOR FLAP FACING

PATCH POCKET WITH SELF-FLAP

1/4" SEAM

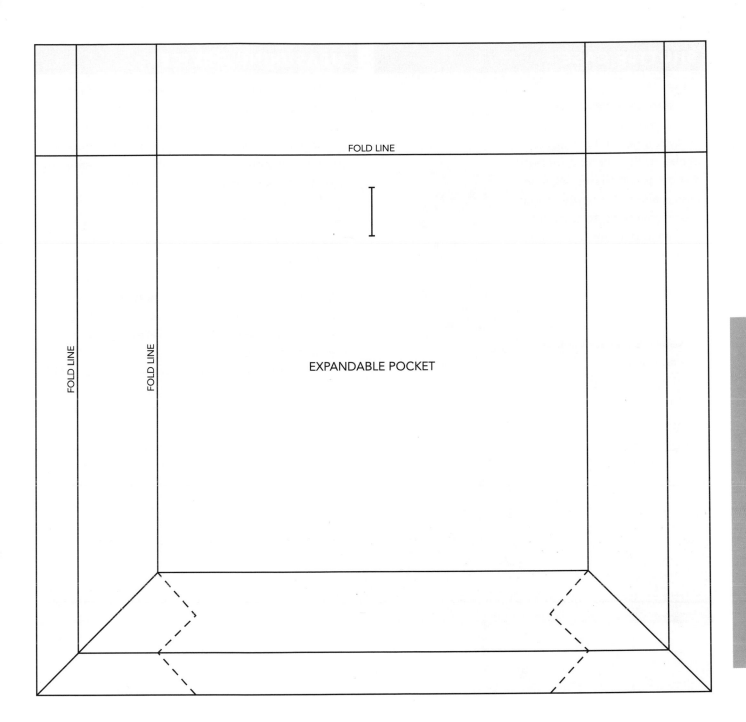

FOLD LINE

FOLD LINE

FOLD LINE

EXPANDABLE POCKET

Intricately carved ivory or tortoiseshell cases held 6 to 8 ivory shuttles and gauges to make mesh or netting for bed hangings and shawls. Women also made nets to protect fruit trees from birds, to catch fish, as well as delicate coats to go over a ball gown.

Netting Shuttle Case, 5 inches long, c. 1800.

Measurements varied widely in early days. Ribbon tape measures that wound into small cases, such as shells, were used early in the 17th century. Early ribbons were marked with embroidery or ink; stenciled or printed ribbons came into use at the beginning of the 19th century.

Long before accurate yardsticks came into being, housewives had their own marked wooden measuring sticks. These were used to mark new ribbons for their needlework as well as to check that they received accurate measures from traveling peddlers from whom they bought ribbons and laces. From this usage we derive the meaning of the word "yardstick" to mean receiving a full measure of value.

Until the metric system was adopted in 1799, the whims of kings determined measurements. Henry I decreed that an English yard should be as long as his arm. A cloth-yard was equal to the length of a hunting arrow. Edward VI decreed that each yard of cloth should have 37 inches in it—an inch equaled the length of the first joint of the thumb. In some instances, an inch equaled three barleycorns laid end-to-end. How's that for accuracy?

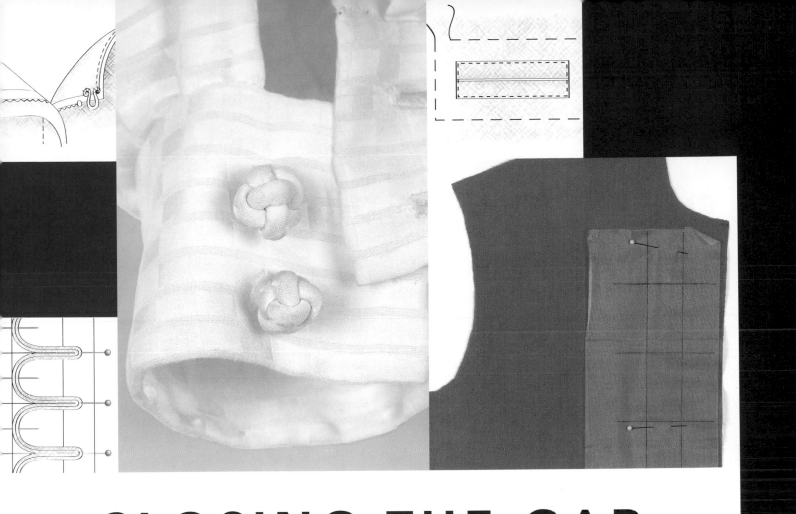

CLOSING THE GAP

6

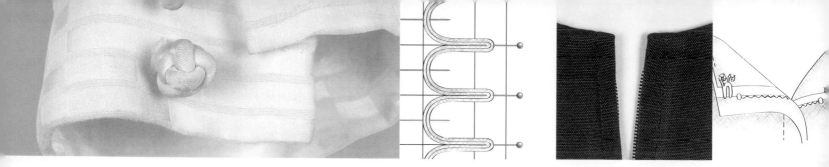

Chapter 6: Closing the Gap

ZIPPERS can have a custom look rather than the home-sewn look you get when using standard zipper instructions. The following techniques are not the ones found in ordinary sewing directions. These methods will help you obtain the professional results you want, and they are just as easy, or easier, than the procedures you have been using.

Help is here because the following zipper techniques are not those found in ordinary sewing directions. These methods will help you achieve the professional results that you want.

ZIPPERS

First, a few words about zippers in general. There are various types of zippers on the market today, and you should know about them so that you can choose the correct one for the garment and fabric with which you are working. Lightweight fabrics need lightweight, flexible zippers. Heavyweight sport and outerwear fabrics require heavy-duty zippers. Zippers are made from both metal and synthetic material, the most common of which is polyester.

Invisible zippers give the home sewer an alternative to the traditional zipper closing. These are perfect for printed fabrics that don't need the "busyness" of extra rows of stitching. They offer the ideal solution to the problem of zipper color when making a multicolored garment. A lightweight, polyester-coil invisible zipper is a must for lightweight knits and other thin fabrics. Regular zipper application on these fabrics may leave a puckered appearance along the zipper seams.

Invisible zippers do have some disadvantages, though, of which you should be aware. Do not use them in center-front seams of fitted or semi-fitted garments. Unless you sit or stand very straight at all times, they bulge out, giving your figure an unattractive line. This does not happen in loose, flowing garments such as robes or caftans, so invisible zippers can be used in these

garments without any problems. Stitching an invisible zipper into a striped or plaid fabric requires very careful sewing so that the design matches perfectly the zipper opening. The metal pull of the zipper is painted, which means that its color may chip off during the life of the garment. Painting the pull with several coats of clear fingernail polish before the zipper is sewn into the garment can slow this down.

ZIPPER KNOW-HOW

For best results, stitch both sides of the zipper in the same direction—bottom to top for regular zippers and top to bottom for invisible zippers. Stitching one side in the opposite direction makes for matching problems and uneven ends at the top of the zipper.

Center a 1/2"-wide strip of drafting tape down the zipper seam, on the right side of the garment, when inserting a center-slot zipper. The edges of the tape will be guidelines for the final machine or hand stitching. Just be careful that you don't stitch into the tape with your needle. This may coat the needle with a sticky substance and interfere with your stitching.

Stabilize the seam area of a knit garment with strips of tape before you stitch an invisible zipper in place. Place long tape strips down each side of the opening so that they are about 3/4" from the cut edge. This keeps the fabric from stretching and makes sure that the seam edges are even when you get to the end of the zipper and lower garment edge.

Garments that have collars or some sort of binding at the neckline should have the zipper positioned so that the top of the teeth end at the neckline seam.

Garments with faced necklines should have the zipper positioned so that the top of the teeth end 3/8" below the finished edge. This gives room for the hook-and-eye closure that keeps the edges neat.

Did you know that you can shorten both metal and polyester zippers? Therefore you can use up all those odd zippers in your sewing drawer that always seem to be the right color but the wrong length. Shorten the zipper by hand or machine stitching across the teeth at the desired length. (Careful—stitch slowly across the teeth so as not to break the needle.) Trim away the excess zipper 1/2" below the bar tack. Long zippers can be used for fly applications without having to shorten them first because the excess zipper will be cut off at the top once the waistband has been stitched in place. Unfortunately we haven't figured out a way to use zippers that are too short.

Insert zippers into the garment before you do any other sewing. It is easier to work on flat pieces of the garment rather than waiting until after the shoulder and side seams have been sewn. This works only if the pattern has been adjusted for fit so that no fitting has to be done in the finished zipper seam. Of course, garments with yoke and waistline seams in the zipper area should have those seams stitched and pressed first.

Note the labeled diagram of a zipper and refer to it when reading the following instructions.

CORDED EDGE

ZIPPER PULL

ZIPPER TAPE

ZIPPER STOP

CENTER-SLOT ZIPPER

The center-slot zipper is used in the back or front of garments. Occasionally you see it at a side seam, but the lapped zipper is really the preferred zipper application there. There should be a 5/8" seam allowance when inserting a center-slot zipper.

Center-Slot Zipper With Facing

Pin the garment pieces together, right side to right side, and mark the bottom of the zipper opening with a pin. Allow a seam allowance plus 3/8" above the top of the zipper teeth when measuring the length of the zipper opening. Machine-baste from the top to the pin; change to a normal stitch length, backtack to secure and finish sewing the seam. Snip the basting threads on both sides just above the pin mark. Now snip the bobbin threads at 1" intervals for easy removal later. Press the seam open.

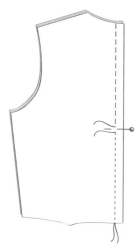

Place a strip of Wash-A-Way Wonder Tape along one edge of the wrong side of the zipper, overlapping the zipper by just 1/8". Position the right side of the zipper to the wrong side of the garment so that the zipper teeth run straight down the seam line. Finger-press tape firmly against the fabric. Using a zipper foot, edge-stitch along the untaped side of the zipper catching the zipper tape **just to the seam allowance**. Stitch from top to bottom (**Fig. 1**). Remove the tape and edge-stitch the other side of the zipper to the other seam allowance. Make sure

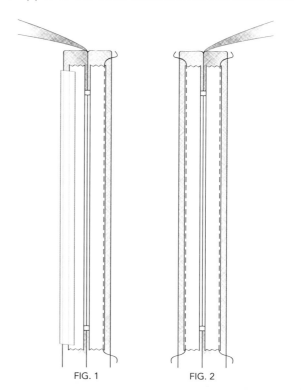

FIG. 1   FIG. 2

that the seam stays pressed open flat and stitch from the top to the bottom (**Fig. 2**).

Remove the basting from the top 2" of the center seam and open the zipper to that point. Clip the neck edge of the garment 5/8" from the edge of the seam allowance on both sides of the neck opening.

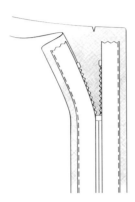

Stitch the shoulder seams of the garment together and press. Prepare the facing by stitching the shoulder seams together, pressing them open and clean-finishing the outside edge of the fabric. Trim 1/2" from both ends of the facing.

Stitch the ends of the facing to the edge of the garment seam allowance, right sides together, with a 1/4" seam. Make sure to catch the edge of the zipper tape in this stitching. Now the zipper is sandwiched in between the facing and garment at this point.

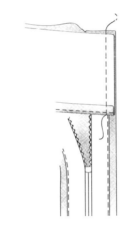

Pin the facing in place at the garment edge, matching up construction marks and seam lines, and fold the garment fabric at the 5/8" clip so that the facing fold is a scant 1/4" short of the garment fold. Stitch the facing to the garment with the given seam width, making sure the seams are the same width on each side of the zipper.

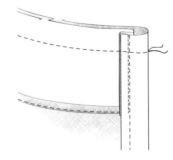

Grade and clip the neckline seam, trimming away excess fabric at the top corner of each side of the zipper. Turn the facing to the back, understitch and press.

Machine Finish: On the right side, mark the bottom of the zipper with a pin so that you won't hit it with the machine needle. Using a zipper foot, begin stitching at the seam line just below the zipper stop. Stitch for about 1/4", pivot the fabric under the needle and stitch up the side of the zipper. When you get to within 1" of the top edge, raise the presser foot and needle until the needle is just barely "in" the fabric. Carefully open the zipper down below the needle, removing a few more basting stitches if necessary, then continue stitching to the top of the opening. Make sure the seam fold just covers the zipper teeth in the open section of the seam. Stitch the other side of the zipper in the same manner, from the center bottom of the zipper to the top. Pull the threads through to the wrong side at the bottom of the zipper and tie. Remove the basting stitches and lightly steam-press the zipper from the wrong side. Sew a hook and eye in place at the top edge.

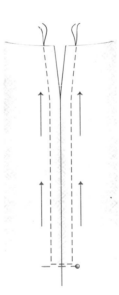

Hand Finish: Making the final stitching of the zipper by hand is well worth the extra time because it gives a custom look to the finished garment. The stitching process is called hand picking and is done with a small backstitch. This is the easiest finishing technique for stripes or plaids to be sure everything is lined up perfectly.

Hand-baste around the zipper opening about 1/4" from the seam. Using the basting stitches or a strip of tape as a guide, hand pick with a single thread around the zipper with small, even backstitches. Remove the basting stitches and steam-press lightly from the wrong side. Sew a hook and eye in place at the neck edge.

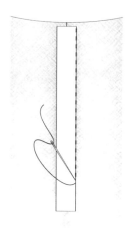

Center-Slot Zipper With Lining

The neckline facing can be eliminated on garments that are fully lined, letting the lining take the place of the facings. Use the following instructions for applying the center-slot zipper in this situation.

Follow the instructions in the previous zipper section up until the edge stitching of the zipper has been completed. Trim 1/2" from the center back edge of the lining pieces. Stitch the trimmed edge of the lining pieces to each side of the zipper tape. The zipper will be sandwiched between the garment and the lining seam allowance. Do this stitching with a zipper foot so that you can get right next to the zipper teeth.

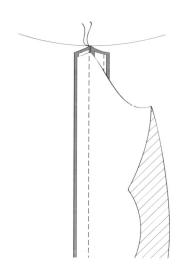

Remove the basting from the center seam for about 1 1/2". At the neckline edge, fold over the zipper along the corded edge so that right sides are together. The garment fabric should extend a little beyond the lining fabric. Pin the lining in place around the neckline and stitch the neckline seam to within 1 1/2" of the shoulder seam. Grade, clip and trim the neckline seam then understitch. Turn the lining to the wrong side of the garment and carefully press the edge.

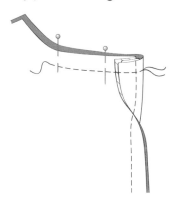

When attaching the lining to a sleeve edge, push or "crowd" the lining into the armhole so that it extends 1/8" beyond the garment edge. This allows the neckline and armhole seam to roll to the underside. There is no need for topstitching or hand picking the zipper. Sew a hook and eye at the neck edge, and now you have a truly invisible zipper finish.

Center-Slot Zipper With Waistband

Apply the zipper to the garment the same as for the first center-slot zipper except position the zipper so that the top of the teeth are just a seam width below the cut edge of the garment. (The top edges of the zipper tape will be enclosed in the waistband.)

LAPPED ZIPPER

The lapped zipper is used in the back of a dress or top, or on a skirt or pants at the side or center back. It is never used in the front of a garment. A 5/8"-wide seam must be allowed for this zipper application.

Because this type of zipper can be used at both the center back and side seams, we will refer to the garment sections as right and left, rather than right back and left back or back and front. Make sure the garment fits before inserting the zipper so you won't have to do any alterations. The zipper is applied to each of the garment pieces **before** they are sewn together.

Lapped Zipper With Facing

Place the right side of the closed zipper down on the right side of the right seam allowance so that 1/8" of the fashion fabric extends beyond the edge of the zipper tape. The top of the zipper teeth should be a seam width plus 1/2" down from the top edge of the garment. Using a zipper foot, stitch from the bottom of the zipper stop to the top of the zipper as close to the teeth as possible. Pivot, stitch across the top of the zipper tape, then down the outside edge to the bottom of the stop.

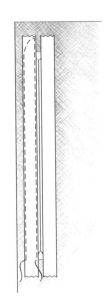

Stitch the facing pieces together; press the seams open and clean-finish the outside edge.

Unzip the zipper. Insert a pin from the wrong side of the garment so that it comes through the zipper tape precisely at the seam line and is on the tape side of the corded edge of the zipper. This will be the pivot pin.

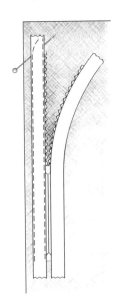

Pin the right facing in place along the top edge of the garment, right sides together. Push the pivot pin through the facing so that it comes out at the seam line.

Extend the lower edge of the facing 1/2" out beyond the edge of the seam allowance. This distorts the facing a bit, but makes it lie flat when the garment is completed. Stitch from the bottom of the facing, starting in the center of the zipper tape, and stitch up to the pivot pin.

Remove the pin and take one diagonal stitch across the corner and continue stitching along the top edge of the side to within 1 1/2" of the side seam. (Remember, the garment pieces have not been joined at this point.) Grade, clip and trim the seam allowance. Turn the facing right side out and press the faced edge and the zipper area. The underside of the zipper is now finished without any stitching visible on the right side.

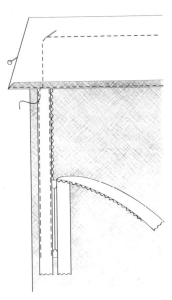

Note: *When working with heavy fabrics, angle the stitching up into the seam allowance a tiny bit after turning the corner and then gradually come back to the given seam line. This gives a smoother line to the finished edge.*

Next position the free side of the zipper on the seam allowance of the left garment piece, right sides together, so that the edge of the zipper tape is even with the seam edge. The top of the zipper teeth should be a seam width plus 1/2" down from the top edge of the garment. **Note:** *It is very important that this side of the zipper be positioned on the garment precisely as the first side is so that the top edges of the finished zipper will meet exactly. Edge-stitch the zipper to the seam allowance as shown.*

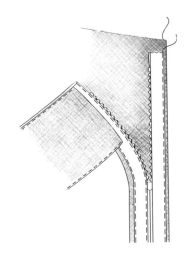

Close the zipper and stitch the garment seam below the zipper, starting just slightly above and to the left of the zipper stop. This stitching should be approximately 1/8" to the left of the visible stitching. Stitch all the way to the bottom of the garment taking a 5/8" seam. Press the seam open, forming a little "pleat" at the bottom of the zipper on the right seam allowance. The "pleat" allows for the finished zipper's slight overlap.

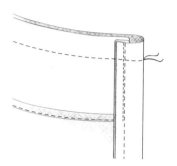

Note: *If the zipper is in the pants center back seam, you should stitch the crotch seam to within 1" of the inseam and then backstitch. This then allows for the continuous stitching of the crotch seam **after** the inseam has been completed.*

Make a clip into the top edge of the left garment piece 3/4" from the seam edge (**Fig. 1**). Trim away 3/8" of the free end of the facing, then stitch the edge of the facing to the edge of the garment's seam allowance with a 1/4" seam (**Fig. 2**). Make sure you catch the zipper tape in this stitching line.

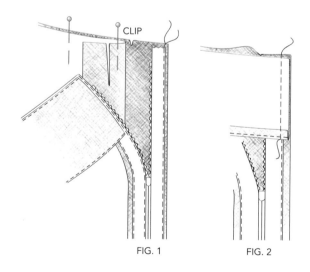

CLIP

FIG. 1   FIG. 2

Fold the garment back on the 3/4" clip so that the facing and zipper are sandwiched in between the garment layers. The garment should extend a good 1/4" beyond the corded edge of the zipper. Stitch the facing

in place with the given seam width ending 1 1/2" short of the garment's seam (shoulder or side seam). Turn the facing to the right side and close the zipper to see that the finished edges meet **precisely** at the top of the garment. Adjust the seam width if necessary. Grade, clip, trim and turn the facing to the finished position. Press lightly from the wrong side.

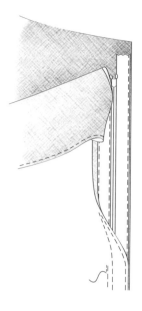

Close the zipper and pin the lap in place making sure that the right side is covered by 1/8". (This lap is important so that the zipper doesn't show when the garment is worn.)

Machine Finish: Place a pin at the zipper stop so that you know where it is and won't hit it with your machine needle. Place a 1/2"-wide strip of drafting tape along the folded edge of the zipper lap to act as a guide for the final stitching. Using a zipper foot, stitch the left side of the zipper, starting just below the zipper stop and continuing up the side, creating a 1/2"-wide seam. Pull the thread ends through to the wrong side at the bottom of the zipper and tie.

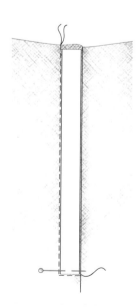

Sew a hook and eye at the top of the opening.

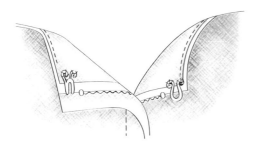

Hand Finish: For the professional touch, hand-pick the side of the zipper with small, even backstitches. Mark the stitching line with a line of hand basting or a strip of 1/2"-wide Magic Tape.

Hand finishing the zipper is the best method to use when working with stripes or plaids. Handstitching makes it so much easier to match up stripes across the zipper opening, and really doesn't take much more time than machine stitching. Finish by sewing a hook and eye at the top of the opening.

Join the garment seams (shoulder or side seam) and complete the faced edge. Understitch the entire faced edge for a perfect finish.

Lapped Zipper With Collar or Waistband

Follow the instructions for the lapped zipper with facings, except position the zipper on the seam allowance so that the top of the teeth are just a seam width down from the top edge. Of course, you won't be using facings, so just ignore those instructions. Lap the left side of the zipper over the right side 1/8" and finish with machine or hand stitching.

INVISIBLE ZIPPER

The zipper is applied to each side of the seam **before** the two pieces of garment are stitched together. Stabilize the seam area of stretchy fabrics by finger-pressing a strip of tape down the seam about 3/4" in from the cut edge.

Uncoil the zipper coil by pressing lightly with a steam iron or with your fingers. Position the zipper face down on the seam allowance so that the top of the zipper teeth are 1" down from the top edge of the garment when using a facing finish, and a seam width down from the top edge when applying a collar or waistband. The teeth of the zipper should run right along the garment's seam line.

Backstitch at the top of the zipper tape and hold the zipper in position with your fingers or pins while stitching with an invisible zipper foot. The coil of the zipper should run through the left side groove on the zipper foot, and the needle should be positioned in the center of the foot. Stitch as far down the zipper as you can, then backstitch.

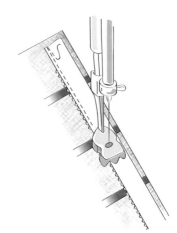

Note: *You get better results on heavy or bulky fabrics if the needle is positioned a little to the left of center. This allows for the thicker fabric and lets the zipper work more smoothly. Stitch thin fabrics close to the zipper teeth and thick fabrics farther away from the teeth. When the zipper is closed, you should not be able to see **any** of the zipper in the opening. If you do, that means that you didn't stitch close enough to the teeth. This problem can be corrected easily by restitching both sides of the zipper.*

Close the zipper and position the unstitched side of the zipper on the opposite seam allowance with the zipper face down. It is important that both sides of the zipper be positioned identically so that patterned fabrics will match across the zipper opening and the garment edges will meet after the rest of the seam has been closed. Matching plaids, stripes or patterned fabrics across the zipper opening can be done quite easily if you make some light pencil marks across the wrong side of the zipper at key matching points. Match these marks to corresponding points on the other seam allowance. Pin in place.

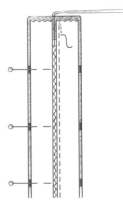

Open the zipper, position the coil in the groove on the right side of the foot and stitch that side of the zipper for a perfect match.

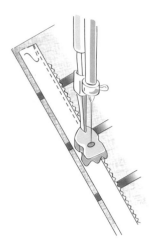

Close the zipper and complete the garment seam by pushing the zipper foot all the way to the left, pull the end of the zipper out away from the seam area and start sewing about 3/8" above the end of the zipper stitching and a scant 1/8" to the side. Backstitch at the beginning and close the remainder of the seam, making sure the edges are even at the bottom.

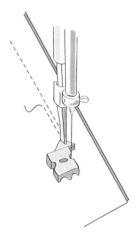

Pull each seam allowance out away from the garment and stitch the ends of the zipper tape to the seam allowance only. This controls the ends of the tape and keeps them flat after repeated washings.

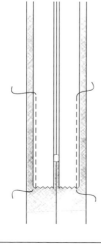

Clip a mark at the top edge of the garment 5/8" from the open edge. Trim 1/2" from the back edge of both ends of the facing. Stitch this trimmed edge to the garment edge. Make sure the stitching catches the zipper tape (the zipper will be sandwiched in between the garment and the facing).

Pin the facing in place at the neck edge, folding at the 5/8" clip mark. There will be a 1/8" extension of the folded garment beyond the folded edge of the facing. Stitch the neckline seam with the given seam width. Grade, clip and trim the seam allowance and turn the facing into the finished position.

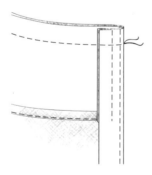

Invisible zippers are perfect for Ultraleather skirts and slacks, as no topstitching is needed. Use glue stick to hold the seam allowance flat or secure it with Wash-A-Way Wonder Tape and carefully finger-press it in place.

Invisible zippers **can** be put in with a regular zipper foot instead of a special zipper foot! The secret is to unzip the zipper and press the coil **away** from the tape. (Use an iron set at wool.) The teeth don't show, as they're pressed to the right side.

Now simply line up the inside edge of the zipper

coil on top of the seam line. Have the right side of the zipper facing the right side of the fabric. Hold in place with Wash-A-Way Basting Tape. Stitch close to the inside edge of the coil. Use a regular presser foot to ride on top of the zipper coil. (You will be stitching on the seam line.)

Note: *Experiment with how close to stitch and still be able to unzip the zipper. (If you get too close you have to rip!)*

ZIPPER IN A SLASH

The zipper in a slash is used only on knit fabrics. This is because you will be working with a very narrow seam allowance, 1/8". Woven fabrics ravel too easily to handle this narrow seam. The slash zipper leaves one less seam to sew and match, which is especially welcome when working with striped or patterned knits.

A polyester zipper rather than a metal zipper is the best choice for this application. First of all, it is lightweight and more flexible than is a metal zipper. Second, polyester zippers are more attractive as they look more delicate and don't have the paint-chipping problems of metal zippers. **Note:** *Cover the chipped paint of zipper pulls with model-car touch-up paint available at craft shops.*

You must decide what type of neckline finish you are going to use on the garment. If you are just going to turn under and topstitch the neck edge or bind it with a Chanel trim, then insert the zipper **before** the neck edge is finished. If you choose to apply a mock or full turtleneck collar, insert the zipper after the collar has been stitched to the neck edge.

Garment Preparation

Stitch the shoulder seams and press. The neckline seam allowance should be left intact if you are topstitching or binding the neck edge. Trim the seam allowance to 1/4" if you are applying a turtleneck collar.

Turtleneck Collar Preparation

There are three types of turtleneck collars that you can use on your garment. For a mock turtleneck that stands up around the neck but does not fold over on itself, cut a 5" wide piece of fabric across the stretch of the fabric and about 16" long.

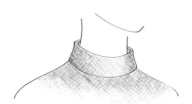

A full turtleneck or a prefolded turtleneck collar folds down around the neck. These look the same in front but the zipper treatment in the back is different. The zipper in the full turtleneck goes all the way up through the collar and turns back down on itself when the collar is worn.

For a prefolded turtleneck, fold the collar down into position and then insert the zipper. The zipper goes just to the fold of the collar, but does not turn back down on itself. This makes for a less bulky finish at the back of the neck. Cut the full or prefolded turtleneck collar 10" wide across the stretch of the fabric and about 16" long.

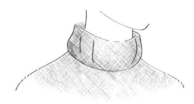

Determine the finished length of the collar by folding the collar strip as it will be when it is worn, once for the mock turtleneck and twice for the full or prefolded turtleneck. Wrap it around your neck until it looks good to you and feels comfortable. You will find that soft, stretchy knits need less length than firm, heavy knits. Cut the collar so that the ends just meet at the center back. Do not allow for a seam allowance. Collar length should never be more than the neckline measurement. Clean-finish one long edge of the collar piece with a wide zigzag stitching.

Collar Application

Fold the garment in half and press a crease down the center back the approximate length of the zipper less the finished width of the collar. Cut down the exact center back of the garment for about 1". Stitch the unfinished edge of the collar to the neck edge of the garment with a 1/4" seam. The collar will usually be smaller than the neck edge so you will have to distribute the collar evenly around the neckline. This will be an easy matter if you first divide the collar edge and neck edge into four equal sections and then stitch just a section at a time, stretching the collar to fit the neck edge.

The finished top fold of the collar should be marked with a pin. Find the top fold of the mock turtleneck by folding the collar piece back down on itself, wrong sides together, so that the edges meet. Place a pin at the fold.

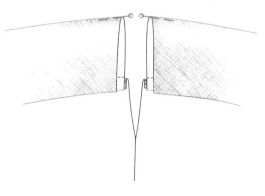

The first fold of the full turtleneck is determined in the same way; however, the width of each folded section will be approximately twice that of the mock turtleneck. Mark the fold with a pin.

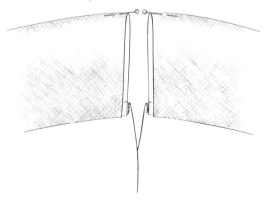

The finished top fold of the prefolded turtleneck is found by folding the collar in half so that the cut edges are even, wrong sides together. Now bring the fold down so that it covers the neckline seam by about 1/2". Put a pin in just the top layer of fabric at the top fold line. Pull the back section of the collar out away from the rest of the turtleneck and pin the three sections of collar into the finished position at the neckline seam shown below. Baste along the edges to hold everything in position. The pin marks the top folded edge of the collar, while the back section that is free acts as a facing for the turtleneck and will be stitched in place after the zipper has been applied. (The reason for folding the collar down below the neckline seam is so that the seam will be covered all around the neckline when the garment is worn.) It is important that you don't make the turtleneck collar too tight when measuring it around your neck. Tight turtlenecks tend to ride up and expose the neckline seam.

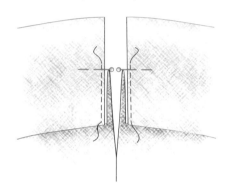

Zipper Application

Measure the length of the zipper from the top of the pull to the **top** of the stop at the bottom. If you measure to the bottom of the stop it is exposed in the finished garment and becomes unsightly after the paint chips. Mark the zipper length on the crease with a pin, measuring down from the neckline seam if no collar is used, or from the fold pin if a turtleneck collar is used.

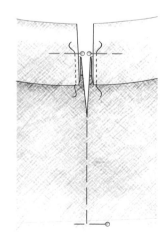

Place strips of tape down both sides and across the bottom of the center crease as illustrated. Keep the edges of the tape 1/2" from the crease. This is a "stay tape," not a stitching guideline. It prevents stretching of the cut edges of the knit while stitching the zipper in place.

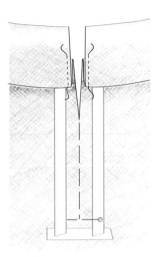

Stay-stitch a box around the center back crease that is precisely 1/4" wide. The stitching line is 1/8" to each side of the crease line. Draw stitching guidelines on the wrong side of the garment if desired. Use a zipper foot when stitching along these lines for greater visibility, or you swing your needle all the way to the right and run the edge of the zigzag foot along the center crease. This gives you a box 1/4" wide. The bottom of the box is at the pin-mark. Slash down the center back line to within 3/4" of the bottom pin, then cut into each corner to the stitching, forming a good-sized wedge.

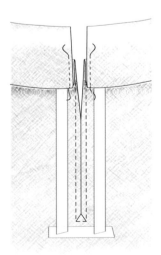

Position the zipper as shown so that the right side of the zipper is against the right side of the garment. The stop at the bottom of the zipper should be completely above the bottom of the stitched box. Secure the zipper to the garment by stabstitching across the zipper teeth to the corners of the box. Make sure that this stitching is done **between** the teeth and the stop so that the stop doesn't show after the zipper is completed.

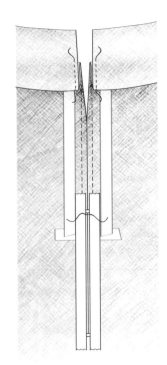

Bring the zipper up along the slash edge into the finished position. Pin the right side of the garment to the right side of the zipper so that the stay stitching line is next to the teeth of the zipper. Using a zipper foot, stitch along the stay stitching line from the bottom of the zipper to the top, so that you don't end up with an unsightly pucker at the bottom of the zipper. Stitch to the top of the pull only, not to the end of the tape.

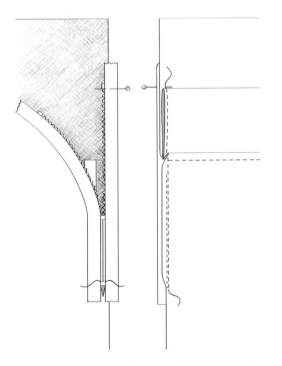

Be sure that the neckline seam is turned up into the collar as you stitch across it. If you have measured and stitched correctly, the top of the zipper teeth should end at the pin that marks the top fold of the collar. If you are not using a collar, the top of the teeth will end at the neckline seam.

Note: *When you come to within 1" of the top of the zipper, you must lift the presser foot, raise the needle and hold the zipper tape in position while you unzip the zipper. It is impossible to stitch neatly around the zipper pull if you don't do this. Move the garment back two stitches (do not backstitch) so as to take up the excess loop of thread that forms when you pull the needle out of the fabric. This loop would easily catch in the zipper and eventually break. Finish stitching just to the top of the pull.*

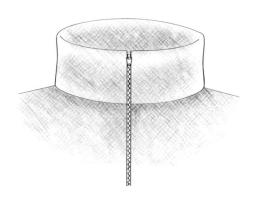

Unzip the zipper all the way. With the zipper tape flat, turn down the excess tape at the top, at right angles to the garment as shown. Wrap the back or facing half of the collar over the zipper, right sides together. The teeth of the zipper should extend into the collar at this point, and the cut edges of the collar should extend approximately 1/4" below the neckline seam. Stitch down through the collar section on the first stitching line. Trim away the excess tape at the top of the zipper.

Finish stitching this side of the zipper as you did the first side, from bottom to top. If you are using a collar, finish the inside neck edge by hand-stitching the edge of the collar to the neckline seam, or you can tack it in place by "stitching in the ditch" on the right side of the garment. Collarless necklines are finished by binding the edge with bias or Chanel trim, or just by turning under the seam allowance and topstitching in place.

FLY ZIPPER

Putting a fly zipper in a pair of pants is really a simple procedure. You will find various methods in pattern instructions, but the one found below is the easiest and can be adapted to any pattern.

Pattern

First of all, examine your pattern to see what pieces are used in the fly construction. Some patterns have the fly facing cut as one with the pant front pattern. This is preferred.

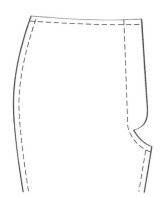

If your pattern has a separate fly facing, you must make it into a cut-on facing by overlapping the facing pattern and the pant front pattern so that the seam lines match. Pin the pattern pieces together and use this new pattern to cut out your fashion fabric.

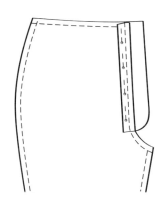

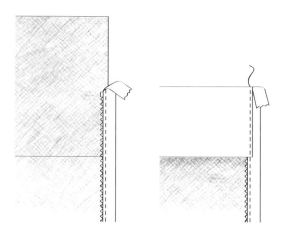

Close the zipper and pin the other side of the slash to the zipper tape, right sides together, making sure that the stitching line is precisely along the zipper teeth and the neckline seam matches exactly across the zipper. It is suggested that you hand-tack the zipper to the garment at the neck seam to make sure it doesn't shift in the final stitching process. Mismatched seams at the neckline are a sure way to achieve that "loving hands at home" look.

Zipper Construction

Before removing the pattern from the cut out garment pieces and from the wrong side of the fabric, mark the center-front stitching line with a small clip as well as marking the "dot" at the bottom of the zipper seam with a small pencil mark.

Apply some fusible interfacing to the wrong side of the left fly facing, as shown. This interfacing stabilizes the fly area and keeps it looking smooth. This is especially important when working with knit fabrics. Mark the center-front stitching line on the wrong side of the fly facing.

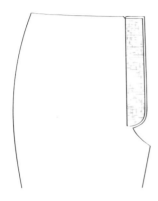

It is also advisable to edge-stitch a piece of pre-shrunk twill tape to the left fly facing, next to the fold line, on knit garments. This stabilizes the fold of the fly and keeps it neat.

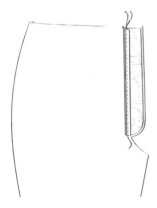

The fly zipper is completed after any front pocket detail is sewn, but **before** any other sewing is done on the pants.

With the right sides of the pants front together, machine-baste down to the dot at the bottom of the zipper. Clip the bobbin threads at 1" intervals for easy removal of the basting stitches after the zipper has been completed.

Stitch the seam below the "dot" with a regular or straight stretch stitch, stopping 1" before the end of the seam. If you are using just a plain straight-stitch, double-stitch this lower seam for strength. (This seam area is very difficult to repair if it pulls out later in the wearing process.) Clip to the seam line at the bottom of the fly facings as shown.

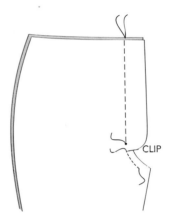

On men's pants, the fly is always on the left side. On women's pants there is no consistent rule, the fly can be found on the right as well as on the left side depending on the designer. The instructions given have the fly on the left side. Just substitute right for left if you prefer the fly on the right-side.

With right sides of fabric together, pull the right fly facing out away from the garment's front and press the seam open.

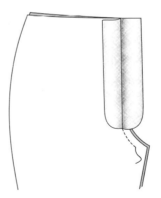

Use a zipper that is at least as long as the distance from the "dot" to the waistline seam. If the zipper is longer, it can be easily cut off **after** the waistband has been stitched in place. Metal trouser zippers are good for heavy-duty use, but most polyester zippers will serve just as well in everyday clothes, and the color selection is greater.

Place the zipper face down on the right fly facing so that the bottom of the stop is 1/4" above the dot. If you want the narrow fly finish that some patterns call for, you should place the edge of the zipper teeth right along the center seam line. Make the regular-width fly finish by placing the left edge of the zipper tape along the center seam. Using a zipper foot, stitch down the right zipper tape close to the teeth. Stitch again along the outside of the tape.

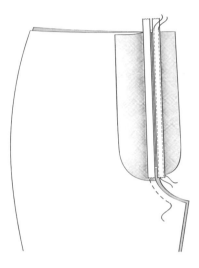

Turn the zipper over, right side up; pull it out to the side so that it faces up and press.

Now, rearrange the pants front so that the left fly facing is pulled out to one side. Position the zipper face down on that facing, making sure that the zipper is pulled over as far as it can go. Secure with a few pins and stitch down the left zipper tape just to the side of the teeth. Stitch a second time along the edge of the zipper tape. Both sides of the zipper should be stitched from top to bottom.

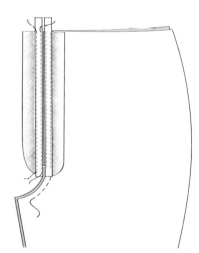

Open up the pant fronts and place them right side down on a table. Fold over the fly facings onto the left pant front, making sure they are pulled over as far as they can go, and pin in place. If your zipper stitching is straight, and your machine's bobbin stitching is perfect, it is best to do the final stitching from the wrong side. Stitch along the edge of the zipper tape, curving smoothly over to the center front line. Or, pivot the fabric under the needle at a point just above the end of the zipper teeth and then stitch down to the "dot" at an angle. Backstitch at the end of this stitching line for strength.

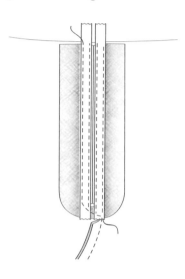

The final stitching can also be done from the right side of the garment, if you prefer. First, machine-baste along the edge of the zipper tape from the wrong side. This holds the fabric layers securely so that they don't drag against each other during the final topstitching. (Use glue stick to hold the two layers in place to avoid a drag.) Mark the stitching line with a sliver of soap, 1 1/4" from the fold for the wide fly finish, or 3/4" from the fold for the narrow finish. Topstitch down the side of the zipper; curve or angle the bottom of the fly to the center front as desired.

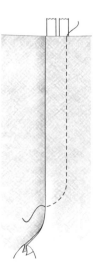 

Press the entire zipper assembly from the wrong side using a steam iron, then remove the center-front basting.

Zipper guard

A zipper guard is a layer of fabric that is stitched in place behind the zipper. It protects your skin or shirts and blouses when the zipper is zipped up. While you won't always see a zipper guard on ready-to-wear garments, it is a custom touch and is an absolute **must** for snug-fitting pants in order to prevent painful pinches.

The guard is easily made from a piece of fabric cut 2" longer than the zipper and 3" wide. Use your fashion fabric or cut it from a matching lightweight fabric if you prefer. Fold over 1 1/2" along one long side and press with the wrong sides together.

Open the zipper and position the guard so that the top edge is even with the top edge of the pants and that approximately 3/4" extends beyond the edge of the zipper teeth. Stitch down the fold of the fabric to the left of the teeth. If you don't use a zipper guard, edge-stitch this fold to hold the zipper in the proper position.

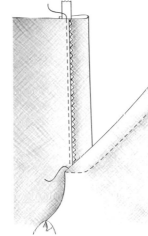

Close the zipper. Turn the pants to the wrong side and trim the right fly facing so that it is even with the edge of the zipper guard. Trim the cut edges of the guard close to the edge of the zipper tape underneath it.

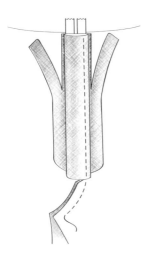

Make a small bar tack at the end of the zipper stitching on the right side of the pants front.

Fold over the left pant front until you expose the edge of the left fly facing, which should be directly on top of the folded edge of the zipper guard. Make a small bar tack through all these layers of fabric about 1/4" above the zipper stop. (This bar tack prevents you from tearing out the bottom of the zipper.) It is especially important on snug-fitting pants.

Trim away any excess guard-fabric at the bottom of the zipper and your fly zipper is finished. If the zipper you used was longer than the fly opening, just trim away the excess **after** the waistband has been stitched in place. Don't do it now; otherwise the zipper slide might just slip off the cut end, leaving you in a real fix!

Zipper guard Variation

Cut down on bulkiness in the zipper area by making the zipper guard from a single rather than a double layer of fabric. This works only if your fashion fabric is firm enough to hold its shape and does not fray badly. Use this technique for most double knits because you don't have to worry about the cut edges raveling. Woven fabrics should have the cut edge zigzagged or serged in order to prevent fraying.

The single-layer zipper guard is made by adjusting the fly extension of the pattern so that it is at least 1 3/4" wide.

Construct the fly zipper as described above, except when you get to the zipper guard instructions, just wrap around the right fly facing along the edge of the zipper tape so that it forms the guard. Open the zipper and stitch through this fly facing close to the edge of the fold of the fabric so that the facing is held in position.

Trim the left fly facing close to the edge of the zipper tape. Close the zipper and trim the guard even with the left fly facing.

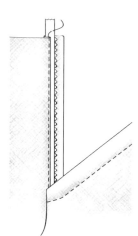

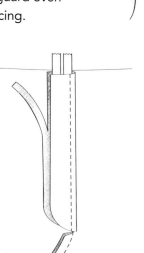

Bar-tack the zipper as described above and trim away excess facing fabric at the bottom of the zipper.

FAKE FLY

Many times you will want the look of a fly zipper on knit pants but want to eliminate the bulk that it creates. The solution is a fake fly. Of course, it works only on pants that can be pulled on over the hips without an opening of any kind. It is the perfect fly to use on men's and boys' swim trunks.

The pattern should have a cut-on facing at the fly instead of a separate facing. Adjust your pattern according to the instructions in the fly zipper, if necessary.

Baste and permanently stitch the center-front seam as described in the fly zipper, and clip to the seam line just below the dot (**Fig. 1**). Using a regular straight stitch, sew a second seam 1/2" from the basted center-front seam, stitching all the way down to the clip (**Fig. 2**).

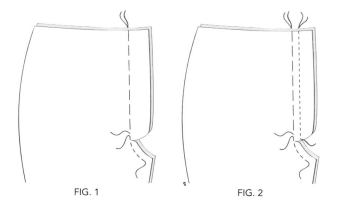

FIG. 1   FIG. 2

Press the fly facings over onto the left pant front and pin in place. Turn the garment to the right side and topstitch approximately 1 1/4" from the fold, curving down to the "dot" at the bottom of the fly opening. Steam-press from the wrong side, trim away any excess fly-facing and remove the center-front basting.

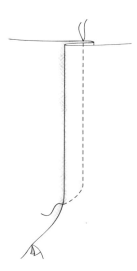

EXPOSED ZIPPER WITH DECORATIVE TRIM

It's fun to spice up your wardrobe with fancy trimmed zippers. There are so many beautiful ribbons and trims available, you will find it difficult to make a choice. The techniques for applying trimmed zippers are easy to do and the result is impressive. They can be put in a seam or slash opening.

Buy enough ribbon-type trim to line both sides and across the bottom of the zipper. Preshrink the trim.

Stitch the trim to both sides of the zipper tape, mitering or creating a point at the bottom. The edge of the trim should be as close to the zipper teeth as possible without interfering with the zipper slide.

Bring the seam allowance through to the right side and press along each seam line so that the fabric is right side to right side. Trim the seam allowances if they are going to extend beyond the edge of the zipper trim.

Position the trimmed zipper on the right side of the garment so that the top of the zipper teeth is a seam width down from the top edge of the garment. Sew the zipper in place by edge stitching along the trim.

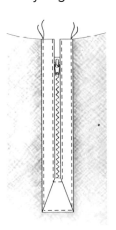

Turn the garment over and slipstitch the edge of the seam allowance to the zipper tape.

Zipper in a Seam

Stitch the seam closed below the zipper opening. Clip the seam allowance at the end of the stitching line on the diagonal. Press the seam open.

Zipper in a Slash

Press a crease that is the length of the zipper plus a seam width down the center of the garment. Stitch a long box around the crease so that it is precisely 1/4" wide.

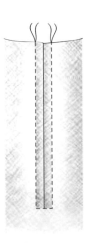

Position the trimmed zipper on the right side of the garment so that it is centered over the "box." The zipper stop should be at the bottom of the box. Edge-stitch the trim to the garment.

Turn the garment to the wrong side and slash down the center of the "box" to within 3/4" of the bottom. Clip into the corners forming a wedge.

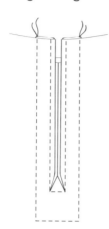

Turn under the cut edges along the machine-stitching line and slipstitch to the zipper tape. This technique can also be used with the zipper that has its own wide decorative tape.

BUTTONS & BUTTONHOLES

Have you ever given much thought to the hows and whys of buttons and buttonholes? Have you ever wondered how fashion designers figure out where to place the buttonholes on a new creation so that the buttons complement the design and fit of the garment? Surely they must have some guidelines, but what are they?

Since most of us usually follow a commercial pattern, that gives buttonhole locations and button size, we don't run into too many problems. However, as soon as we start to do our own thing, we then need the knowledge that designers have, so that the result is a custom, rather than a homemade look.

You might now be thinking, "Why would anyone need to change the button and buttonhole information on a pattern?" Well, for starters, the pattern might require some alteration that would affect button placement; maybe the fabric selected has such a design that the buttonholes have to be adjusted to complement it, or perhaps you want to use groups of two small buttons in place of large ones.

Button and buttonhole guidelines are also necessary if you are designing your own pattern or using one that doesn't have button and buttonhole information.

Well then, what has to be considered when working with buttons and buttonholes? Some of the things to be taken into account are: the style lines of the garment, whether the garment is fitted or loose, the selected fabric and the size of the buttons.

BUTTON SELECTION

Let's start with the basics of button choice. Buttons should be interesting design features as well as functional. Give some careful thought to your choice of buttons. Many times the right button can turn an ordinary garment into a fashion statement. The wrong button can make an otherwise fashionable garment look "homemade."

Most patterns come with a suggested button size, and as long as you follow this guide you will not have any problems. However, if you decide to use a larger size than recommended, you must change the distance between the closing line and the edge of the garment to accommodate the larger button. The width of the facing must also be changed the same amount. Failure to do this, will place the buttons too close to the edge of the garment when it is closed. Refer to Buttonhole Placement section.

Think about groups of buttons rather than a single button. Two or more small buttons placed close together can take the place of one large button and add interest to the garment.

Consider unusual types of buttons, such as wooden toggle buttons with string or leather thongs serving as buttonholes, Chinese ball buttons or frogs made from matching or contrasting tubing, or don't use buttons at all; instead, apply some decorative gripper snaps.

Select small lightweight buttons for fabrics that are thin or soft. Large or heavy buttons can be used on crisp or thick fabrics.

Buttons should be compatible with the cleaning method used for the finished garment. While most buttons are machine washable, you will find some that should not be washed—or even dry-cleaned! Such buttons are best used on garments that don't require frequent cleaning and can be attached with button-pins instead of being sewn in place.

Buttons should be kept to 1/2" or smaller for blouses or tailored shirts. Larger buttons are sure to give a "homemade" look.

Select nonshank buttons for double-breasted garments that do not have two rows of buttonholes. The buttons will lie flatter against the garment if this is done. Shank buttons "droop" if they are not supported by a buttonhole.

Contrasting buttons up the front of a garment will establish a strong vertical line, which is good for short or heavy figures. The reverse is true for tall or thin figures.

Take a scrap of garment fabric to the store when buying your buttons. Make a buttonhole-size slit in it and place this over various buttons to see how they look on that particular fabric. If you can't find just what you want, then consider covered buttons. They are a snap to make when you buy a covered-button packet and follow the instructions.

BUTTONHOLE PLACEMENT

Most patterns that you will be working with contain complete buttonhole placement information. If you have to make some pattern alterations or are designing your own pattern, you need the following information to help position the buttonholes correctly.

- Buttonholes should start 1/8" beyond the closing line of the garment in order to accommodate the shank of the button. The shank can be either a part of the button or one formed by thread.

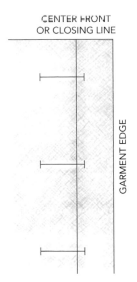

CENTER FRONT
OR CLOSING LINE

GARMENT EDGE

- The distance between the closing line and the edge of the garment is equal to the width of the button, for an average-size button, and equal to one half the but-

ton width plus 1/2" for large buttons. These measurements make sure that the buttons do not come too close to the edge of the garment when it is buttoned.

- The top button on garments that close all the way up should be positioned so that it is the same distance down from the finished edge as it is in from the front edge of the garment.

- The button is always sewn to the closing line of the garment whether it is the center front or some other line, i.e. a sleeve.

- Buttonhole length is equal to the width of the button plus 1/8". The length for an extra-thick, round or bulky button can be determined by wrapping a narrow strip of paper around the biggest part of the button and then using one half of that measurement. Add an extra 1/8" for thick coating-type fabrics.

- Vertical buttonholes are placed directly along the closing line. Button location for vertical buttonholes is 1/8" down from the top edge of the buttonhole rather than the center of the buttonhole. This makes the closing less apt to pull open.

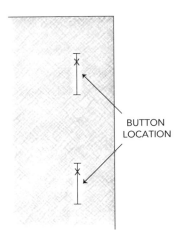

BUTTON
LOCATION

- Buttonholes in plackets or tab fronts should be made vertically, otherwise the button will pull to the edge of the buttonhole and will not be on the center-front line. This includes "false plackets" that are made by topstitching only. **Note:** *Some designer fashions will take exception to this rule.*

- The buttonhole underlap must be wide enough to extend **beyond** the buttonhole opening when the garment is closed. If you follow the above rules for button and buttonhole placement this will not be a problem. However, if you try to make a garment a little larger by moving buttons out, you will run into this problem.

- Fitted garments should have a button at the bustline in order to prevent gapping. This is especially important for large-busted figures. To eliminate gaposis, be sure to check the placement of buttonholes on a dress or blouse **on you**! Just because it's positioned a certain way on the pattern doesn't mean you have to place it there. Place a buttonhole at the strain of the bust; then position other buttonholes up and down from that critically placed buttonhole. If it is impossible to place a button there because of fabric or pattern design, then secure the area with a concealed snap (or use Res Q Tape).

- Fitted garments should also have a button or hook and eye placed at the waistline. If a belt is worn with the garment, use the hook and eye rather than the button in order to reduce bulk at the waistline. Make sure the buttons are spaced equally above and below the belt and are of sufficient distance away so that they don't interfere with it.

- A button should also be placed at the widest point of the hips.

- Never place buttonholes in the hem area of a garment. The last button on a dress or skirt should be placed 4" to 5" above the hemline.

- When using rounded or ball buttons on a shirt that will be tucked into slacks or a skirt, substitute flat buttons for the tucked-in portion. Why? This avoids strange bumps showing through the skirt or pants.

- Loose-fitting garments can have buttons placed almost anywhere for design purposes. However, if they

are widely spaced, it might be a good idea to place snaps between them to make for a perfect closure.

- Patterns for short, heavy figures usually need more buttons than those for tall, thin figures. Small to average-size buttons are suitable for short figures, while larger buttons can be used for taller figures.

- Buttonholes are placed on the right side of the garment for women and the left side of the garment for men. If you ever goof and set women's buttonholes on the left, don't worry, you're in good company. Many European designers place all their buttonholes on the left side. But—if you place men's buttonholes on the right side, you are going to have to think up your own excuse.

- Not quite enough yardage for the blouse you want to make? Use lining fabric or nylon sheer for the shirttails that won't show when the blouse is tucked into the skirt. When using the Chinese knotted buttons for an elegant designer effect, use snaps below the waistline to avoid unattractive bulges.

- Most patterns with a collar-band finish call for a buttonhole in the collar band. However, this is a difficult buttonhole to machine-stitch, as the seam allowances of the band prevent the presser foot from lying flat on the band resulting in a crooked buttonhole. Save a lot of frustration. If you'll never use the buttonhole—don't put it in! If you're making the shirt for your husband, tell him to keep his tie on to cover your problem buttonhole!

BUTTONHOLE TYPES

The type of buttonholes you use on your garment is up to you. Machine buttonholes can be used on any type of apparel, but a beautiful bound buttonhole has long been essential for the custom look on your designer clothes. Bound buttonholes are not used on men's clothes except for leather jackets and coats or corduroy jackets where a bound buttonhole made of leather is used. Believe it or not, bound buttonholes are not difficult to make. The method given below is easy to master and results in gorgeous buttonholes.

Buttonholes don't always have to look the same. They can be varied by placing them on the diagonal, or in the case of bound buttonholes, make the lips of a contrasting fabric or a fabric cut on the bias or lengthwise grain. An entirely different fabric such as silk, or Ultraleather can be used for the "lips" of the buttonhole. Some garment styles require buttonholes in seam lines at a yoke or waistline. These are also easy to make following the instructions given below.

The buttonhole area on garments made from fabrics cut on the bias should be well interfaced in order to keep the buttonhole firm and neat. Machine buttonholes on bias cuts tend to ripple if not interfaced adequately. This problem can be easily prevented by placing the buttonholes on the straight grain so that the buttonholes run at an angle to the edge of the garment. This makes for neater buttonholes and also adds a fashion touch.

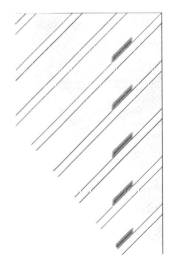

It is a good idea to make a complete machine- or bound-buttonhole sample on a scrap of your fabric, before you begin to make them on the actual garment. This is important even if you have made lots of buttonholes be-

fore as it lets you double check the buttonhole size. It also shows how the fabric will handle that type of buttonhole. Make the trial buttonhole from the same fabric and number of layers of fabric that are used in the actual garment. This will give you a true picture of the finished buttonhole.

MACHINE BUTTONHOLES

Machine buttonholes are made after the garment has been completely assembled. Marking the placement of the buttonholes is done at this time if the tape method is used, or it can be done just after the garment has been cut out if you use the basting method.

Most zigzag machines have the ability to make a good machine buttonhole. Today's machines utilize a built-in mechanism that automatically stitches both sides of the buttonhole without having to turn the fabric. Follow the directions in your machine instruction book for perfect buttonholes.

Machine buttonholes should be reinforced with some type of interfacing. If possible, color-match the interfacing to the fashion fabric; this eliminates the problem of having white interfacing threads showing in the buttonhole opening. If you have no choice as to interfacing color, camouflage the white line by marking it with a colored pencil or felt-tip pen.

Marking Buttonholes

Perfect buttonholes are the sign of an expert seamstress. Buttonholes of unequal length and separation detract from the overall look and ruin an otherwise perfect garment. There are several ways of marking the garment for machine buttonholes, but the easiest one makes use of 1/2" wide strips of drafting tape (or Wash-A-Way Wonder Tape). Drafting tape is preferable to transparent tape because it is visible on all types of fabrics. **Note:** *Test a piece of tape on a fabric scrap before placing it on the garment to see if it pulls off the fabric without leaving a mark. Tape cannot be used on napped fabrics because of this problem. Mark these fabrics with machine or hand basting. Never leave the tape on the garment for an extended period of time, as it is possible for a sticky residue to transfer to the fabric.*

Note: *Some machines may have difficulty feeding when tape is used to make buttonholes. The presser foot gets hung up when it runs along the tape. Use machine or hand basting to mark buttonholes if your machine exhibits this problem when making a test buttonhole.*

Tape Marking: Place the paper pattern in position over the completed garment and stick pins through both ends of the buttonhole lines. Make sure the pattern is positioned so that the **seam line** rather than the cut edge is along the finished edge of the garment. Carefully pull the pattern away from the fabric, leaving the pins in place. A cardboard cutting board will give you something to stick your pins into, making this marking process easier. Double check the pins with a ruler to make sure they are accurately placed. You don't want drunken buttonholes!

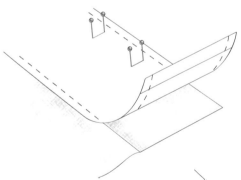

Place long strips of tape along the outside edge of each row of pins. Place short strips of tape (cut approximately 1/2" wider than the buttonhole length) across the two long strips. The short strips should be placed **above** rather than below the pins.

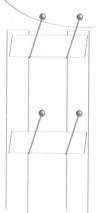

Start the buttonhole by putting the needle into the fabric where the two strips of tape cross. Start at the front edge of the buttonhole when using a machine that moves forward when stitching the first side of the buttonhole. If your machine backstitches the first side, then place the needle in the fabric at the other end of the buttonhole. It is important that you adjust the position of the needle in the fabric so that it never sews into the tape. This may put a sticky coating on the needle causing it to skip stitches.

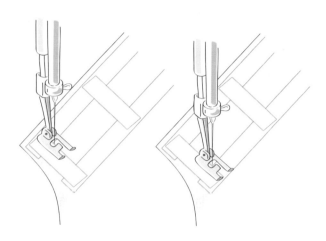

Complete the buttonhole, using the tape strips as guides for equal lengths.

Thread Marking: Transfer the buttonhole marks to the wrong side of the cut-out garment piece. Use the pattern-and-pin technique described above, except mark each pin with a pencil dot rather than tape strips. Using a ruler, connect the dots, then hand- or machine-baste the lines through to the right side.

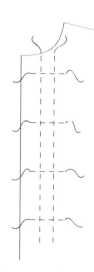

Many times you can use the lines on striped or checked fabrics as guides for buttonholes. Use tape strips as needed, or just make a light pencil mark at the beginning and end of each buttonhole. If the last stitch at each end of the buttonhole just covers these marks, you will never see them.

Easiest Making Method

Draw the buttonhole "ladder" onto a piece of water-soluble stabilizer such as Dissolve or Solvy. Pin this pattern to the right side of your garment and stitch the buttonholes. Now, they are all of identical length and are perfectly parallel.

Buttonhole Thread

Garments made from fabrics other than lightweight wovens and knits look best if the buttonholes are stitched with buttonhole thread instead of regular thread. There are two types of buttonhole thread on the market today. One is made from silk and the other from polyester. Polyester thread has a greater color selection and is usually easier to find since most fabric stores carry it. Use it for topstitching and for sewing buttons in place. Silk buttonhole thread looks elegant on the finished garment but is somewhat difficult to find.

You will need a larger machine needle when stitching with the thicker buttonhole thread. (See Machine Needles, in Chapter 1). Thread both the top and bobbin of your machine with buttonhole thread, then make a sample buttonhole on a scrap of your fabric to see if any machine adjustments are necessary. Some machines need to have the upper thread tension increased. If you still have problems, then try using regular thread on the bobbin and the buttonhole thread on the top.

If buttonhole thread is not available, you can create the same thick-looking buttonhole by using two strands of regular thread on the top. Thread the two strands through the machine and needle just as though they were one thread. This technique makes the buttonhole strong, and it stands out from the fabric. This is especially important when the buttonholes contrast with the fabric.

Corded Machine Buttonhole

Corded machine buttonholes add a professional touch to your garments. A soft piece of perle cotton or carpet thread is placed **under** the buttonhole foot, then covered by the "zigzag" of the buttonhole. This type buttonhole is excellent on knit fabrics as it stabilizes the buttonhole edges so that they don't stretch out of shape or ripple. Check your machine instruction book for special helps when making corded machine buttonholes.

BOUND BUTTONHOLES

Bound buttonholes are made on a garment before any other sewing is done. The buttonholes are worked through both the fashion fabric and the interfacing if they are both fairly lightweight. If you are using a heavyweight fashion fabric or hair canvas for the interfacing, the buttonholes should be worked before the interfacing is applied. Once the buttonholes are finished, "windows" are cut in the interfacing at the appropriate places to allow for each buttonhole, then the interfacing is attached to the garment.

Fashion fabrics that fray easily should always have the buttonhole area backed with fusible interfacing in order to keep the narrow buttonhole seams from fraying away. Fusing interfacing to the entire garment front will take care of this, or use just a lightweight patch of fusible interfacing for each buttonhole if the fashion fabric is very heavy or if a hair canvas is used for the interfacing.

The backs of bound buttonholes, which are in the garment facing, are finished after the facing has been permanently stitched in place.

A well-made bound buttonhole is a work of art. Most ready-to-wear garments use machine buttonholes due to the labor cost of bound buttonholes.

Marking Buttonholes

Precise marking of the buttonhole location and length is very important. Unequal spacing and length of the buttonholes can ruin the look of a garment no matter how professional your actual buttonhole technique is.

The easiest way to transfer buttonhole lines to the garment piece is to use a buttonhole grid. This grid is drawn directly on the wrong side of the garment piece before applying the interfacing, if the fashion fabric is heavy or if you are using hair canvas for the interfacing. Draw the buttonhole grid on the wrong side of the garment piece of lightweight fabrics, using lightweight or fusible interfacing, after the interfacing has been applied. Follow the instructions below for making the grid.

Place the paper pattern over the wrong side of the garment piece. Stick pins through each end of the buttonhole marks. Starting at the bottom edge, carefully lift the paper pattern and put a small pencil dot where each pin pierces the fabric. Remove the first two pins and work on up the buttonhole line. Remove the pattern and double check your pencil dot spacing with a ruler.

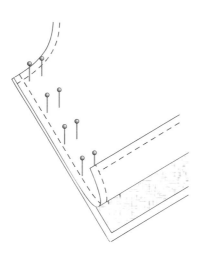

Connect the vertical rows of dots with a pencil line, extending the lines approximately 1" beyond the top and bottom dots. Draw the horizontal buttonhole lines, from dot to dot, extending them approximately 1" beyond the vertical lines. Check to make sure they are parallel.

Transfer the grid marks to the right side of the garment by machine-basting along each line with a contrasting thread. Stitch both vertical lines and all horizontal lines from the same direction so that the grid stays square. Double check the grid at this point to make sure every line is in the proper place. Make any necessary corrections.

A single bound buttonhole should be accurately marked with hand basting. Insert a pin straight through the fabric at the exact ends of the buttonhole mark. Using a needle and thread, secure the thread at one pin with a few stitches. Wrap the thread around the opposite pin, bring it back to the first pin, then take small stitches between the pins, using the loose thread as a guide. Secure the end with a few stitches.

Buttonhole Construction

It is recommended that you do the same step on all the buttonholes at the same time rather than make one complete buttonhole, then go on to the next one. This speeds up the sewing process and also makes it much easier for you to "catch" a sewing or size mistake before it is too late.

The buttonhole method given below is what we consider the ultimate bound buttonhole. It isn't harder than any other method; in fact, we think it is the easiest, and it makes the best-looking buttonhole.

Cut a strip of fabric 1" wide and long enough to have two strips for each buttonhole. Each strip should be 1" longer than the finished buttonhole length. Cut these strips on the bias, unless the bias cut isn't attractive when using with patterned fabrics. Bias cuts are easier to handle as the edges don't fray easily.

Fold the strip lengthwise down the middle with wrong sides together and press. Stitch the length of the strip 1/8" from the folded edge. It is important that this stitching line be accurate as this is what determines the width of the buttonhole "lips." If the fabric tends to fray, make several more rows of stitching as illustrated. **Note:** *Garments made of bulky fabrics such as coatings should have 1/4" rather than 1/8" allowed for the "lip" width. Cut the buttonhole strip 1 1/2" wide to allow for this extra width.*

Stay-stitch a box around each horizontal buttonhole mark. The stitching should be 1/8" on each side of the basting line and directly **on** the vertical lines. Count the stitches as you sew across the ends of the box so that the vertical sides will be of equal width. **Note:** *When stitching boxes that are to be cut open and turned, start stitching awaw from the corner. This prevents a buildup of thread in the corner which will interfere with a perfect turn.*

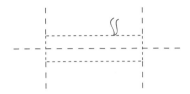

Cut the long prepared buttonhole strips into equal pieces that are at least 1" longer than the buttonhole's width. Position one strip on the right side of the garment so that the stitching line on the strip lines up with the stay-stitch line as shown. Hand-baste the strip in position. Secure the strip by machine-stitching just **below** the bottom stitching line, beginning and ending precisely on the verticals.

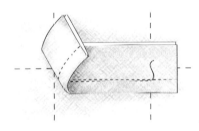

Pull the strip down out of the way and position another buttonhole strip along the upper line with the folded edge up. Hand-baste and secure this strip by machine-stitching along the hand-basted line, beginning and ending precisely at the verticals.

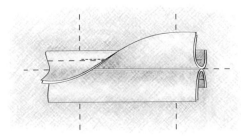

These two lines of stitching must be accurate for perfect buttonholes. Count the stitches as you sew to make sure each stitching line is the same length. Do not backstitch at the beginning or ending of each line. Pull the threads through to the wrong side and tie them in a square knot.

Cut between the stitching lines, as shown, being careful not to cut into the buttonhole strips. Leave a good-sized wedge at each end of the buttonhole.

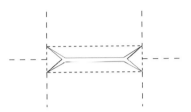

Turn the strips through to the wrong side and you will see the "lips" of the buttonhole begin to take shape. Straighten everything out, making sure that the little wedges at each end are tucked to the wrong side. Baste the "lips" of the buttonhole closed and steam-press from the wrong side.

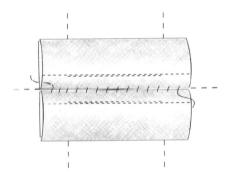

Fold back the right side of the garment along one edge of the buttonhole until the wedge is exposed. Machine-stitch across the base of each wedge, catching it to the "lips" of the buttonhole. Important: This stitching line should curve slightly in toward the center of the buttonhole to square up the ends. Backstitch to make sure this stitching is strong.

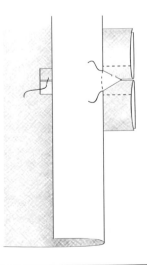

Repeat the process on the opposite end. Steam-press from the wrong side.

Trim the excess strips to about 1/4" from the wedge. Hold the scissors at an angle so that they "grade" the edge of the strips rather than make a blunt cut.

The front side of the bound buttonhole is now finished. Construct the rest of the garment and finish the back of the buttonholes after the facing has been sewn in place. Use one of the methods given below.

Method #1: Baste the facing in place between the buttonholes. Insert pins through to the wrong side at each end of the buttonhole. Slash the facing open between the pins. Turn under the raw edges, forming a curve, and slip stitch in place to the wrong side of the buttonhole.

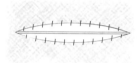

Method #2: Baste the facing in place between the buttonholes, then stick pins through all four corners of the buttonhole.

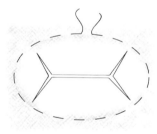

Slash open as illustrated. Turn under the raw edges, forming a "box", and slipstitch in place to the wrong side of the buttonhole.

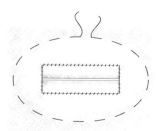

Method #3: Use this method for fabrics that fray easily. Pin the facing in place between the buttonholes and stick pins through the ends of the buttonholes.

Transfer these marks to the right side of the facing with light pencil marks.

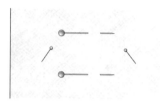

Pull the facing away from the garment, and make a clean-faced buttonhole opening using a lightweight fabric that doesn't ravel, such as sheer tricot. Stitch as illustrated and cut open the length of the stitching. You have now "faced the facing."

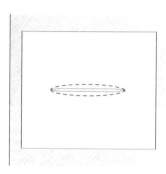

Turn the facing patch to the wrong side of the facing and press, rolling the facing patch under so that it doesn't show on the right side. Catch the faced opening to the wrong side of the buttonhole.

Method #4: This method is good for knits. Baste the facing in place around the buttonhole. Working on the right side, stitch in the ditch all around the buttonhole. Use a short stitch length so that the machine will feed slowly and bury the stitches in the fabric. On the facing side, carefully trim the facing fabric close to the box that was stitched in a ditch.

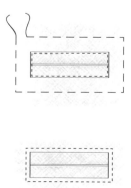

Corded Buttonholes

Corded bound buttonholes are an elegant touch to any garment. Not only does the cording give a raised appearance but it adds strength and stability to the buttonhole "lips." Corded rather than regular bound buttonholes are a good choice for knit fabrics as they control the fabric stretch across the buttonhole opening.

Use a #9 cotton cord or a heavy string for the filler. Place the cord along the fold of the buttonhole strip and stitch close with a zipper foot. The distance between the folded edge and the stitching line should be about 1/8". Use this corded strip for the buttonhole "lips" following the instructions given above.

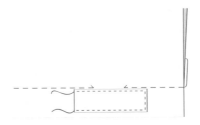

Press open the seam and secure each end of the buttonhole with a small bar tack made by machine or hand.

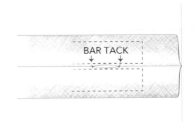

SEAM BUTTONHOLE

This buttonhole is found at waist and yoke seams of garments. It is very simple to do and looks much better than trying to work a machine buttonhole close to a seam line. The front and back of the buttonholes are worked the same if the facing has a seam in the same place as the garment does. Otherwise, the back of the buttonhole is worked as for the back of a bound buttonhole. (See above.)

Mark the buttonhole width on the seam line and leave this area unsewn when stitching the seam. Backstitch at both ends of the opening for added strength.

Reinforce and give stability to the fabric on the sides of the opening by stitching a strip of seam binding to each seam allowance above and below the opening. Extend this strip about 1/4" on both sides of the buttonholes opening.

BUTTON LOOPS

Some fashions call for button loops instead of machine or bound buttonholes. These are fun to make and you get quite a sense of accomplishment when you complete a perfect line of button loops down a bridal dress or some other such fine gown.

Select a ball or half-round button when using button loops. But, why not go all the way and make your own Chinese ball buttons with matching tubing? Instructions for tubing and buttons follow.

If you decide to put button loops on a pattern that has been designed for conventional buttonholes, you must make a few pattern changes to accommodate the different closure. The side of the garment to which loops are sewn will need to be altered. The button loops will be sewn to the closing line, which is usually the center-front or center-back line. Adjust the garment and facing pieces so that there is only a seam width to the side of this closing line. **Note:** *Button loops require the pattern to have a separate facing.*

Make either self-filled or corded tubing for the button loops. Lightweight fabrics should be corded, while heavier fabrics can use the self-filled technique. Cut bias strips 1" to 2" longer than the amount of tubing that you need and six times as wide as the desired finished width. Trim one end of the strip into a sharp point.

Self-Filled Tubing

To make the turning process easier, securely stitch a string or narrow cord to the pointed end of the strip. The string should be a few inches longer than the bias strip. Fold the bias strip in half, right sides together, and position the string **inside** the fold so that at least 1" extends beyond the other end of the strip. Start stitching from the end opposite the point a little bit wider than the desired seam width. Then taper back, as illustrated, so that the tubing will have some extra room to start the turning process. Stretch the fabric slightly as you sew or use a small zigzag rather than a straight stitch. The seam will then have some give so that you won't break stitches when turning the tubing. For average-weight fabrics trim the seam allowance so that it is the same width as the distance from the fold to the seam line. Sheer fabrics can have a much wider seam allowance in order to fully "stuff" the tubing. Carefully turn the tubing by pulling the string and working the tubing back over the string. Remove the string and trim the ends even.

Corded Tubing

Proceed as for the self-filled tubing except use a piece of cord the desired size in place of the string. The cord should be twice the length of the bias strip plus 1". Position it inside the fold of the strip so that half its length extends beyond the end of the strip. Secure the cord to the strip. Stitch as directed above and then trim the seam allowance close to the stitching. To turn the cord, pull on the short end of the cord and work the tubing back over the other section of cord. Use a zipper foot during the stitching to allow you to stitch quite close to the cord. Remember to **stretch** the fabric slightly as you sew otherwise you'll have popped stitches.

Bias Tubing

Bias tubing in various fabrics is available by the yard. Use this tubing for your button loops if you can find some that matches or complements your garment's fabric.

Button-Loop Construction

Draw a button-loop grid on a piece of paper that is as long as the closure area and about 3" wide. Line A is the seam line. The distance between lines A and B is approximately one half the button diameter plus the width of the cord. The distance between the horizontal lines is the button diameter plus twice the width of the cord.

Pin the loops within the guidelines on the grid, adjusting them so that the seams of the loops are **up**. The loops can be placed separately or as a continuous series.

Hold the loops in place with a strip of drafting tape and stitch them to the paper just outside the seam line.

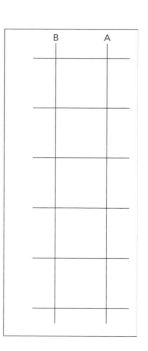

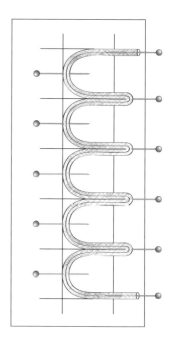

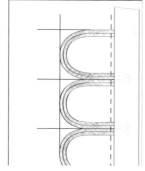

Remove the tape and pin the loop grid in place on the garment (paper side up). Line up the edge of the paper with the edge of the garment. Stitch the loops to the garment along the seam line. Remove the paper. Trim the open ends of the loops at an angle in order to reduce bulk.

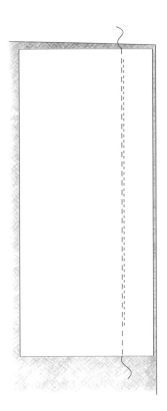

Finish the button-loop area by stitching on the garment's facing. Adjust the button location by pinning the garment together along the closing lines, then marking the buttons at the ends of the loops.

CHINESE BALL BUTTON

A Chinese ball button, made from the same tubing as the button loop, is an elegant touch to any garment. The size of the button is determined by the thickness of the tubing. Tubing made from lightweight to medium–weight fabrics should be corded, as previously shown. Each button will take approximately 10" of tubing.

Form the button following the diagrams. Be careful to keep the **tubing seam up** while forming the button so that it won't be visible on the right side of the finished button. Make sure the tubing does not twist. Carefully tighten and mold the button until it is round. Trim away the excess tubing and fasten the ends to the underside of the button with a needle and thread.

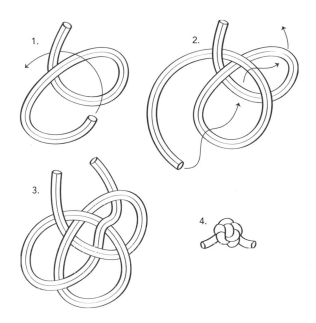

FROGS

Frogs are another type of closing that can be made from tubing. They look the best when made with corded tubing. Two basic frog designs are given below, but you can make your own if you wish. Attach Chinese ball buttons as desired to the sides of the frog.

Draw the frog design on a piece of very thick cardboard or plastic foam. Lay the tubing along the lines, holding it in place with pins. Tack the tubing together where it meets and/or laps. Remember to keep the tubing **seam up** so that it won't show on the right side of the "frog". Tack the finished frogs and ball buttons in position on the garment.

SEWING ON BUTTONS

Proper technique is just as important when sewing a button to the garment as it is when making the buttonhole. The button should be correctly positioned with a long enough shank so that the garment will close smoothly.

Buttons are sewn to the closing line of the garment. This is usually the center-front or center back line, but not always. Check your pattern to be sure. Lap the garment in its closed position and mark the first button by sticking a pin through the buttonhole end closest to the edge of the garment. Carefully lift the top layer of the garment and mark where the pin enters the fabric. Sew the first button to this mark. Button the garment after the first button has been sewn in place, then mark the next button's position with a pin. Stitch the second button in place and follow this procedure for the rest of the buttons.

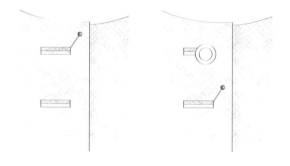

All buttons should have a shank that is the same thickness as the garment is at the buttonhole area. This makes for a smooth closing. Many buttons come with attached shanks. Other buttons need to have shanks created for them with thread. This is done while the button is being sewn in place. If the attached shank of a button is not long enough to accommodate the thickness of the garment, it should be made longer with a thread shank.

Buttons without attached shanks or with very short shanks are the best choice for lightweight fabrics. Long-shanked buttons droop when the garment is buttoned because the fabric is not thick enough to support the button in position. This is an obvious problem on double-breasted suits, where there is no bulk to hold the "button-only" button from drooping.

Sew buttons to the garment with buttonhole thread or doubled regular thread. Run the thread through beeswax before sewing in order to strengthen the thread and keep it from tangling. Waxed dental floss can be used to sew buttons in place. It is very strong as it is made of nylon. It is recommended to use for metal shank buttons that tend to cut ordinary thread. **Note:** *Use dental floss to sew on pant hooks and eyes. Regular thread wears through quickly and you need to resew it.*

Create a thread shank for flat buttons by stitching over a toothpick or matchstick. Remove the stick and wrap the thread around the shank threads several times, then fasten it to the garment.

Create a longer shank on a button that already has an attached built-on shank by placing the stick between the garment and the button and then stitching over it.

Sometimes a jeweled button on a dressy garment tends to snag the fabric when it is buttoned. Avoid this problem by stitching the button to the top side of the buttonhole, then placing a snap underneath each buttonhole to close the garment. **Note:** *Do not cut open machine buttonholes, and do not finish off the back of bound buttonholes when using this procedure.*

Tuck-in shirts and blouses should always have flat buttons placed below the waistline to avoid unattractive bulges.

COVERED SNAP

Covered snaps give a custom-finish touch to your dresses, jackets and coats. These garments require a #3 or #4 snap, which is fairly large, so don't try to use them on lightweight garments. Uncovered snaps do just fine for them.

The fabric used to cover the snaps should be a matching piece of lining or some other lightweight fabric. Cut two circles of fabric that measure about twice the diameter of the snap. Stitch a series of small stitches around the very edge of each fabric circle with a needle and thread. Keeping the threaded needle attached to the fabric, center the snap section, wrong side up, on the circle, then pull the fabric up tightly around the snap.

Secure the fabric in position by taking several stitches across the snap, to flatten the fabric.

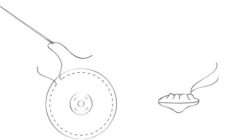

Cover each half of the snap by using the same method. Sew the snaps in place by carefully feeling for the stitching holes with the needle. Holes will soon wear in the fabric in the proper place when the snap is closed.

THE STORY OF CLOTH

Yes, we've come a long way in the art of dressmaking. Our sewing sisters of long ago spent many days and even weeks creating their simple everyday wear or elegant evening fashions. We are fortunate that we can make a new outfit in a matter of hours, thanks to our modern sewing machine and the large variety of sewing tools available in every fabric store. While none of us would want to return to the good old days of dressmaking, we felt you would be interested in the story of the cloth and sewing tools we so casually take for granted. It is a fascinating as well as educational part of the history of mankind.

From the earliest of days, the manufacture and sale of cloth has been of primary importance. The processes of producing it were closely guarded, and the sale of cloth was strictly regulated. Death by torture was the penalty for anyone revealing the secrets of silk making outside the borders of China. During the Middle Ages, exile was the penalty for anyone caught smuggling wool out of England. It was a capital offense in England in the 1790s to export plans or parts of textile machines.

Sumptuary laws, or laws of dress, were enacted to keep the lower classes separate from royalty and the very rich. These laws prohibited the imitation of the styles of dress of the nobility. In ancient Rome, only free citizens were allowed to wear the long toga.

An elegant French mother-of-pearl sewing box c. 1820. Needlecase, bodkin, thread winders, scissors, scent bottle and delicate thimble with the Palaise Royale insignia are set in a fitted tortoise shell box lined with velvet, and is complete with lock and key.

Simple short tunics were worn by all non-citizens such as foreigners and slaves. The all purple toga was permitted to be worn only by the emperor or by conquering generals. However, priests and magistrates could wear a purple border on their togas.

Plain togas were worn by the ordinary free-citizen. If he wished to run for public office, he dusted his toga with chalk to show his intentions. The chalky white color was called "candida;" thus the office seeker became a "candidate."

During the Middle Ages in France, members of the nobility were allowed only four garments, while unmarried women were restricted to one gown! In 13th century France, laws governed the length of the hood adornments, the length of a train and the cost of fabrics. In the 14th century, long pointed toes were fashionable. A commoner was limited to a 6-inch toe, a gentleman could have a 12-inch toe, while a nobleman could have a 24-inch toe—these extended toes were held up by long chains attached to the waist.

For centuries, wool has been of major economic importance in England. In 1326, Edward II ruled that commoners had to wear wool—only the nobility, clergy and those who paid forty pounds a year for rent were permitted to wear imported cloth. Even bastard sons of nobility had to wear wool only! In 1331, Edward III gave liberal franchises and protection to Flemish weavers to lure them to England, thus virtually destroying the Flemish wool industry. Elizabeth I ruled that every man, woman and child over the age of 6 had to wear a woolen cap when out of doors on Sundays and holy days, or pay a fine.

In 1600, Elizabeth I chartered the East India Company and its ships that brought back spices and calico from India in limited quantities. (The word "calico" is a derivative of Calcutta, as the calicos initially came from that part of the world). The imported calicos were used as cheap clothing for servants and as bed linens. However, in 1662, when Catherine of Braganza of Portugal married Charles II of England, the woolen industry met a formidable foe—calico. The Portugese particularly liked the painted calicos or chintz (chint is the Hindi word meaning spotted or variegated). A favorite pattern was the brightly colored "tree-of-life" design. As part of Catherine's dowry, England was given free trading rights in Brazil and the Portugese East Indies; also, Tangiers and Bombay were ceded to England. Therefore, with Catherine's marriage to Charles, and the increase in trade, calicos became very popular, making huge inroads into the English woolen market. Calicos became the rage in England, and by 1685 even the queen wore them. Calicos were hand-dyed and painted by a very slow, tedious process until block printing came into use in the 18th century. They were used everywhere, for gowns, petticoats and bedclothes, including the draperies around the bed. Naturally the woolen interests protested vehemently.

To protect the wool, in 1678, Parliament ruled that all corpses should be wrapped in a woolen shroud; this

law remained in effect until 1814. In 1700, Parliament ruled that buttons and buttonholes had to be made of wool thread instead of silk. A treaty with Portugal in 1703 tried to encourage the wool trade by giving low duties on its imports. In exchange, England received oranges and port. As a result, Englishmen who had been drinking claret turned to port!

Finally, in 1722, Parliament forbade the importation of Chinese silks and cottons from India—any use of calicos was strictly banned. These restrictions remained in effect for the next 52 years. Not even cotton printed in England could be worn or used in the home! Therefore, the East India Company had to sell its chintz and calicos to the American colonies. In England, it became the fashion for ladies to do crewel embroidery on all sorts of garments using the popular "tree-of-life" pattern, thus simulating the forbidden calicos.

The width of English cottons was determined by the distance the shuttle could be thrown while weaving the cloth, approximately 36 inches. In 1733, John Kay invented the "fly shuttle" to compete with the three-yard width of India cotton. On his loom, the shuttle was jerked by a thong attached to the weaver's wrist. Now the shuttle was thrown across the loom farther than a man could ordinarily throw the shuttle. Kay was hated and feared by the weavers who were afraid of losing their jobs. He fled to Paris where he died in poverty. It is now considered that his "fly shuttle" was the device that started the Industrial Revolution.

In 1771, Richard Arkwright made the first coordinated spinning mill that was driven by water power. Now English cotton could finally be spun fine and strong, enabling it to compete with Indian cottons. In 1790, the textile industry was begun in the American colonies by a runaway apprentice from the Arkwright spinning mill. He carried the plans for the water-powered spinning mill in his head to the new world. With Eli Whitney's invention of the cotton gin in 1793, an ample supply of raw material was available, and the American textile industry was off to a running start.

TAILORING TACTICS

7

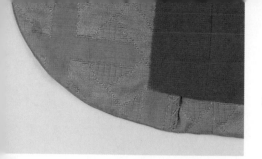
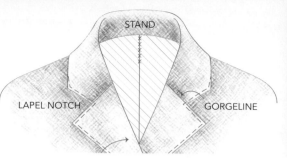
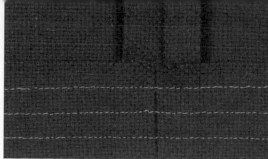

Chapter 7: Tailoring Tactics

TAILORING a coat or jacket has always been the ultimate test of the home sewer. Many hours of construction steps, including lots of detailed hand work, were required. Now the tailored garment is a much quicker and simpler project, thanks to modern sewing aids.

TAILORED GARMENT

The biggest tailoring time-saver is fusible interfacings. How much easier it is to fuse the interfacing to the garment front, the under collar and the hem areas. Applying interfacing this way cuts your construction time in half.

Using this time-saving technique doesn't mean you are making a less-than-first-quality garment. Examine designer suits, in both men's and women's fashions; you will see that the majority use fusible interfacings. You are in good company, so take advantage of this help.

Occasionally a nonfusible interfacing or hair canvas on a tailored garment is needed. For example, velvet requires hand-applied interfacing because fusing an interfacing in place would ruin the nap. However, fusible interfacing is ideal for velveteen.

It is possible to purchase preformed coat interfacing that can be hand-stitched into the garment front. This is called a "canvas front," or coat hymo, and is available at tailor's supply houses. You must trim the hymo to fit your particular garment, but it saves much handwork.

Pattern instructions are better written than the ones we used years ago, and they use many new construction techniques that simplify the whole process. A tailored garment is now an enjoyable undertaking, rather than something to be endured and overcome.

While we don't plan to guide you step-by-step through the construction of a tailored jacket, we do want to give you the tailoring tips and alternate construction methods that we use in our own sewing.

PATTERN NOTES

Look at the ready-made tailored jackets, suits and sport coats that you have hanging in your closet.

The men's garments have the under collar applied by hand, and the back lining goes all the way up to the collar, thus eliminating the back neck facing. Some women's garments are made the same way, while others have a stitched-and-turned collar, with or without a back neck facing.

As you are making your own clothes, you have the choice of construction methods. We recommend that you use the man-tailored way of applying the under collar for both men's and women's garments. This method can be used with any jacket or coat pattern—except heavy outerwear—and it results in the best rolling collar and lapel, with the flattest finish. It also gives you very good control of the under collar, so that you get an accurate roll and identical collar points.

A hand-applied under collar should have all seam allowances trimmed away, and should be interfaced with a fusible, nonwoven interfacing. Trim the interfacing slightly smaller than the under collar, so that it will not peek out around the finished edge. An extra layer of interfacing applied below the collar roll line adds extra support to the collar stand.

If your pattern calls for a back neck facing and you are going to use the man-tailored method, eliminate the facing by pinning it to the back lining pattern. Overlap the back facing and lining pattern pieces until the seam lines meet. Add extra width at the center back of the facing to allow for the back pleat. Now cut the lining fabric from this altered pattern.

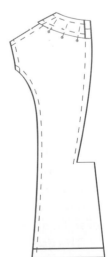

Whether using the man-tailored back lining method or some other collar method, we still suggest that you eliminate the back neck-facing from tailored garment patterns. This reduces bulk at the back of the neck and prevents a facing line from showing through on the right side of the garment.

FITTING

Test your pattern in muslin or other similar-weight fabric (i.e., denim or corduroy) before cutting into expensive fabrics. This allows you to work out any fitting problems in a cheaper fabric.

The actual garment should be tried on periodically during the construction process to check the fit. Baste the main garment pieces together after the front-interfacing has been applied. Baste the shoulder pads in position and the under collar in place, but omit the sleeves at this point. Check the fit and length; make any necessary adjustments.

Do another fitting just before you stitch the sleeves in place. Baste the sleeves in position then check the fit and sleeve hang. Make any necessary adjustments. Then permanently stitch the sleeves in place.

INTERFACINGS

Use a fusible interfacing of a woven, nonwoven or hair canvas type. Choose the weight that gives the desired finished look to your fashion fabric. Thin fabrics will need heavier interfacings than do bulky fabrics.

Apply interfacing to the entire garment front, collar, pocket flaps and sleeve hems. Thin fabrics can also have interfacing applied to the front facing. Sometimes the entire garment will benefit from being totally fusibly interfaced. Certain fabrics, such as cotton velveteen, will always look unpressed unless you add some extra support. Interfacing can be fused to **all** jacket pieces when made of cotton velveteen, raw silk or linen. The finished look stays crisp and fresh-looking dry cleaning after dry cleaning. (But, remember to always preshrink the interfacing!)

Trim away all seam allowances from the interfacing pieces before fusing. Apply interfacing to the wrong side of the upper pocket flap pieces, and to the under, rather than upper collar piece, when the man-tailored method is used. Interfacing can also be applied to the upper-collar if a thin fashion fabric is used.

The use of fusible interfacing makes it easy to re-duce bulk in the dart area. Fuse the interfacing to the garment piece except for in the dart area. Transfer the dart marks to the interfacing using the paper pattern as a guide. Cut away the interfacing along the dart lines and complete the fusing process.

Stitch the dart using the cut edges of the interfacing as a guide.

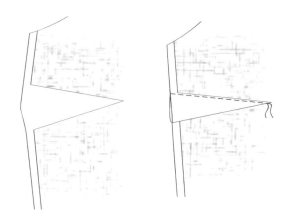

An extra piece of interfacing applied to the lapel point will add firmness and help so that the lapel will lie flat.

Construction marks, such as pocket locations, should be transferred to the wrong side of the garment piece after the interfacing has been fused in place.

Interfacing should be applied to sleeve hems. Use either a fusible or nonfusible type.

Cut fusible interfacing the same width and shape as the hem allowance, and fuse it in place before stitching the sleeve seams.

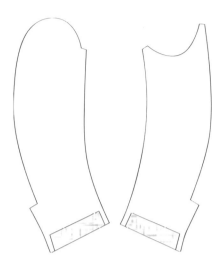

Cut nonfusible interfacing 1/2" wider than the hem, and stitch it to the hem edge with a straight or zigzag stitch. Hand-baste along the hemline. If you are using a woven interfacing, cut it on the bias. Nonwoven interfacing should be cut the same shape as the hem edge.

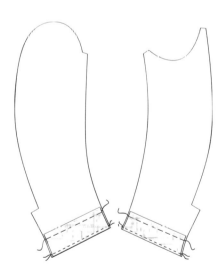

POCKETS

Pockets add interest to your tailored garment as well as serve a functional purpose. There are many pocket styles from which to choose, and you can substitute one pocket style for another on any given pattern.

Directions for various types of pockets are found in in Chapter 5. Just remember, as you construct the pockets, they should match perfectly in size and shape. If the pocket calls for flaps, make the flaps first, then construct the pocket opening to fit the flaps. This makes sure there are no gaps between the flap and the end of the pocket opening. Make sure each set of pockets and flaps are the same size. **Note:** *Sometimes the pocket flap is 1/16" wider to ensure coverage.*

If you are using a patterned fabric for your garment, make sure the pocket or flaps match the pattern perfectly, or cut them on the bias for a definite contrast.

TWILL-TAPE APPLICATION

Twill tape is used in tailored garments to stabilize certain areas. It keeps things from stretching out of shape and adds strength. Use 1/4" or 1/2" twill tape that has been preshrunk. Apply it to the following areas.

Lapel Roll Line

Twill tape is applied just **behind** the roll line of the lapel in order to keep it firm and help the lapel to roll properly. Pull it taut as it is applied, so that the lapel will assume a slight curve. Apply the tape after the front interfacing has been fused in place.

Starting the twill tape at the neckline seam (about 1/8" behind the roll line), pull the tape taut as it is machine-basted down the center. End the tape 1 1/2" above the front edge. Hand-catch both edges of the tape to the interfacing. Remove the machine basting.

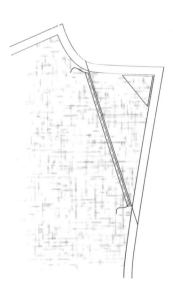

To set the roll line, position the garment front over a tailor's ham and firmly press the lapel in the finished position.

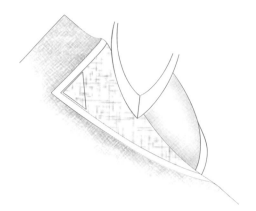

Back of the Neck

Twill tape should be applied to the neckline seam allowance of the jacket back. This stabilizes the area and adds strength. Apply the tape after the center back seam has been sewn and pressed, but before the shoulder seams are stitched.

Measure the distance between the shoulder and center back seam of your pattern. Cut a strip of twill tape twice this length.

Position the twill tape on the wrong side of the neck seam allowance, so that the lower edge is just slightly above the seam line, and the edges of the tape end at the shoulder seam. Machine-stitch in the center of the tape with a regular-length stitch.

When you finish the neck edge of the garment, be careful **not** to catch the tape in the seam line as this would add unnecessary bulk.

Pockets

Garments that have set-in pockets rather than patch pockets should have the back corner of the pocket supported with a strip of twill tape that has the other end

attached to the armscye seam allowance. This is to keep the pocket from sagging.

Stitch one end of the tape to the pocket's seam allowance at the inside back corner. Attach the other end of the tape to the armscye seam allowance, as shown. Be careful that the tape is long enough so that it doesn't create a "pull" on the garment.

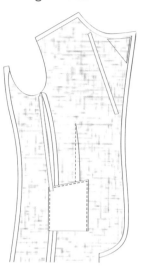

BACK VENT

Most tailored garments have either a center back or two side-back vents. The corner of the upper vent can be mitered or faced to finish. Directions for both methods follow, and you can choose the one that works best for you.

Apply a 1 1/2"-wide piece of fusible interfacing to the facing portion of the upper vent. This adds support and keeps it flat.

It is a good idea to check the lower edge of the vent before you begin the finishing process. A little trimming done at this point results in an even line across the finished vent edges.

Lay the garment, wrong side up, on a flat surface, and arrange the vent layers in the finished position. Trim all the layers of the vent so that they are even with the garment's edge. Trim the under vent slightly shorter so it doesn't peek out.

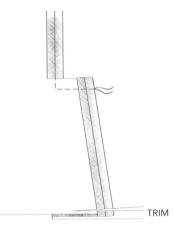

Miter the corner of the upper vent or make a simple faced finish. Either method gives a neat, flat vent.

Mitered Vent

Press the vent facing over into its finished position, then press up the hem allowance. Clip the two layers of fabric where they meet. Mark the corner with a pin.

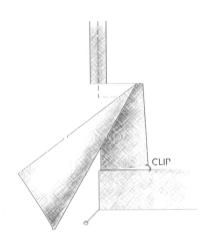

Refold the vent along the diagonal, with right sides together, matching the clip marks. Stitch from the clips to the corner pin.

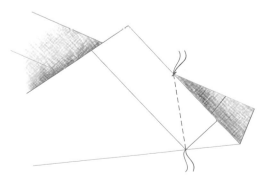

Trim the seam; turn and press from the wrong side. Slip an envelope in between the layers of fabric so that seam impressions won't show on the right side.

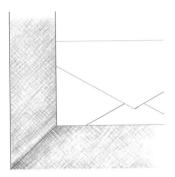

Faced Vent

Fold the vent facing against the garment's back, right sides together. Position the facing so that a scant 1/8" extends below the edge of the garment. Stitch across the bottom of the vent, along the hemline.

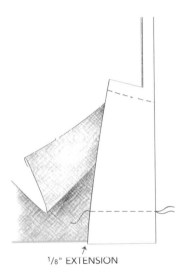

1/8" EXTENSION

Trim the seam allowance. Turn the vent to the right side and press. Roll the seam to the inside. Use an envelope as a shield between the fabric layers.

Fuse the upper vent facing to the jacket with fusible web to keep it from drooping.

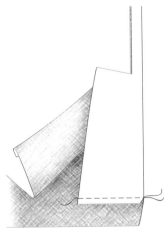

SLEEVE VENT

Some jacket and coat patterns use this construction technique, seen on designer garments, for the sleeve vent. It consists of an extension below the hem allowance on both the upper and under sleeve pattern pieces. This extension acts as a facing for the vent and gives a smooth, flat finish.

You can modify any sleeve pattern to take advantage of this technique. The modified patterns require a few extra inches of fabric to accommodate the length of the extensions. If you are short of fabric, then use the sleeve pattern as given, and follow the instructions for the mitered vent.

In this section you will find two methods of handling the sleeve vents. One involves a change in the shape of the pattern at the lower edge. Read through the sleeve-vent instructions before cutting the fabric, so you can decide which method you want to use.

Extended Facing

Measure the length of the vent extension on the upper sleeve pattern from the hemline to the top of the extension. Make note of this measurement, then trim away the extension as indicated.

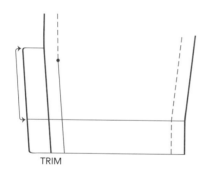

TRIM

Add an extra length at the bottom of the sleeve pattern that is 3" wide. The distance from the hemline to the bottom of the extension should be the same as the measurement of the vent extension you have already taken.

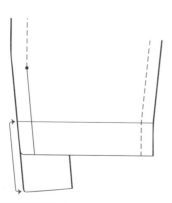

Now, add the same-size extension to the vent area of the under sleeve. Leave the side-extension intact on this pattern piece.

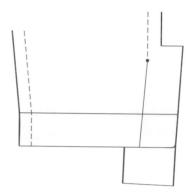

Cut the fashion fabric using the new sleeve pattern pieces. Apply interfacing to the hem allowance, as previously described. Stitch and press the front sleeve seam.

Turn up the sleeve hem with right sides together, pulling the sides of the vent out a little beyond the sleeve edges. Stitch along both vents with the given seam allowance. Trim the seam; turn and press, rolling the seam to the inside for a "clean" finish. Remember to slip an envelope in between the layers of fabric when you press.

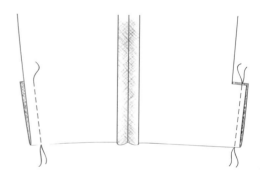

Stitch the upper sleeve seam with the given seam allowance. The upper vent extension should be opened up and pulled out of the way during this stitching process. End the stitching 1/2" below the top edge of the vent extension.

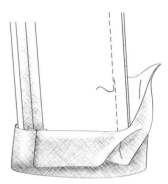

Clip the under vent extension to the seam line and press open the upper sleeve vent. Secure the sleeve hem with a loose catchstitch, or fusible web.

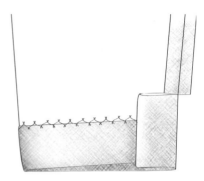

Mitered Vent

Use this finishing technique on sleeve vents that don't have the lower extensions.

Interface the sleeve hem as previously described. Stitch and press open the front sleeve seam. Fold the hem up in its finished position and press.

Press over the upper sleeve vent extension along the seam line. Clip into the vent and hem edge where they meet. Mark the corner with a pin.

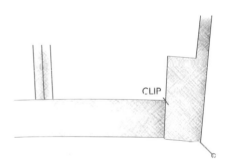

Refold the vent along the diagonal, right sides together, lining up the clip marks. Stitch from the clips to the corner pin. Trim seam; turn to the right side and press using an envelope as a "shield."

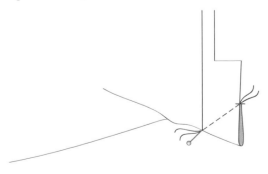

Finish the other side of the vent by folding the hem up, right sides together. Pull out the hem edge just slightly beyond the sleeve edge. Stitch the length of the extension with a 1/4" seam. Trim, turn and press. Secure the sleeve hem with a loose catchstitch or fusible web.

Note: *If you anticipate any sleeve length adjustment on the garment at a later date, **don't** trim away the excess fabric at the mitered corner. Just squash it out flat with your fingers and turn it to the inside of the sleeve hem. The sleeve length can now be adjusted without any danger of your running out of fabric. The most expensive men's suits have "working" buttonholes on the sleeves. And of course, the wearer leaves several open to show that this is a **very** expensive suit.*

TAILORED SLEEVE

Set-in sleeves, in a tailored garment, require absolute control of the sleeve cap ease, with no tucks, gathers or puckers along the seam line.

Easestitch the sleeve cap before pinning the sleeve into the armscye. Match up all construction marks and pin, making sure the pins enter the fabric right at the seam line. Stitch with the given seam allowance. Trim the sleeve seam to 3/8" around the top and 1/4" between the notches. Do not press the seam.

Shoulder Pads

Tailored garments usually require padding in the shoulder area. Some garments will need thicker padding than others, depending on the style and the person's figure and posture. (Fashion often dictates the thickness of shoulder pads.)

Men's suits and coats and women's outer coats need more padding than lightweight jackets. Padding is sometimes added to the shoulder area of a tailored dress.

The pad may consist of one or many layers of padding material. Whatever the thickness, padding helps the garment hang better and gives a professional look.

Shoulder pads can be purchased ready-made in various sizes and thicknesses. Pads for menswear are usually thicker and larger than pads for women's wear. The thickness of purchased shoulder pads can be reduced by pulling out some of the middle layers of padding before placing the pad in the garment. The outside edges of many pads can be trimmed if you find them too large for your purpose.

You can make your own shoulder pads so that you get just the right size and thickness that you need. This saves quite a bit of money as well. Buy a yard of polyester fleece and keep it handy in your sewing supplies for pad making.

The pattern for the pad is made from the garment pattern. Overlap the front and back pattern pieces at the shoulder seam. Draw a pad outline on the paper pattern. The sleeve edge of the pad should extend 1/4" into the seam allowance for dresses and lightweight jackets, and 3/8" into the seam allowance for suits and coats. The back of the pad should be longer than the front. Mark a notch on both edges of the pad pattern at the shoulder seam.

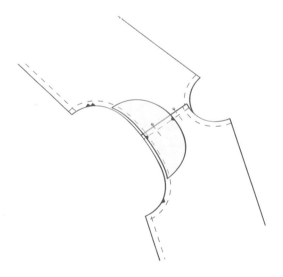

Construct the pad by cutting the number of layers of polyester fleece needed to build up the desired thickness. Cut them all the same size and mark the notch- es with a small clip.

Pads made of mul- tiple layers should have the inner layers trimmed in order to reduce bulk at the outer edges. Trim as indicated.

Stack the padding layers so that the sleeve edges and notches are even. Roll the pad over your fist and pin the layers together as they fall. You will notice that the outside edges are now uneven. Secure the padding lay- ers in this rolled position with hand stitches.

Holding your scissors at an acute angle; trim the edges of the pad so that you create a beveled edge. Do this so that the top layer of the pad is the longest.

Shoulder pads are inserted after the sleeve is perma- nently stitched into the armscye. Trim the sleeve allow- ance to either 1/4" or 3/8", as directed above.

With the sleeve seam allow- ance turned out into the sleeve, position the pad so that the edge of the pad is even with the trimmed sleeve seam. The gar- ment should be turned right side out when positioning the pad so that it will assume the proper curve. Place the pad and garment over your knee during this pro- cess to obtain the desired curve.

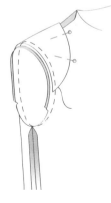

Remember that the longest part of the pad is placed toward the back of the garment. Match up the notches with the shoulder seam, and pin in place. Secure the pad by stabstitching through the pad's edge and the sleeve's seam allowance. Do not pull the stitches tight. Secure the free edge of the pad to the shoulder seam allowance.

Sleeve Padding

Sleeve padding is often used in tailored dresses, jackets and coats to support the top of the sleeve. It prevents the seam allowance from showing through to the right side and gives a soft roll to the sleeve cap. Used alone or in combination with shoulder pads, sleeve-padding is added to the sleeve after any shoulder padding has been stitched in place.

Sleeve padding is made of a bias strip of soft material that is cut long enough to go around the top half of the sleeve. Lambswool makes excellent padding for garments that are going to be dry-cleaned. Polyester fleece or other similar fabrics can be used for garments that are to be washed. Sometimes it is possible to buy preformed sleeve padding at tailor's supply houses. These are referred to as sleeve heads. They are usually quite thick and should be used for tailored coats and jackets, rather than lightweight garments.

Cut a bias strip of padding fabric 3" wide and about 8" long. Fold over 1" and baste.

Permanently stitch the sleeve into the armscye and trim the seam allowance to $1/4$" or $3/8$", as directed above. With the sleeve's seam allowances turned out into the sleeve, position the sleeve padding so that the fold goes along the seam line. Slipstitch the fold to the seam line of the sleeve cap.

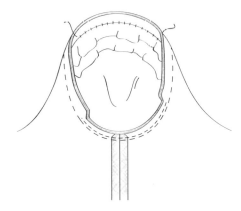

Turn the garment to the right side and mold the sleeve cap over the padding for a smooth look. Holding a steam iron several inches away from the sleeve cap helps in the molding process. Do not touch the garment with the iron.

LINING

Always select a slick-finished lining fabric for your tailored garments. This makes it easier to slip the garment on and off. Choose either a solid color or a patterned fabric. (Make a coordinated outfit by using the lining fabric for a blouse or matching tie.)

Linings should have a pleat at the center back to allow for wearing ease. The pleat should be $3/4$" to 1" deep. Hand-stitch the fold of the pleat with cross-stitches for a professional touch.

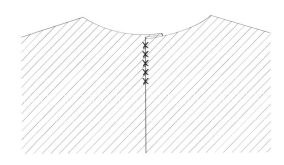

Expensive ready-to-wear blouses have a center back pleat for added ease and elegance. The pattern must have a yoke for this design.

Place the center back fold line of the pattern $1 1/2$" away from the fold of the fabric, thus adding 3" for a pleat. Make a box pleat by loosely basting the center back together on the pattern's center back line. Pleat the remaining 3" of fabric as shown. The yoke now holds the top of the pleat in place. To hold the bottom of the pleat in place, stitch a triangle 1" below the waistline. Leave the loose basting in to hold the pleat in position when ironing the blouse.

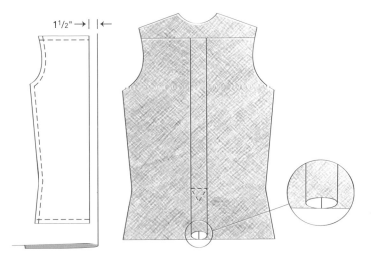

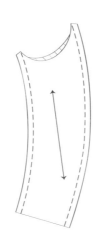

Cut the sleeve lining 1/2" higher in the underarm area. This allows for the extra fabric needed to go up and over the underarm seam allowance.

Hand-baste the lining to the garment's armscye seam allowance before sewing the sleeve lining in place. Place the basting stitches in the seam allowance next to the seam line.

Easestitch the cap of the sleeve lining; use a regular stitch along the seam line for the rest of the sleeve before stitching the sleeve lining in place. Use the stitching line as a guide for turning under and basting the seam allowance. Transfer the construction marks to the folded edge with a chalk or soap mark. Trim and clip the seam allowance in the underarm area to release the curve.

Turn the sleeve lining inside out and pin it to the garment, matching up the construction marks. The folded edge of the lining should just cover the basting stitches. Hand-stitch the lining in place using small stitches for strength.

FRONT FACING

The front facing should always be cut slightly wider and longer than is the garment front at the top corner of the lapel. This gives ease at the lapel point so that it will roll toward the body and lie flat. Thick fabrics require more ease than thin fabrics. Since patterns are designed with average fabrics in mind, you may find that you have to increase or decrease this ease when working with certain fabrics.

The lapel ease must be preserved when stitching the facing to the garment's front. Control it by folding the corner of the facing along the diagonal, right sides together, then weaving a long pin or needle along this fold. Leave the pin in position while stitching around the lapel point.

The lower edge of the front facing should be cut slightly **shorter** than the garment front. This makes it easier to roll the seam to the inside when pressing the garment front. Thick fabrics require more shortening than thin fabrics.

Well-designed patterns allow for the above size differences between the garment front and the front facing. However, it is a good idea to compare the two pattern pieces by lining up the notches on the front edge before cutting your fashion fabric, to see just how much has been allowed. Adjust the differences if you don't think they are correct for your fabric. If you do any pattern designing or changing, this knowledge is essential for a professional finish.

Important: *Think of a curve, rather than a straight line, when stitching across the top of the lapel. The finished lapel will then have a straight top edge, rather than the slight downward curve or dip that so often happens. (The dip is caused by gravity!)*

Garments requiring two or more bound buttonholes should have the buttonhole side of the garment left about 1/4" longer than the button side. This allows for the slight drawing up that occurs when buttonholes are made. And, it makes sure the underlap doesn't extend below the garment front when the garment is buttoned.

Press open the front edge seam allowances before they are graded. This pressing makes it easier to turn and press the front edge.

Use a point presser to help you press the seams open, or press them open as described in Chapter 2.

Understitch the lapel area if you are not going to topstitch the garment edges. This gives a hard edge on which to turn and press, and also keeps the lapel facing from peeking to the right side.

COLLAR APPLICATION

The diagram below identifies the various parts of the collar and lapel area. Seam allowances are always trimmed and pressed open in the gorgeline, no matter what application method you use. The seam allowances around the back of the neck are pressed **up** into the collar to add support to the stand.

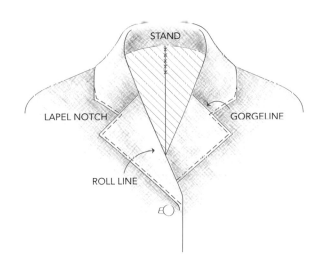

Follow your pattern instructions for applying collars, since they are usually quite complete.

Accurate cutting and marking are critical for a perfect collar finish. The "circles" on the collar and jacket pattern must be marked at the precise position, as they determine the width of the collar and the width of the lapel. The "circles" must be marked in such a way that you can still see the marks when it is time to stitch the lapel area.

ULTRASUEDE UNDER COLLAR

Take the fears and tears out of tailoring by using an Ultrasuede under collar. Men's jacket under collars are made of melton, which is difficult (sometimes impossible) to find in many areas of the country. An Ultrasuede under collar is the perfect solution. It can be used with **all** jacket fabrics, is washable and results in a professional look. There is no bulk at the collar notch as all under collar seam allowances have been removed. The bulk of the center back under collar seam allowance is eliminated and the collar looks elegant when it is worn standing up.

Since the cross grain of Ultrasuede has more stretch than does the bias, the under collar is cut from an 18" x 3 1/2" piece of Ultrasuede (or less depending on the size of the collar).

Fold a 3 1/2" x 18" piece of tissue paper in half. Trace the **finished** size of the under collar pattern, including the roll line and the shoulder marks.

Use this pattern to cut the Ultrasuede under collar. Cut the interfacing, using Armo Weft, Tailor's Touch, Pel-Aire or similar weight interfacing. Trim 1/16" from all edges (you don't want any peek-a-boo interfacing to show at the finished edge) and fuse in place. Cut a second piece of interfacing just the size of the collar stand and fuse it in place. You now have two layers of interfacing in the "stand" area. Fold on the roll line, pin to a ham and steam-shape the under collar.

Stay-stitch the neck edge of the jacket. Place the wrong side of the under collar to the right side of the jacket, lining up the center back, shoulder and collar notch marks. Place the neck edge of the under collar on the seam line, pin and fellstitch in place.

On the inside, catchstitch the jacket seam allowance to the under collar.

Miter the corners of the upper collar as shown in Chapter 5. Turn under 5/8" seam allowance and baste; wait to trim.

Stitch the upper collar to the facings.

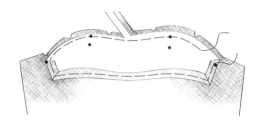

Pin the facing/ upper collar unit to the under collar/jacket unit. Stitch the front facing and lapel edges. Press open. (It's easier to press open 5/8" seams than trimmed seams.) Now, trim and grade.

Turn right side out. Check that both lapels and collars are of equal width. On the inside, sew the upper collar seam allowance to the jacket's neck seam allowance loosely by hand.

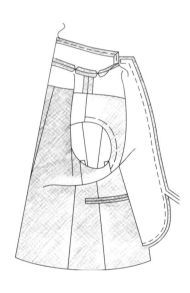

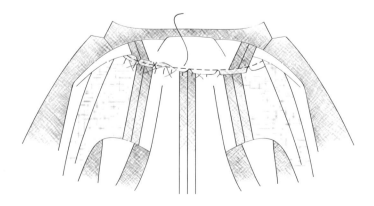

With wrong sides together, pin the collars in position. Shape the collar into the finished position, making sure the collar rolls correctly. Tailor-baste the entire roll line of the lapel and the collar as this holds all the layers in position. Check that there is sufficient "fall" in the upper collar and that the collar does not ride up exposing the back neck seam (see Chapter 8). **Now** trim the upper collar seam allowance to 3/8". Hand-whipstitch the upper collar to the Ultrasuede under collar.

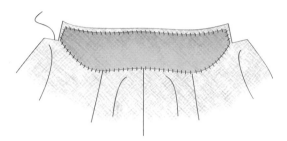

Step back and admire your beautiful collar!

STITCHING TIPS

When stitching the upper collar/facing unit to the under collar/jacket unit, **never** stitch across the neckline seam (also called the gorgeline). Hold the neckline seam allowances away from the collar notch. Align the facing and the jacket collar notches **perfectly**. Leaving a 3" tail of thread and stitching **away** from the collar notch, stitch the facing to the jacket. Remove the pins and again holding the neckline seam allowance away, align the collar notches of the upper and under collars. Leaving another 3" tail of thread, stitch **away** from the collar notch. Why? It is easier to stitch away from the notch than towards it. When stitching toward the notch, the presser foot obscures the critical stitching point.

Always directionally stitch collars and jacket fronts, otherwise one side may have a strange distorted look or "pull," to the collar and lapel.

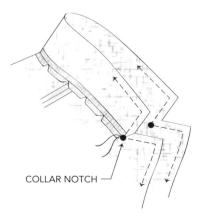

COLLAR NOTCH

Before pressing the outer edges of the jacket, tailor-baste the entire roll line and neckline to hold it in position. Tailor-baste (also called diagonal basting) using silk thread so as not to leave an impression after pressing. Eliminate knots from basting threads, as they leave an impression on the garment. When tailor-basting, baste from the side of the jacket that shows when worn. Insert the needle perpendicular to the finished edge, thus rolling the under layer ever so slightly to the underside into its correct position. Notice that from the top side, the stitches are diagonal, but they are straight on the underside.

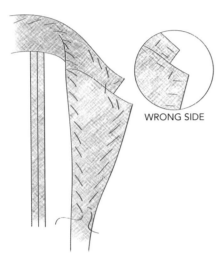

WRONG SIDE

If the jacket is not topstitched, under-stitch in the lapel area to help hold it in position.

FINISHING TIPS

Press up the hem of the garment and secure it in place by hand or use a fusible web. We like to use the fusible web because it is so quick and adds a little bit of firmness to the garment's edge. Cut the web slightly narrower than the hem width and fuse in place, following the manufacturer's instructions, so that you get a perfect bond.

Lining

The lining should be attached to the garment's hem so that there is a free fold at the bottom to give wearing ease. Make sure the lining is long enough at the top of the center back vent so it doesn't pull. Check the length of the lining, and trim it so that it is even with the hemmed edge of the garment. Press up a lining hem that is one half the width of the garment's hem.

Baste the fold of the lining hem where it falls against the garment's hem.

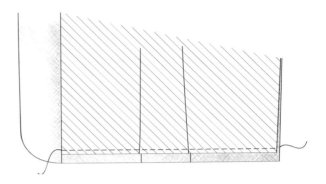

Working through the vent opening, hand- or machine-stitch the lining edge to the garment's hem using small stitches. Remove the basting and hand-stitch the lining to the garment on both sides of the vent.

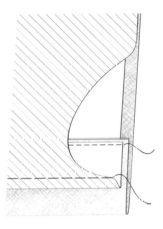

Use a fine catchstitch over the raw edge of the facing that extends below the lining's hem. This holds the edge in place and keeps it from fraying. Never turn this edge under—it's too bulky.

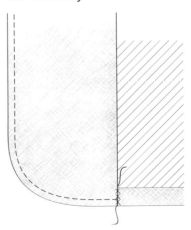

Garments that do not have vent openings require a slightly different technique of finishing the hem. Trim and press up the lining hem allowance, as described above.

Hand baste the lining to the garment about 1/2" above the edge of lining. Fold back the edge of the lining and catch only the turned-under section to the garment's hem. Remove the basting.

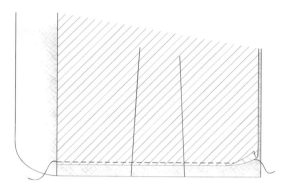

Sleeve lining

Trim the sleeve lining so that it is even with the edge of the sleeve and press under a 1/4" hem. Position the folded edge 1" above the sleeve edge, matching up the sleeve and lining seams. Slipstitch in place. This allows a 3/8" free fold of lining around the sleeve's edge when the garment is worn.

Pressing

The finished lapel is never hard-pressed farther than 1" below the gorgeline. It should have a soft roll. The roll line of the collar can be steamed and pressed to set it. Place a tailor's ham in the neckline of the garment and use it as a body-form during the pressing process.

Topstitching

Topstitching is the finishing touch used on many tailored garments. Not only does it add interest, but it keeps the garment edges flat and the facings in their proper position. Use topstitching thread or two strands of regular thread, so that it will show up well. See Chapter 2 for more topstitching helps.

For perfect topstitching, draw a "road map" on the garment using an air erasable marking pen and a plastic see-through ruler for precise marking. Now you know **exactly** when to pivot at the collar and lapel points. No more ripping out of stitches because you've gone one stitch too far! Use the air erasable pen to draw curves ac-

curately on patch pockets as well as curved jacket edges. Now you know when to start turning the machine for smooth, even curves.

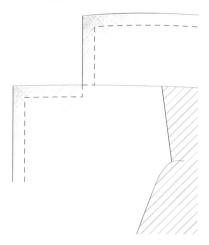

When topstitching, help your machine around corners and points by taking a stitch through the edge of the garment with a threaded hand-needle. Use the thread ends as a "handle" to help ease the fabric around the needle. Without this "handle" the presser foot has no traction and stitches in place or makes shorter stitches, thereby ruining the look of the topstitching. Be careful to avoid a skipped stitch, make sure the needle is on the upstroke.

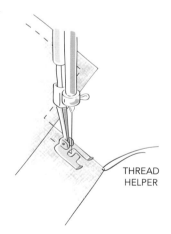

THREAD HELPER

Buttons and Buttonholes

Machine buttonholes are used on men's garments. The keyhole style is preferred. A standard machine buttonhole can also be used, but it should be made with buttonhole thread or with two strands of regular thread on the top. Insert both threads through the needle's eye. Or, take the finished garment to a tailor's shop to have them made.

Women's tailored garments use a standard machine buttonhole. Heavy fabric garments, such as coats, need a keyhole buttonhole. See page Chapter 6 for more button and buttonhole helps.

TAILORED STYLES

The cut and style of tailored garments changes with the current fashion, just as do other types of clothes. Lapels are wider or narrower, jacket lengths shorten or lengthen, waistlines go in and out. You can follow the current fashion, but this tends to date your clothes, and sometimes the current style is not what looks best on your figure.

Women with wide hips look better if the jacket is longer than the length a slim person might choose. A heavy, mature figure will find a princess line, minus the center back seam and vent, a good choice for the larger figure. (Vertical lines divide the figure and are slimming.) This is also a good pattern for a person with a swayback and large hips.

A good length for both men's and women's jackets and coat sleeves is found by standing erect, with the arms hanging in a relaxed position, and cupping the fingers around the hem. The fingers should cup without causing the sleeve to wrinkle.

The sleeve length for both men's and women's garments is a matter of choice. However, a recommended length is determined by letting the arm fall in a relaxed position, and then extending the thumb up and out, as far as it will go. Adjust the sleeve length until no break occurs in the fabric. A sleeve worn with French cuffs should be cut 1/2" shorter so that more of the shirt cuff will show below the edge of the sleeve.

Of course, your personal preference takes precedence over the above suggestions, but we feel you should consider them when making your tailored garments.

SEWING TIPS

* Fold up the lining that extends below the dot at the bottom of the facing before stitching the lining and facing together. This makes it easier to finish the lower edge of the lining.

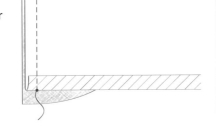

* Before cutting the lining away from the left side of the vent, lay the lining against the garment in the finished position to make sure you are trimming the correct side.

* Topstitch the collar, as shown. Shorten the stitch length as you stitch in the seam well of the gorgeline so the stitches bury down in the fabric. This short line of stitching flattens the gorgeline and makes the collar notch lie perfectly flat.

FINISHING TOUCHES

Hems and edge finishes add the final touch to your garments. Hems should never show on the right side unless you are making a decorative finish. Various fabrics and garment styles require different hem techniques. Some of the edge finishes given in this section can be used around sleeveless armholes, necklines, and the front edges of coats and jackets.

HEM WIDTHS

The first thing to consider once you have marked the proper hem length is the hem width. Suggested widths are given in the chart below. Trim your garment accordingly.

Dress or skirt	Straight	2 1/2" – 3"
	A-line	1 1/2" – 2"
	Full	1/2" – 1"
Pants		1 1/2" – 2"
Shirts and Tops	Tuck-in	1/4" – 1/2"
	Pullover	1" – 1 1/2"
Sleeves		1" – 1 1/2"
Jackets and Coats	Lightweight	1 1/2" – 2"
	Heavyweight	2" – 3"

BASIC HEM

After determining the proper length, trim the hem to the desired width. Trim any seam allowances below the hem fold to 1/4". This reduces bulk in the hem area.

Fold the hem up in position, basting along the fold. Press from the fold up, placing a strip of paper or large envelope between the fabric layers to prevent hem edge impressions on the right side.

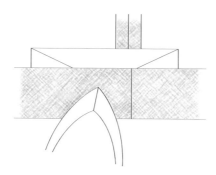

Small amounts of fullness at the top edge of the hem can usually be steamed out. The fullness found on A-line or flared hems should be controlled with a line of ease-stitching 1/4" from the hem edge.

Make the proper hem finish for your particular fabric and garment, and secure the hem using one of the techniques given below.

Hem Edge Finishes

Pinked and Stitched: Use this finish on fabrics that don't ravel very much. Straight-stitch 1/4" below the raw edge of the hem, then pink the edge.

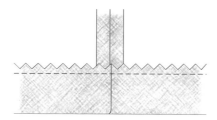

Turned and Stitched: Use only on lightweight, woven fabrics as it is too bulky for most other fabrics. This finish is commonly used on washable cottons. Turn under 1/4" of the hem edge and edge-stitch. If you are working

with a sheer fabric, eliminate the edge stitching and just baste the fold in place.

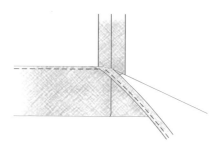

Overcast: Used on fabrics that tend to ravel. Straight-stitch 1/4" from the edge, then overcast by hand or machine.

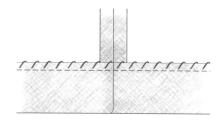

Bound Hem Finish: Loosely woven fabrics and washable garments use this finish where a turned and stitched hem would be too bulky. Use ribbon seam binding or stretch lace for straight hems and bias seam binding for flared or curved hems. Hem can also be finished with Seams Great, which is nylon sheer cut on the bias. This gives a soft, flat finish to all hem edges.

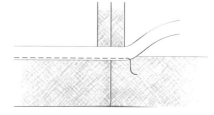

Hong Kong Finish: Bulky fabrics that tend to fray can be finished with an elegant Hong Kong finish. This finish is used on expensive silk dresses made in Hong Kong—hence its name. This is a good method to use if the garment is unlined. Cut 3/4"-wide bias strips of lightweight lining fabric to use for the binding. Stitch the bias strip to the hem edge with a 1/8" seam, right sides together. Turn the strip over the hem edge to the wrong side. Secure the bias strip by hand or by stitching in the ditch.

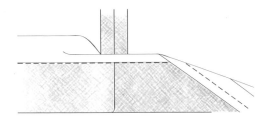

Hem Techniques

There are two basic hemming techniques, the flat finish and the inside hem. The flat finish has the hem edge sewn flat to the garment. The hem is stitched in place with a blind stitch, catchstitch or slipstitch, depending on the hem finish.

The other hem technique is referred to as an inside finish. The hem stitches are done **between** the garment and hem fabric, using either a catchstitch or blind stitch. This is the method to use with fine knits and wovens. Because the garment and hem are lightly layered together, the hem edge never shows as a ridge on the right side of the garment and is invisible on the wrong side.

Whatever technique is used, never draw the hem threads up tightly, or else the hem will show on the right side. (This is your one chance to get away with sloppy sewing!)

Hemming Stitch: This stitch is worked from right to left by taking a stitch in the hem edge, then just catching a thread of the garment, as shown.

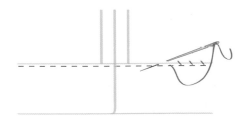

Catchstitch: Very strong, this hem is a good choice for children's clothes. It is also quite flexible and can be used on very lightweight knits that tend to ravel.

Work from left to right, and catch just a thread or two of the garment and hem edge.

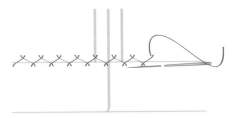

Slipsitch: Use this technique only on a flat finished hem that has been turned and stitched. Work from right to left. The needle runs along the fold of the hem, coming out periodically to catch a thread of garment fabric.

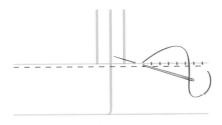

Tailor's Hem: The tailor's hem is the inside hem that is used on fine knits and wovens. It makes an invisible hem finish on both sides of the garment.

Pin the top edge of the hem about 1/2" from the hem edge; place the pins parallel to the hem edge. Fold the hem back as illustrated. Working from left to right, stitch a catchstitch between the hem and the garment fabric. Insert the needle into the fabric opposite to the direction you are hemming. The threads will cross over each other, locking each stitch. If one stitch breaks, the others stay in place until you can make repairs.

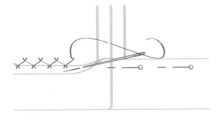

You can also use a locked, blind stitch for the tailor's hem. Pin the hem in place, as directed above, and roll back the hem edge 1/4". Working from right to left, catch several threads of the rolled-back hem. Next, insert the needle just behind the thread, taking a small stitch that won't show on the right side of the garment. Cross over the thread and insert the needle in the hem fold about 1/2" to the left. This is my favorite hem technique as it gives a bit and doesn't "glue" the hem edge to the garment.

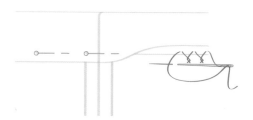

Double Hem: A double hem is another version of the inside hem. It is used on wide hems of garments made of knit or heavy fabrics—wherever a regular hem would sag and "pull" on the garment. It is also used on wide hems of lightweight fabrics to keep them from spiraling and ballooning out.

Fold up and baste the hem edge, then finish with the proper edge finish. Baste down the center of the hem; turning back the hem along this basting line then catch-stitch the hem to the garment. Turn up the rest of the hem and secure as directed for the tailor's hem.

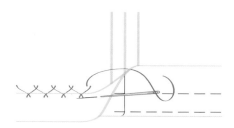

Machine Hems

Hems on fine garments are always done by hand; however, a machine hem is useful for children's or non-dress-up clothes. Machine hems can be done with a machine blind hem or by topstitching.

Each machine has different settings for a blind-hem stitch. Check your machine manual for blind-hem stitch instructions.

The topstitched hem is quick to do and adds design interest as well as finishing the edge of the garment. Many casual sport clothes call for topstitched hems; it is a good choice for knits, as you don't have to worry about

finishing the hem edge first. A hem finish that was used by the designer Jean Muir is done as follows.

Mark and press up a 1" to 1 1/2" hem; finish the hem edge as indicated by the fabric. Topstitch as desired on the right side of the garment. Do one or more rows of stitching using a matching or contrasting thread. Multiple rows of stitching add firmness to the garment edge, which is desirable on most fabrics.

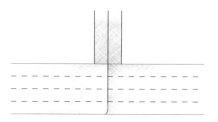

Topstitched hems can be padded for a designer look. Place a strip of polyester fleece between the hem and garment before stitching the hem in place. Cut the fleece so it is 1/4" narrower than the hem width. The padded hem works best if it is basted together before the final stitching.

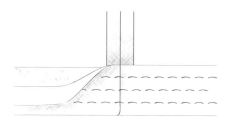

Fused Hems

Narrow strips of fusible web such as Steam A Seam 2 can be used to hold hems in place. Have the strip be 1/4" narrower than the hem, or use precut web strips. Insert the web between the hem and the garment, making sure it is just below the hem edge. Follow the manufacturer's instructions for fusing. Fusible web adds body to the hem, which is an advantage on many garments. Before using on your fashion fabric, test-fuse a hem on a scrap of fabric to see if the fused web will be invisible on the right side. You don't want to have a "glued" look or a line of demarcation.

SPECIAL HEMS

The following hems can be used in place of conventional hem finishes. They also add design interest to the garment.

Fake-Cuff Hem

This hem finish can be used on both woven and knit fabrics. It gives the appearance of a separate cuff, although it is just a special way of turning and stitching the hem. Use it on short-sleeve shirts (it's also a perfect finish for long-sleeve shirts with worn-out elbows), the bottom edge of a casual shirt or top, and at the lower edge of pant legs for a no-trip cuff, wherever you want a cufflike finish. The fake-cuff hem is also attractive when used across the top of a patch pocket (see Chapter 5).

This hem finish works best on garments with little or no flare at the hem edge. The hem width should be 1¹/₄". Allow more if you want a wider cuff finish.

Fold the hem up into position, wrong sides together, and pin. Fold the hem again in the same direction, making a double hem. Stitch ¹/₄" from the fold. Unfold the hem and press from the wrong side. Stitch along the lower edge if desired.

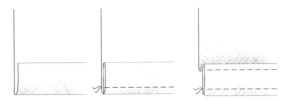

Fake-Band Hem

The fake-band hem can be used on the sleeves and lower edges of sport shirts and casual knit tops. It gives the appearance of a separate band finish. The hem width should be 1¹/₄", or more, if you want the look of a wider band.

Fold up the hem into the finished position and pin. Turn the folded hem back against the right side of the garment so that the hem edge is even with the garment fold. Stitch the folded edge on the garment side with a ¹/₈" seam. (If you stitch on the hem side, you may have problems with the cut edge of the narrow seam; as it tends to curl up into the presser foot.) Unfold the hem and press from the wrong side so that the seam allowance goes up into the garment.

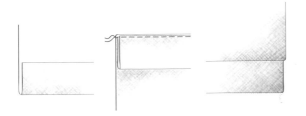

This is a good sleeve finish for a top with a mitered or crossover V-neck. Make the band finish the same width as the V-neck band.

Rolled Hem

Here is an ideal for lightweight knits such as polyester interlocks. It gives a narrow roll finish to the hem edge, which eliminates the shadowing through of a regular hem. It also prevents the pulled, drawn look that a regular hem gives to these luxury fabrics. It is a hem finish you will see on many designer clothes, and is very easy to do. Allow a hem width of 1¹/₄".

Fold up a 1¹/₄" hem, right sides together and machine-stitch ¹/₄" from the fold. Unfold the hem and wrap it over the seam allowance to the inside of the garment. Do not press—as you want a soft rolled edge.

Finish the back of the hem by folding under the edge ¹/₄". Pin the folded edge so that it just meets the stitching line. Make sure the roll is an even width all around the hem. Catch the folded edge just to the stitching threads with a loose backstitch.

The edge can also be finished by stitching in the ditch from the right side. You can either turn under the raw edge ¹/₄" or leave it extending up behind the rolled edge. Shorten your stitch length and pull the roll down out of the way of the needle so the fold doesn't get caught in the stitching. If you turn under the raw edge, make sure you have it pulled up high enough so that it becomes caught in the stitching line.

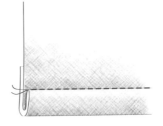

Note: *Don't use the rolled hem finish around the lower edge of tuck-in tops. It will show a ridge through your pants or skirts.*

The following is a simple hem finish seen on an expensive silk dress. It can be used on a bias as well as on the straight edge. It is an excellent finish for taffeta, chiffon or georgette dresses. However, it is not recommended for machine-washed garments.

Allow 5/8" for the seam finish. Stay-stitch 1/2" from the edge using 14 stitches per inch. Fold this to the wrong side on the 5/8" line and press. Edge-stitch 1/16" from the fold (this stitching will be between the stay stitching and the folded edge). Trim close to the stay stitching. This stay stitching keeps the fabric from fraying. The seam edge does not ripple, even on a bias edge. Do not turn it over again and stitch as the hem starts to roll in a "barber pole" fashion.

Stitching Hints

When hand rolling a scarf edge, stay-stitch 1/4" from the edge. This gives a guideline to roll to and keeps the bias edge from stretching.

Shirttail hems can be a real problem to stitch evenly and smoothly. However, Wash Away Wonder Tape makes it so-o-o easy. Place the 1/4" tape on the **right** side of the fabric edge. Remove the paper backing. Fold over twice and finger-press the narrow seam in place. Check that the width is even and that there are no puckers on the right side. Now stitch through all layers—nothing sticks to the needle and the tape washes out in the first laundering. Because the tape is flexible, it does not need to be washed out before the garment is worn.

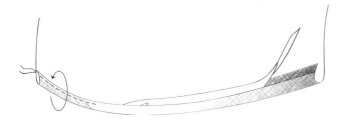

EDGE FINISHES

Try some of the following edge finishes on your woven and knit garments. These are a change from the conventional hem and facing, and add interest to the garment. Many of these finishes are found on expensive ready-to-wear.

The rolled look can be duplicated around a scoop neckline or sleeveless armhole by using a separate strip of self-fabric. It is also the method to use if you want a contrasting color at the bound edge. Use the Chanel-trim technique found in this chapter if you want a light look for the rolled edge. Use the bound-edge technique if you want a heavier look or are working with lingerie fabric. The bound edge is also a good finish for sheer swimsuit cover-ups or chiffon dresses.

Bound Edge

Trim away the hem or seam allowance from the edge to be bound. If you are binding a scoop neck, leave one shoulder seam unsewn. Leave the underarm seam unsewn for a sleeveless armhole and one side seam unsewn if you are making a hem finish.

Cut a 2"-wide strip of self or contrasting fabric for the binding piece. Cut it across the stretch for a knit, or on the bias for a woven or for a knit with very little stretch.

Fold the strip in half, lengthwise, wrong sides together, and pin the cut edges to the right side of the garment edge. Stitch with a 1/4" seam, stretching the trim strip slightly around curves.

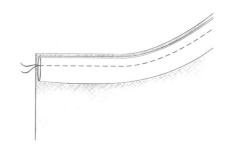

Close the unsewn seam, stitching through the trim, making sure the seam allowances are pressed up into the trim as you stitch across them.

Fold the trim up over the seam to the inside and pin, making sure the roll is an even width around the entire bound edge. Stitch the folded edge of the trim to the first stitching line with a hand backstitch, or stitch in the ditch on the right side. If you stitch in the ditch, pull the folded edge **beyond** the seam so that the machine's stitches will catch it.

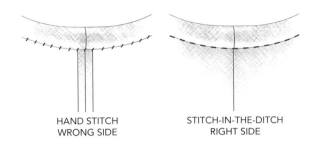

HAND STITCH
WRONG SIDE

STITCH-IN-THE-DITCH
RIGHT SIDE

This technique can be done in reverse. Stitch the trim to the wrong side of the garment first, then turn it over to the right side. Topstitch the fold using either a straight stitch or zigzag. This gives the look that is popular on T-shirt garment edges. Stitch with a 1/4" seam, stretching the trim strip slightly around curves.

Note: *Don't use this finish on the lower edge of tuck-in tops as it shows a ridge through your pants or skirts.*

Piping Edge

This edge finish can be used around sleeveless armholes, scoop or jewel necklines, or even at sleeve and hem edges. Use a matching or contrasting fabric for the trim strip.

Cut the trim strip across the stretch for knits, or on the bias for wovens or nonstretchy knits. The trim strip should be 1" wide.

Trim away the seam or hem allowance of the edge to be piped. Leave one garment seam allowance open.

Fold the trim strip in half, wrong sides together, and pin to the right side of the garment. Then cut edges even and stitch with a 1/4" seam. This is easy to do if you let the edge of the wide zigzag foot run along the fabric fold (**Fig. 1**). Turn the raw edges of the strip to the inside, leaving a

narrow fold of fabric extending beyond the garment edge. Press lightly from the wrong side, and close the open garment seam. Press the seam open and hold the piping-strip in place by machine-stitching 1/8" from the garment's fold. Making the final stitching with a contrasting thread gives a decorative effect (**Fig. 2**).

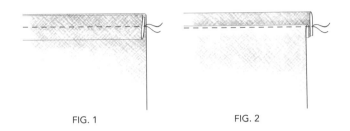

FIG. 1   FIG. 2

Lettuce Edge

For a very delicate, ruffled look, use this edge finish. It is suitable for stretchy knits only, such as interlocks, tricots, ribbings and jerseys.

Trim away the entire hem or seam allowance from the edge to be finished, or for a firmer edge, leave a 3/8" hem allowance. Try both ways on a scrap of your fashion fabric to see which method gives you the desired look.

Set your machine for a narrow to medium-wide zigzag, with a short stitch length. The exact stitch combination can be adjusted to your liking on the test scrap.

Stitch along the cut or folded garment edge while stretching the fabric. Hold the fabric in front of and behind the presser foot. **Caution:** *Don't stretch so hard that you cause your fabric to "run." Different fabrics stretch different amounts, and this influences the look of the finished edge. Fabrics that have lots of stretch will ruffle more than less stretchy fabrics.*

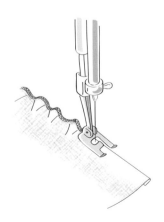

A lettuce edge makes a lovely ruffled edge that is most attractive around the bottom edge of nightgowns and peignoirs. Use it around necklines, sleeves and hem edges of dresses and tops, and for the bottom edge of pajama-type pants. It can also be used on the edge of ribbing that is being applied to the neckline and sleeve of a T-shirt. Just cut the ribbing half the regular width, "lettuce edge" one side and apply to the garment.

Satin-Stitched Edge

A satin-stitched edge finish is often seen on designer fashions. It is quick and easy to do, and gives the garment an elegant touch. It is most suitable for wool flannels, gabardines and double knits. You do not want this edge to ripple, like the lettuce edge, so test stitch a scrap of your fashion fabric before you decide on this finish to see if it will be satisfactory.

The satin-stitched edge finish can be used at hem edges, sleeveless armholes, necklines, and collar and pocket edges. Experiment with it for other applications.

Turn under the hem or seam allowance and zigzag along the folded edge. Adjust the stitch so that it is about 1/8" wide and quite close together. Miter corners and points for a clean finish. Easestitch curves to help them turn under neatly. Re-stitch along the edge so that you build up a smooth satin-stitch look. Trim the seam or hem allowance close to the stitching, being careful not to cut the stitches. Steam-press to remove any ripples.

Chanel Trim

Chanel trim is a matching or contrasting strip of fabric used to bind the edges of a garment. It derives its name from the famous French designer, Coco Chanel, who used it extensively on her suits. This technique can be used on both knit and woven fabrics. The initial trim application is the same for both types of fabrics, but the finishing is slightly different.

Trim away all seam or hem allowances from the garment edge that is to be bound. If the garment has a front facing, pin the facing to the garment wrong sides together. Now trim all seam and hem allowances at the same time preparatory to binding the edges. Leave one seam unsewn when applying this trim to the garment. The seam will be closed after the trim has been stitched in place, but before it is turned and finished.

Cut the trim from the desired fabric, across the stretch for knits and on the bias for wovens and firm

knits. The width of the trim-strip should be four times the width of the finished trim.

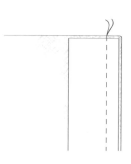

Apply the trim to the cut edge of the garment, right sides together, cut edges even. Stitch with the desired seam width. The width of the finished trim will be the same as the initial seam width. It can be 1/4" to 1" wide. Stitch accurately so that the finished trim is even.

Press the trim out over the seam allowance and close the unsewn seam. Cut the seam allowance and turn the trim to the inside of the garment. Secure in place using one of the following methods.

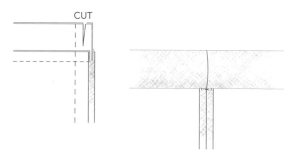

Knit Fabrics: Secure the trim by stitching in the ditch on the right side. Use a short stitch length so the machine feeds slowly; this also helps the stitches to bury down into the fabric. Trim away the excess seam allowance close to the stitching.

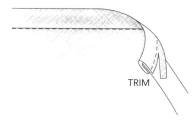

Woven Fabrics: On the wrong side, turn under the trim strip so that the fold barely covers the stitching; slipstitch it in place so that seam and hem are "bound" at the same time.

When applying Chanel trim around curves, stretch the trim slightly around the inside curves (neckline, armhole) and ease it around the outside curves (rounded corners of jacket fronts—patch pockets). This makes the trim lie flat and neat in those areas.

SLACKS CONSTRUCTION TIPS

Women's slacks instructions make installing the zipper a bit tricky. They say to stitch inseams and outside seams together and then to install the zipper. Instead of "wrestling" with your zipper and having problems topstitching a perfect fly, try this sequence.

Stitch the crotch seam leaving it unsewn 1 1/2" from the inseam. Now install the zipper while both fronts are flat. It's much easier to topstitch a perfect fly now.

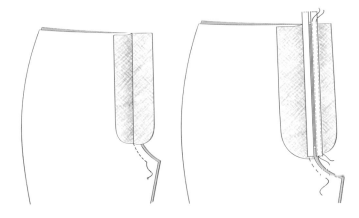

Next, stitch the inseams together, and then finish sewing the crotch seam.

It's always easier to stitch a smooth crotch curve when you "stuff" one pant leg down inside the other leg, right sides together as shown above.

Here's another tip for better fitting slacks made out of any fabric. Scoop out the back crotch seam an additional 1/2". You'll be amazed at how much more comfortably these "scooped out" slacks are. This "scooping out" allows for the actual curve of the body.

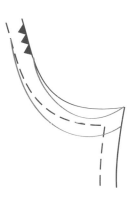

BELT LOOPS

Many garments require belt loops. They can be basic, straight loops or shaped loops. Basic loops are stitched to the garment before the waistband is stitched in place. Shaped loops are added after the waistband has been completed.

Basic Belt Loops

Cut a lengthwise strip of fabric, three times as wide as the finished loop. **Tip:** *Use the selvage edge for one side of the belt loop strip.*

Fold the loop strip, as shown, and stitch along each edge.

Cut the strip into even lengths, twice the length of the finished loop. Pin the strips to the waist of the garment before the waistband is stitched in place.

Apply the waistband and stitch the belt loops to the garment below the waistband. Place the stitching so that the finished loop will be wide enough to allow the belt to slip through it easily.

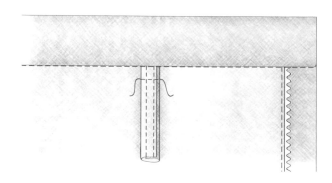

Fold under the end of the belt loop and stitch it to the top edge of the waistband. Backstitch for strength. Trim away any excess loop fabric.

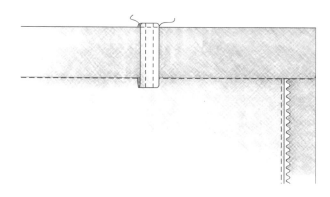

Shaped Belt Loops

Shaped belt loops are applied after the waistband has been completed. The top edge is folded under and stitched to the top of the waistband. The bottom edge is topstitched in place below the waistband, leaving enough space for the belt.

Shaped, western belt loops are very popular on men's and women's clothing. Use the pattern on the next page for a popular version of the Western belt loop. Use the following instructions for construction.

Fold the belt loop piece right sides together and stitch a narrow seam across the bottom. Stitch the side

to the dot (**Fig. 1**). Turn to the right side, push out the point and fold the lower end as illustrated (**Fig. 2**).

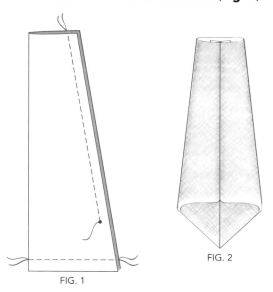

FIG. 1

FIG. 2

Stitch in place as directed above.

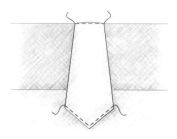

Support the ends of the belt loops that are stitched to just a single layer of fabric by placing an extra piece of fabric behind them on the wrong side of the garment. Stitch through all the layers.

HEM TIPS

- Hems that have to be let down usually leave a crease. A half-and-half solution of white vinegar and water helps to remove the crease. Apply the solution to a press cloth and steam-press, or use a Rajah Press Cloth, which removes 90 percent of the line.

- Pleated garments keep a sharper look at the hem edge if you edge-stitch the back of each pleat on the wrong side. Stitch just the depth of the hem.

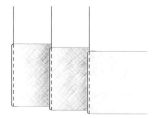

- Never use the turn under 1/4" and stitch method to finish knits. It is too bulky and not necessary, as knits don't fray. Never use seam binding on knits either. This makes a hem ridge that shows on the right side. The tailor's hem or some form of topstitched hem is the best method to use.

- Stretchy knits, such as stretch-terry and velour, should have the edge finished with a wide zigzag before they are hemmed. In order to keep the edge from stretching out of shape when zigzagging, use the following technique.

  Attach a thread to a garment seam at the hem edge by wrapping it around a pin, as shown. Leaving the thread attached to the spool, hold the thread taut along the edge of the fabric and zigzag over it. This keeps the hem edge from stretching out of shape. Remove the pin, pull the thread away after stitching and rewind it around the spool to use again.

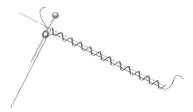

- Place a fine cotton cord along the inside fold of the hem on fine wool garments. This softens the hem edge for a nicer look. Hold the cord in place with large running stitches.

- Do not use a machine blind hem on pile fabrics such as corduroy, velour or velvet. The needle tends to pick threads out of the fabric, leaving visible marks or holes on the right side.

- Never use a double thread when hemming. You may think you are making it stronger, however, if you ever catch your heel in the hem, the thread will hold, but the stitch may pull out of the garment, leaving a hole.

- When hand finishing Chanel trim or other bound edges, insert the needle under the threads of the first stitching line instead of into the garment fabric. The stitching will not show on the right side, and the machine stitching line is covered on the wrong side.

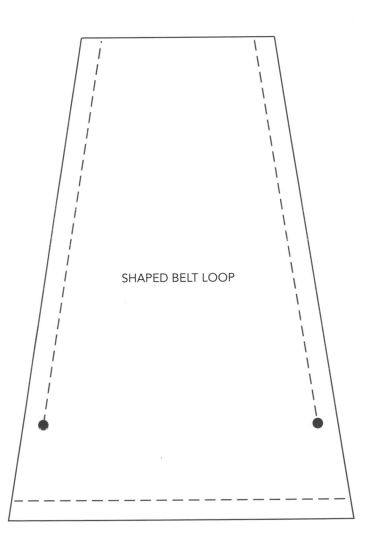

SHAPED BELT LOOP

NEEDLEMAKING

Needlemaking began in London in Queen Elizabeth's time. Needles were made in Threeneedle Street. This street was named for the coat-of-arms of the needlemakers guild, which consisted of three needles. The name today has been corrupted into Threadneedle Street. Due to economic restrictions, the needlemakers moved to the country and finally centered in Redditch, England, where there was the needed water power to run the stamping machines. Redditch is still a needle center of the world.

In Queen Anne's time, steel needles were in relatively good supply. At that time needles were kept in needlebooks with embroidered covers; however, the flannel leaves gathered moisture and the needles rusted. Tightly closed cylindrical needlecases were found to solve the problem of rust. These cases were made of many materials—wood, silver, ivory, mother-of-pearl and tortoise-shell; many were beautifully carved and inlaid.

Self-threading needles were available by the 19th century. They had a V-shaped notch at the blunt end to carry the thread. By now needles were plentiful and were sold in packets of special blue paper to prevent their rusting.

18th century Dutch needlecase carved from a Coquilla nut. 4¼" long

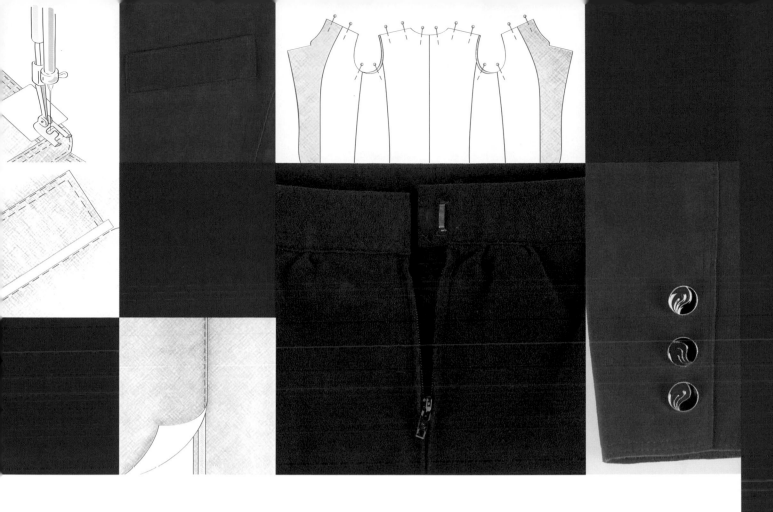

FAUX LEATHER

8

Chapter 8: Faux Leather

ULTRASUEDE is featured in the following instructions, however many of the same techniques can be used for Ultraleather and other synthetic suede fabrics.

Ultrasuede fabric is easy to sew! Yes, that's really true! It's easier to sew than most woven fabrics and lots of knits. One of the most luxurious fabrics available today, it is used in high-fashion clothes by top-name designers.

Why don't more people sew it at home? For one thing, it is quite expensive and most home sewers are afraid of making a mistake on such an expensive fabric. However, as soon as you read through these instructions, you will see that Ultrasuede really is easy to sew. Those designer clothes that you have dreamed about can easily be yours at a fraction of their cost.

ALL ABOUT ULTRASUEDE

Ultrasuede is a nonwoven fabric made from 60 percent polyester and 40 percent nonfibrous polyurethane. It does not have a lengthwise or crosswise grain, but it does have an up and down nap. It has all the advantages of real suede leather and none of the disadvantages.

It is completely machine washable and dryable and does not shrink. Washing makes the fabric softer and helps eliminate the rustling sound that it has when new. Machine-wash in warm water and dry at medium heat, being careful not to overdry. For best results, remove the fabric from the dryer immediately. It is not necessary to preshrink this fabric.

Ultrasuede can be dry-cleaned if you prefer, but it isn't at all necessary. Why make your fashion garment that much more expensive with added cleaning bills if you don't have to? This is one of the fabric's big advantages over real suede. **Note:** *While washing softens the fabric, dry cleaning preserves the original firm hand. If you want to retain a crisper look, dry cleaning is the answer. Most ready-to-wear Ultrasuede garments are marked dry-clean only. This is usually because nonwashable linings and bindings have been used in the construction, not because the fabric is not washable.*

Garments made from Ultrasuede will not shrink, ravel, pill, peel, lose their nap or crock (meaning the color doesn't rub off as with real suede). It is wrinkle-proof and lightweight, making it ideal for travel. You won't feel worn out wearing an Ultrasuede coat or jacket as you will with heavier, real-suede garments.

Ultrasuede is warm like a sweater, and it does breathe. You won't perspire in it as you do when wearing other fake leathers. It acts like a windbreaker—the same as real leather—so even though it is lightweight, it keeps you warm on a cool, breezy day.

Jackets and coats made from the fabric are perfect for outerwear. A light-colored Ultrasuede trench coat is a very practical item because it is so versatile and can be machine-washed and machine dried whenever needed. Outerwear garments can be made water repellant by spraying with Scotch-gard. This treatment also makes the lighter colors of suede somewhat dirt repellant.

Ultrasuede doesn't water-spot or stiffen when wet, so you can spot-clean stains on any garment and not have to worry about leftover cleaning marks.

One word of caution—all synthetic suede fabric burns easily. A dropped cigarette ash immediately leaves a permanent mark or hole. Rubbing dry, white scouring powder on the spot can sometimes remove the burn mark if it isn't too deep. Smokers, please be careful, and nonsmokers, watch out for careless smokers at crowded parties.

Now that you know some of the facts about Ultrasuede and are excited about this luxurious fabric, you should be ready to begin your own designer fashion. But, before you rush out and buy your favorite shade, please read through the rest of these instructions. Some planning has to be done before you select the pattern and buy the fabric. Since Ultrasuede does involve a sizeable investment, you should inform yourself with its

FAUX LEATHER

cutting and stitching techniques. As was previously mentioned, Ultrasuede is easy to sew, but it is different from woven fabrics, and you should be well aware of these methods before you begin.

ABOUT ULTRALEATHER

Ultraleather is a wonderful synthetic looks-like-leather fabric. It's soft-as-butter, easy to sew and so practical. No one will believe it's not the "real thing"—until you throw it into the washing machine. Ultraleather has all the benefits of real leather, such as suppleness, beauty and comfort, but none of the negatives—such as expensive leather cleaning bills! Real leather "pouches out" at elbows and knees. Collar points tend to curl up unattractively instead of lying flat. Not Ultraleather—it behaves! When stretched, it recovers perfectly, collar points lie flat, skirts don't "bag out" in the hip area and the fabric doesn't split at the seams—even in straight, unlined skirts and slacks.

Ultraleather is different from Ultrasuede in more than its surface looks. It has no nap—Ultrasuede does. You'll save fabric by using a "without nap" layout when cutting out the pattern. Ultraleather has good crosswise stretch but unlike Ultrasuede, it also stretches lengthwise. This stretch in both directions makes it super-comfortable to wear.

Ultraleather is 48" wide and definitely should be pre-shrunk. (Ultrasuede doesn't shrink one iota.) Ultraleather doesn't shrink in the washing machine but the dryer heat does cause shrinkage. A 1⁵/₈" yard piece shrank 1/2" in the length and 7/8" in the width.

The information in this chapter is written for Ultrasuede sewing with specific notes on Ultraleather considerations included.

SELECTING PATTERNS

Ultrasuede looks best in jackets, vests and coats, and, of course, the traditional shirtwaist dress made so famous by Halston. It does not drape or ease well, so avoid patterns with close-fitting curves, lots of gathers or pleats, and eased seams. Remember, Ultrasuede is similar to leather, and garments that are casual and loose fitting, with tailored lines, look best. Styles calling for topstitching show the fabric to best advantage. Choose patterns with yokes, patch pockets and flaps, and extensive topstitching detail.

Most tailored jacket patterns are suitable for Ultrasuede, but some are available that are designed specifically for leather or leatherlike fabrics. These have the lines

that look best with suedelike fabric. You will find that the ease in the sleeve cap is less than normal, so the sleeve can be stitched into the armhole without any puckers.

Whether you use one of the leather-adapted patterns or a standard pattern, it is best to make up a trial garment first so that any pattern alterations can be done before the fabric is cut. It is not practical to alter your garment after it has been cut and sewn due to some of the seam construction.

A heavy muslin can be used for the trial garment, but it's more fun to pick up a denim remnant to use. Denim is good for this purpose because it has the same drape and ease characteristics of Ultrasuede, and you will get a true picture of the fit and any construction problems that you may have with the suede. Of course, a denim trial garment costs a bit more, but with a little more work you will have a wearable garment instead of just a muslin shell that you throw away.

Things to look for when making the trial garment are length in sleeve and body, general overall fit and suitability of the style. It's a lot easier to decide that you don't like a less expensive denim jacket than it is to reject a costly Ultrasuede jacket.

Ultraleather makes up beautifully in any jacket pattern, but it is best to use "leather-look" patterns.

SEAM VARIATIONS

Look at ready-to-wear Ultrasuede garments and you will notice the different seam types used. Manufacturers use the conventional, topstitched, lapped and slot seams, and you have the same options. Your choice is governed by the desired finished look. Some garments are made using one seam method exclusively, while others are made with a combination of two seam types. For example, we saw a beautiful man's sport coat, by Halston, that was made with the conventional seam method except for the lapel, collar edges and pocket flaps. These were finished with just the cut edges topstitched together. This coat was also fully lined and was truly an elegant garment.

While all seam types work for Ultrasuede, we have found through experience that the lap method gives a smoother more leatherlike look to the garment and saves you fabric in the pattern layout. The conventional seam is recommended for armholes and can also be used for other seams, except, some method must be used to keep the seam pressed open flat if you are going to wash and dry the finished garment. We do not recommend conventional seam techniques for faced edges such as lapels, pocket flaps, etc. The edge will be quite bulky and tend to ripple after machine washing and drying. Read through the Seams section in this chapter to get more information on the various techniques for Ultrasuede.

YARDAGE REQUIREMENTS

Always check the amount of fabric needed before purchasing your Ultrasuede. Yardage requirements given on pattern envelopes are usually more than actually required, and with the fabric being so expensive, it doesn't make sense to buy more than you need. For example, a trench coat made from a Vogue pattern called for 4 3/8 yards of 45" fabric with a nap layout. The actual Ultrasuede garment needed only 3 1/4 yards when the flat method of seam construction was used. The pattern wasn't shortened, so you can see how much fabric and expense was saved.

For Ultraleather you will not need to use a napped layout, so even more fabric expense can be saved.

After you have completed your trial garment, made any pattern alterations and decided on the seam method, you should then lay out the pattern pieces on a marked cutting board or another piece of 45"-wide fabric. Follow the cutting tips given in the Cutting the Fabric section of this chapter to help position the pattern pieces to save fabric. Measure precisely how much fabric is needed and then purchase your Ultrasuede.

SEWING NOTIONS

You don't have to use lots of special sewing notions when working with Ultrasuede. However, we want to review your usual sewing equipment, with some comments on a few items that can make construction easier.

Scissors

A good pair of sharp scissors is a must for cutting so that you get smooth rather than jagged edges. This is especially important when using the lap seam method as the cut edge is visible on top of the garment. Long, sharp bent-handled shears enable you to make smooth, long strokes for straight cuts. A pair of 6" trimming shears is useful for the many trimming jobs involved with Ultrasuede. Appliqué scissors make it easy to trim the underside of lapped seams without having to worry about cutting the garment.

Pins

Pins can be used without leaving holes as they do in real leather. Use sharp dressmaker pins. Extra-long pins (1 1/2") with the large heads are excellent, as they can be pushed into the fabric much more easily than the small, metal-headed pins. Regular pins soon make your fingers feel as though they have holes in them.

A word of caution about pins: While you can use dressmaker pins in your Ultrasuede or Ultraleather with no leftover pinholes, this doesn't hold true for decorative pins or the pins used on the back of convention badges. Their large size puts holes in your garment!

When working with Ultraleather it's best to use pins only in seam allowances. (Don't ever pin into real leather as every pin hole remains forever.)

Thimble

A good-fitting thimble should be used to protect your finger. If you are one of the many who say they have never been able to use a thimble, you will become an immediate convert. Ultrasuede is resistant to hand needles, and you need the help of a thimble to push the needle through.

Machine Needles

Use a size Schmetz Universal 11/75 or 12/80 machine needle when sewing. If you use topstitching thread, you will have to use a larger needle, probably a size 16/100.

Occasionally you may have some trouble with skipped stitches. Try using a needle one size larger. Sometimes changing from one brand of thread to another will solve the problem. Increasing the pressure on the presser foot and/or using the straight-stitch throat plate with the small hole can also help.

Do **not** use leather machine needles, as they tear the fabric.

Hand Needles

Use fine hand needles when basting. As we mentioned above, a thimble is a must.

Fine leather needles, available at most notions counters, penetrate Ultrasuede fabric much more easily than regular needles because they have a fine, sharp wedge at the point. These needles will really save your fingers. If you buy leather needles in a package of assorted sizes, use just the fine ones on your garment. The larger ones may leave marks in the fabric.

Thread

Use polyester thread when sewing. It has good tensile strength. Standard thread can be used for the flat seam method as well as the conventional seam method. You may prefer to use topstitching thread for flat seams because of the heavier look it gives. That is fine if your machine can handle it, but there are some machines that just don't make good seams with this heavier thread. Make some seam samples using four to six layers of Ultrasuede before beginning your garment to see how it is going to stitch. Sometimes topstitching thread works on two layers of fabric but balks at the thicker seams found at the neck, collar, pockets and flaps. You may have to decrease the bobbin tension when using this thread for both the top and bobbin thread. Ultrasuede tends to grab the needle as it goes through the fabric, thereby throwing off the timing and causing skipped stitches and looping underneath. Don't be too concerned if you can't get good results with topstitching thread. Regular thread looks just fine on Ultrasuede and works a lot easier.

Iron

Do not allow a bare iron to touch Ultrasuede. You will end up with an iron mark. Always use a press cloth. Always test iron and press cloth on a scrap of fabric to be sure iron is not too hot and press cloth is not too thin. A Rowenta iron or one with a Teflon soleplate is best. A Rajah Press Cloth protects your fabric. Use a light pressure, there's no need to press hard. Steam and a little heat do the job. **Note:** *Do not iron Ultraleather without a heavy press cloth to protect it.*

Ruler

A plastic see-through ruler is a great help for the precise marking of seam allowances. The best kind to use is 2" wide and 18" long. It has red grid lines at 1/8" intervals over the entire surface of the ruler.

Sewing Tape

Wash-A-Way Wonder Tape, a basting tape, makes sewing Ultrasuede even easier than before. It can be used during garment construction when making conventional seams instead of hand basting. It can be stitched through and disappears in the first washing. It also eliminates any possibility of drag developing as the double rows of topstitching are stitched. The 1/4" width is perfect to hold lapped seams in place.

This tape can also be used to mark the wrong side of the cut garment pieces. This is necessary so that you put your garment together properly. It can also be used to hold small detail pieces in place on the right side of the garment while stitching.

Glue Stick

A glue stick, available at art supply stores and many fabric stores, is a "must" when using the flat method of seam construction. This water-soluble glue makes basting the seams quick and easy and even allows you to do some simple fitting with glued rather than stitched seams. Product Note: We have found Dennison's glue stick or Collins glue stick to be the best glue sticks when working with Ultrasuede. Other brands are available but they don't seem to be sticky enough for this napped fabric.

Do **not** use liquid fabric glue on Ultrasuede. It is not water soluble and leaves a permanent mark if you happen to get it on the right side of the garment.

MARKING THE FABRIC

Construction marks should be transferred to the fabric wherever possible. Notches can be marked with small clips (never snip deeper than the notch) when seam allowances are left intact. Notches should be marked with a soft pencil or chalk on the wrong side when the lap seam method is used. A sliver of hand soap can be used to mark construction marks on the right side of the fabric.

Other construction marks should be marked on the wrong side of the fabric and transferred to the right side of the garment by running a threaded needle through the mark and leaving a long thread in the fabric.

When using the lap method of seam construction, seam lines can be marked on the right side of the underneath layer with pins, Wash-A-Way Wonder Tape or a sliver of soap.

Water-Erasable Marking Pen

Another marking method suitable for this fabric is the water-erasable marking pen. Marks put on either the right or wrong side of the fabric can be easily removed with a drop of water. The purple ink, air-erasable pen fades automatically within 48 hours. So be sure to sew the seam before it disappears!

SEAMS

All Ultrasuede seams must be basted together in some manner before they are machine-stitched in order to prevent "creeping" of the top layer of fabric. This can be done by hand basting, using a glue stick or with Wash-A-Way Wonder Tape.

Conventional Seams

If you choose to use conventional seams, you must be careful that the seams don't look bulky and unpressed when you finish. Special care must be taken to make all seams flat. Follow these instructions below to help you achieve this look.

Stitching Seams: Use one of the following methods when making conventional seams:

- **Hand-baste** the seam together just inside the seam line. Machine-stitch, holding the fabric taut. Remove the basting after the stitching has been completed.

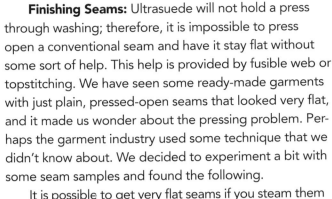

- **Tape-baste** the two layers of fabric together using Wash-A-Way Wonder Tape. Place the tape between the two layers of fabric about 1/8" short of the seam line so that it will not be caught in the stitching. Machine-stitch the seam, holding the fabric taut. If you do stitch into the tape, never fear—it doesn't gum up the needle and disappears after the first washing. **Note:** *This is the best method for Ultraleather.*

Finishing Seams: Ultrasuede will not hold a press through washing; therefore, it is impossible to press open a conventional seam and have it stay flat without some sort of help. This help is provided by fusible web or topstitching. We have seen some ready-made garments with just plain, pressed-open seams that looked very flat, and it made us wonder about the pressing problem. Perhaps the garment industry used some technique that we didn't know about. We decided to experiment a bit with some seam samples and found the following.

It is possible to get very flat seams if you steam them open and then pound them with a clapper. Use a firm surface under the seam, rather than the padded ironing board, when pounding. A child's wooden block is ideal for this.

However, these seams will not stay pressed flat through the washing and drying process. They will have to be steamed and pounded open after each washing. Sounds like a lot of work, doesn't it? Maybe it would be better to send the garment to the dry cleaners, and let them worry about it.

Since we have been unable to find a way of keeping these conventional seams pressed open without help, we suggest that you use one of the following techniques.

- Place 1/4" strips of fusible web under each seam allowance and fuse so that it stays flat. (Do not fuse Ultraleather.)

- Press both seam allowances to one side and topstitch through all layers 1/4" to 1/8" from the seam line. Or make two rows of topstitching. **Note:** *This is the best method for Ultraleather.*

Note: *Use the width of your presser foot for perfectly even rows of topstitching.*

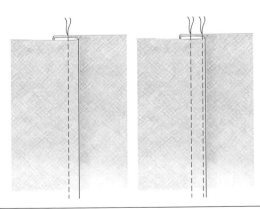

- Press open the seam allowance and then topstitch 1/8" from the seam on both sides.

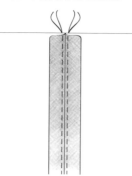

Lap Seam

The lapped method of seam construction gives a flat, leatherlike look to your garment. It is very attractive and is the method used frequently on designer clothes. This method makes it easy to get that professional look with your first Ultrasuede garment, and it is also the fastest method of construction.

We do not recommend the cut lapped seam for Ultraleather, as it would expose the knit underside of the fabric. See Chapter 2, Special Fabrics for seam to use on Ultraleather.

The lap seam is made by trimming away the entire seam allowance from one side of the garment piece and then overlapping the trimmed garment edge over the untrimmed seam allowance until the trimmed-edge lines up exactly with the seam line. It is then hand-, tape-, or glue-basted and stitched with two rows of topstitching. The seam line on the under layer of fabric can be marked using one of the methods given previously.

Stitching Seams: Use one of the following methods when making flat seams:

- **Hand-Basted Seam:** Baste the seams together approximately 1/8" from the cut edge. Position the basting stitches so that they won't be caught in the machine-stitching. Do the first row of machine topstitching just slightly in from the cut edge, holding the fabric taut. Make the second row of stitching 1/4" away from the first. Caution: Always to stitch in the same direction. Remove basting and trim away the excess seam allowance from the wrong side. Holding the scissors at an angle to the fabric makes the trimming job easier. Appliqué scissors are a great help when trimming, as the duckbill blade keeps them from cutting into your fabric.

- **Tape-Basted Seam:** Place a strip of Wash-A-Way Wonder Tape between the layers of the lap seam so that it is 1/8" back from the top cut edge. Make the first row of topstitching just slightly in from the cut edge. Remember to hold the fabric taut. Make the second row of topstitching 1/4" away from the first. Trim away excess seam allowance from the wrong side of the garment. The Wash-A-Way tape can be stitched through and disappears in the first washing.

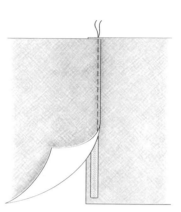

- **Glue-Basted Seam:** Apply glue stick to the wrong side of the fabric edge that has been trimmed. Keep the application about 1/4" wide. Overlap the trimmed and glued edge to meet the seam line of the other garment piece and finger-press in place. Secure the seam with two rows of topstitching sewn in the same direction. Turn the garment to the wrong side and trim away the excess seam allowance. The narrow glue application makes this procedure easy because the under edge will not be glued down. Wide glue application gives problems because you have to pull the fabric layers apart before you can trim.

When sewing multiple rows of topstitching on your garment, it is absolutely necessary to stitch each row in the **same direction**. Otherwise, the layers of fabric will drag against each other, causing ripples between the rows of stitching.

Alternate Lap Seam

This is an alternate lap seam technique that is used when putting in a center-slot zipper (see Zipper section of this chapter), or when stitching darts. Use the following procedure for making this type of lap seam.

Cut a 1"-wide strip of suede fabric as long as the seam or dart to be stitched. Be sure both naps are in the same direction.

Position the suede strip under the garment pieces so that the trimmed edges of the seam or dart butt together in the center of the strip.

Baste the seams together using one of the methods given in the Lap Seam section.

Stitch two rows of topstitching on both sides of the seam, making sure that all rows are stitched in the same direction.

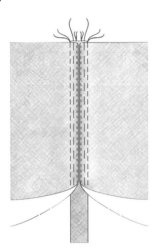

STITCHING TIPS

Sew with a slightly longer stitch length than usual—nine stitches to the inch or a stitch length of 3.5mm. Short stitches weaken the fabric, and the stitch length tends to shorten when sewing Ultrasuede. This problem can be solved by learning to stitch with tension (no, not you—the fabric). Hold the fabric in front of and behind the presser foot and keep it taut while stitching. Don't pull the fabric through the machine—just hold it with a slight tension so that it will feed evenly.

Multiple rows of stitching and all stitching on bands, cuffs and belts must be sewn **in the same direction** because of the creeping problem.

Accurate topstitching is important for that professional touch. Done badly, it can ruin the look of the whole garment, and you can't afford that. Use your machine's presser-foot as a guide for even topstitching. The outside edge of most wide zigzag feet is 1/4" from the needle. The inside edge of the right toe can also be used as an edge stitching guide. Make some sample seams with your presser foot and see if it gives the widths you want.

The seam guide on the throat plate of your machine can be used for wider lines of topstitching. If your machine does not have a seam guide, then make your own with a strip of wide adhesive tape placed to the right of the needle. Measure from the needle and mark the desired measurements on the tape, as illustrated in Chapter 2, The Basic Seam.

The top layer of waistbands, front bands and cuffs tend to push ahead of the bottom layers even though you have basted everything together. This can be controlled by slipping a piece of fusible web between the layers just before you do the topstitching. Fuse the layers together remembering to use a press cloth if you are using a conventional iron. This eliminates the creeping problem and also adds a bit of stiffness to these detail areas, usually eliminating the need for interfacing.

You may backstitch topstitched seams when using regular thread or you may prefer to lockstitch the ends of seams. Some people prefer to tie thread ends. Never backstitch when using topstitching thread. Pull both threads to the wrong side and tie off in a square knot; leave 3" thread ends, thread through a hand needle and weave the threads ends in between the garment and the facing fabric.

Topstitching Tip: When topstitching across thick seams (such as where the collar joins the neck) the machine tends to shorten the stitch length as it approaches the seam. Prevent this problem by following these steps:

1. Stop the machine when the front of the presser foot reaches the seam.
2. Lift the presser foot.
3. Place a folded strip of fabric or cardboard the same thickness as the garment under the presser foot to make it level with the thick part of the garment.
4. Continue stitching until you have gone over the hump.
5. Remove your "helper."

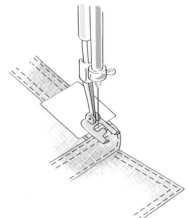

INTERFACING

Interfacing is optional. If you want a soft look, don't use any. If you want a more structured look, use a fusible interfacing. Nonwoven fusible interfacing also works beautifully with Ultrasuede but it should be preshrunk. Just remember not to use too heavy an interfacing or your garment will look too stiff.

Woven fusible interfacing can also be used, but it must be preshrunk before being applied to the fabric. Submerge woven fusibles in a basin of hot water, let stand 10 minutes and then spread flat or hang over the line to drip-dry. Do not preshrink in the machine or dry in the dryer. This causes the fusible material to fall off.

Always test-fuse a piece of the interfacing to a piece of your fabric before applying it to the actual garment pieces themselves. Wash and dry the sample to make sure that the bond is strong and the interfacing doesn't pucker. Carefully follow the fusing instructions that come with your interfacing.

Fuse the interfacing to the wrong side of the part of the garment that shows, i.e., the under collar, the lapel facing, the upper cuff and the upper pocket flap. Use caution when applying interfacing to just part of a garment piece. A visible line of demarcation may show on the right side where the interfacing ends and the garment fabric continues. This is more apt to happen with light rather than dark colors.

Do not include interfacing in the seam allowances. Trim off an extra 1/8" when using interfacing on garment pieces that have had the seam allowances removed so that a line of interfacing doesn't peek out between the two layers of fabric.

To avoid problems with peek-a-boo interfacing after the collar has been applied to the neck edge, rolled into position and stitched, trim the interfacing for the under collar 1/4" smaller than the finished size of the collar around all edges.

One-piece collars can have an extra piece of interfacing added just below the roll line of the under collar,

if desired. This gives more support to the collar stand. If you want a really firm collar finish, apply interfacing to the upper collar as well.

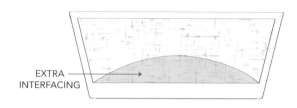

EXTRA INTERFACING

Collar patterns that have a separate band should have both layers of the band interfaced. This gives the extra support needed in this area.

Lapels tend not to lie flat when the facing piece is completely interfaced with a fusible. This problem can be solved by slashing the interfacing along the roll line after you have fuse-basted it in several places; then complete the fusing process. Taping the roll line, as is done in other tailored garments, is not necessary with Ultrasuede.

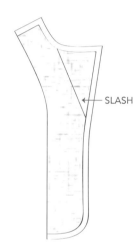

SLASH

Another technique, which can be used for turn-back lapels, is to divide the interfacing at the roll line and apply it to the garment front and the facing. The interfacing should stop 1/8" short of the roll line on each garment piece.

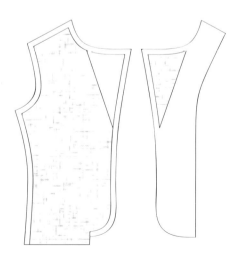

To give additional stability to the chest area of a man's jacket, you can fuse interfacing to the garment front as well as the front facing. Cut the interfacing so it goes just to the first dart and then curves into the armscye as shown. Any line of demarcation left by the edge of the interfacing is masked by the front dart and the patch pocket. If you prefer, you can fuse interfacing to the entire front of the garment, just remember to trim away the interfacing from the dart areas and slash it along the roll line. A woman's jacket doesn't need interfacing on the jacket front—only on the facing.

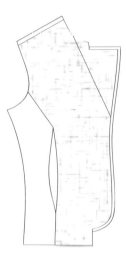

Whether interfacing the garment or not, always back buttonholes with a square of woven interfacing or lining fabric in the same color as the garment. It is best to use a piece of matching lining fabric so that a white line of interfacing will not be visible in the buttonhole opening. Woven fabric keeps horizontal buttonholes from rippling or stretching. Nonwoven interfacing is ineffective.

If you are unable to find a color-matched lining or interfacing fabric, camouflage the white in the buttonhole cut with a colored pen or pencil.

LINING

To line, or not to line, that is the question. Ready-made Ultrasuede garments show a lack of uniformity in lining practices. Some designer fashions are fully lined, some are just partially lined and some have no lining at all. Halston's famous jackets were not lined. He wanted a light sweater-weight garment. In light of this confused state of affairs, we would like to give you some lining

guidelines based on our experience of working with and wearing this luxury fabric.

Ultrasuede is napped on both sides. While this doesn't present a problem in dresses and skirts, it does make putting on jackets, coats and vests somewhat difficult. You will really get "hung up" if you try to pull on an unlined Ultrasuede jacket over a sweater. Linings solve this problem for you and make your garment so much more comfortable to wear.

Ultrasuede will show wear at points of strain (around collars, at elbows and across shoulders) and where it is subjected to repeated chaffing (in underarm and crotch areas). Lining strengthens these parts and prolongs the life of the garment. Linings also cover up inside construction details such as welt pockets and darts on blazer-type jackets and men's sport coats.

After considering all the above observations, we definitely feel that linings (full or partial) should be used in Ultrasuede coats, jackets and vests. Why some designers use lining and others don't, we can't explain, but your garment will be more comfortable to wear and more attractive if you take the time to add some lining. Also, when you consider the cost of your garment, it just makes sense to add lining if that means extending the life of your expensive investment. Follow these suggestions for linings:

- Full linings are recommended for coats and jackets having inside construction details that are best covered up, i.e., darts and set-in pockets. Full linings can be used wherever desired for appearance's sake.

- Vests should be fully lined for comfort. Ultrasuede vests in better stores have just the fronts cut from suede. This type of vest is designed to be worn under jackets. The lining back allows the jacket to slip easily over the vest. Use Ultrasuede for the back of vests that are to be worn without a jacket.

- Partial linings, consisting of the upper back and sleeve lining, can be used on jackets for both men and women. Jackets with front and/or back yokes are especially adaptable to partial linings because only the yokes are lined, and the yoke seams are neatly covered by the lining.

- All jacket and coat sleeves should be lined for comfort and strength. Elbows will soon wear through unlined sleeves if the garment is worn often. If this happens, you can save the garment by adding patches to the elbow area in a matching or contrasting color of Ultrasuede.

Lining Fabrics

Fabrics suitable for lining Ultrasuede garments are lightweight polyester lining fabrics that are machine washable and dryable. Look for something that has a fairly slick surface so that it will slide over your other clothes easily.

CUTTING THE FABRIC

The method of seam construction used on your Ultrasuede garment influences the amount of fabric needed and the pattern layout. The lapped seam method uses less fabric than the conventional seam method because seam allowances are removed from some sections of the pattern. This enables you to place the pattern pieces closer together on the fabric.

You should buy your pattern and make up the trial garment even before you buy your Ultrasuede so that you have all the length alterations made and have decided on the method of seam construction. If you are going to use the lap seam method, you should fold the affected seam allowance out of the way and make a trial layout on your cutting board or another piece of 45"-wide fabric. This gives you an accurate measurement for your yardage and probably saves you quite a bit of money.

General Cutting Tips

Whether you choose the lap or conventional seam method, all pattern pieces should be placed on the fabric so that the tops face the same direction (nap layout). If you cut with the nap running up the pattern pieces, you get a richer color. If the nap runs down, it gives a lighter, glossy look. The choice is yours—just make sure your placement of the pattern pieces is consistent. After repeated washings the nap direction seems to disappear, but initially there is quite a difference. You can cheat a bit on the nap with small pattern pieces. These can be tilted off grain if necessary in order to get a better fit on the fabric.

Ultrasuede can be cut double. Fold the fabric wrong side out and pin the pattern pieces in position.

Mark the wrong side of each cut piece with a strip of basting tape, soap, chalk or soft pencil immediately after it has been cut to help you in the construction process. Position the tape strips so that they will not be caught in any machine stitching.

Mark garment pieces that have **not** had the seam allowance trimmed with small clips at the seam line on each end of the seam line. These clips remind you of what has or hasn't been trimmed when you put the garment together.

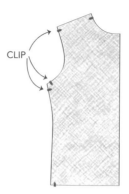

Bias markings on pattern pieces can be ignored. This is a big fabric saver. Place bias pattern pieces on the cross-grain to give them a bit of stretch.

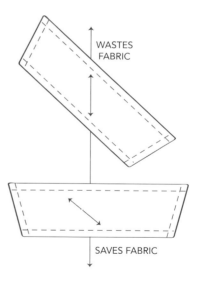

Cut all collar and cuffs on the cross-grain so that they match the nap of the rest of the garment. Positioning all pattern pieces with the print running in the same direction on the fabric gives you the correct layout.

Waistbands should be cut on the cross-grain whenever possible. Some men's jacket patterns, calling for a waistband finish, will be too large to cut the band crosswise. You will have to piece the band at the side seams or cut the band lengthwise on the fabric. Belts should be cut lengthwise if they are longer than 45". Always cut long lengthwise pattern pieces first so that you know how much fabric you have left for the other pieces.

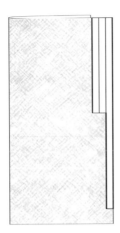

Sleeve and garment lengths should be adjusted before pinning the pattern to the fabric (another reason for making a trial garment). Trim hem allowances to 3/4". If you are going to make a conventional hem, the allowance will just be turned up and stitched or fused in place. If you are going to make a faced hem, you should fold up the entire hem allowance before pinning the pattern to the fabric. Then cut 3/4"-wide strips of Ultrasuede to face the hem edges. If the hem edge is curved, the facing strips must be cut following the same curve. Make sure you allow for enough fabric to cut the facing strips. Hem widths for garments that are going to be fully lined should be 1 1/4" wide. Dress and shirt hems can be left at 2" and hand-stitched using a blind tailor's hem.

Lap Seam Cutting Tips

When using the lap seam method, fold back the affected seam allowances on the pattern pieces before you pin them to the fabric. Figuring out what is going to lap over what is somewhat like working a puzzle, but it is fun to do and isn't difficult with the following guidelines. A good rule to follow when figuring this out is to trim away the seam allowance of the pattern piece on which you will do the topstitching. **Note:** *When pattern pieces show a topstitching line, that seam allowance is the one to be eliminated. Generally, it doesn't matter how you lap the seams, just be consistent within the garment.*

Back shoulder seams are usually lapped over front shoulder seams. Trim away the back shoulder seam allowances. If the back shoulder seam includes a dart, you may prefer to lap front over back.

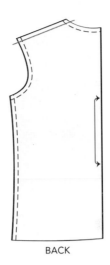

BACK

Yoke seams are always lapped over the body of the garment. Trim away the yoke seam allowances.

FRONT YOKE

BACK YOKE

Side seams are usually lapped front over back. Trim away the side seam allowances on the front pattern pieces.

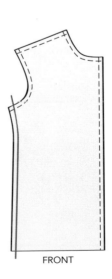

FRONT

Garments with underarm bust darts should usually have the back side seam trimmed so that you can lap back over front. This hides the multiple layers of fabric at the end of the dart. However, if there is a side pocket in a seam, you must lap front over back.

Garments with front and/or back panels should have the seams lap front over back at each seam line. Trim away the seam allowances from the seam line closest to the front of the garment.

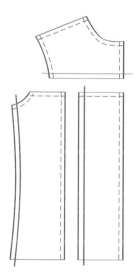

Waistbands, front bands and cuffs overlap the body of the garment. Their cut edges are topstitched together rather than conventionally stitched and turned. Trim away all the seam allowances from these pieces.

Facings for waistbands, front bands and cuffs should also be trimmed, but leave 1/8" of the seam allowance around the outside edges. Leave the complete seam allowance at the edge that joins the body of the garment. This edge will be trimmed after being machine-stitched in place. The 1/8" allowance around the outside edges gives you some extra fabric to work with when you do the final rows of topstitching. This extra fabric helps you make sure that you always catch the underside when stitching and saves your sanity. Other instructions will have you trim both seam allowances equally, but then it is easy to "lose" the under edge when topstitching.

FACING

Patch pockets and patch pocket flaps should have all the seam allowances trimmed away. Leave a 1/8" allowance on the flap facing for the above reason.

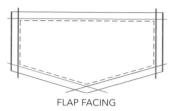

FLAP FACING

Facings for pocket flaps are usually cut from the same pattern piece as the flap itself. However, if you are short of fabric, you can just cut a narrow facing for the pocket, as illustrated. Remember to leave a 1/8" allowance on the outside edges of the facing for ease of construction.

Square flaps can be cut with the lower seam line on a fold, if you have large enough pieces of fabric to accommodate this size pattern piece. Trim the seam allowances from the outside edges of the pocket. Make sure the pocket nap goes in the proper direction when stitching the flap in place.

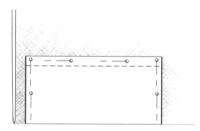

Pocket flaps that will be sewn into yoke seams should have all their seam allowances trimmed except for the seam allowance that goes into the seam. The flap facing should be trimmed the same way, except leave a 1/8" allowance around the outside edges.

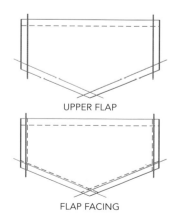

UPPER FLAP

FLAP FACING

Cut the pocket lining pieces from Ultrasuede if you have enough fabric. This looks nicer than using lining fabric, especially if the jacket is to be only partially lined. It also feels good when you put your hands in your pockets.

One-piece collars or collars with a cut-on band should have the seam allowances trimmed from all four edges of the upper collar. Leave all the seam allowances intact on the under collar.

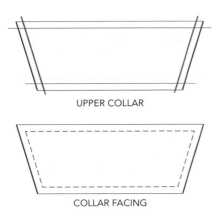

UPPER COLLAR

COLLAR FACING

Upper collars that have separate bands should have all the seam allowances except the lower edge trimmed. The band that goes inside the neck of the garment should have all the seam allowances trimmed away. Trim the collar facing the same as upper collar except leave a 1/8" allowance around the outside edges. Leave the seam allowances intact on the outside band for ease in stitching and placement.

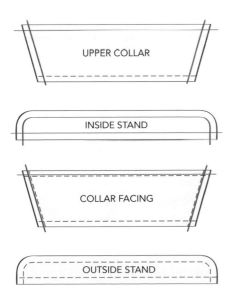

UPPER COLLAR

INSIDE STAND

COLLAR FACING

OUTSIDE STAND

Front-opening garments that do not have a separate front band should be cut without the front seam allowance. The facing for this garment piece should have the front seam allowance trimmed to just 1/8".

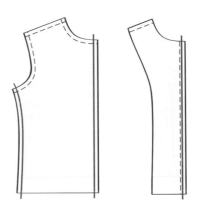

If you are not going to line or partially line the front of a garment with a front band finish, then you should modify the shape of the band facing as illustrated. This helps to prevent wear at the front neck edge, as this area is a point of stress and needs some extra protection.

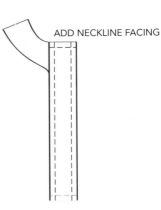

ADD NECKLINE FACING

Patterns having a straight edge at the center front, with either a band finish or a regular finish, can have the facing or band cut all in one so that you have a fold along the front edge rather than a cut edge. Overlap the front seam lines of the two pattern pieces and tape in place, as shown, before placing the pattern on the fabric. This method may create some layout problem because of the size of the pattern piece, so work it out before you buy your fabric.

Garments without collars should have the neckline seams trimmed away. The neckline facing should have the neckline seam trimmed to 1/8".

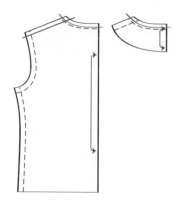

Front-opening garments with a turn-back lapel and collar should have the edge at the top of the lapel trimmed to the point where the collar joins the neck edge. Trim the entire seam allowance from the garment front but leave a 1/8" seam allowance around the edge of the facing.

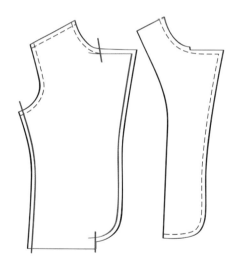

Corners that are to be sandwiched between cuffs, collars and bands should be trimmed as shown.

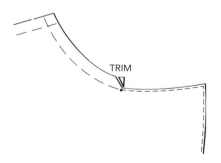

If you are making a two-piece sleeve and are using the lap seam method, then eliminate the seam allowance on both sides of the upper sleeve and leave it intact on both sides of the under sleeve.

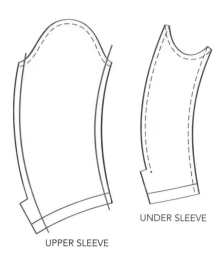

UNDER SLEEVE

UPPER SLEEVE

Many sewers cringe at the prospect of stitching "inside the tube" for the sleeve faced-vent finish as shown in the Sleeve Vents section of this chapter. As an alternative, when cutting the sleeves, remove **only** the upper sleeve vent side-seam allowance.

Make the vent-facing pattern as shown in the Sleeve Vents section of this chapter. Interface the facing for more body. (No more curled-up corners at the vent.) Position the facing against the lower edge of the sleeve, wrong sides together and baste. Remember, the facing is 1/8" larger than the sleeve, so it

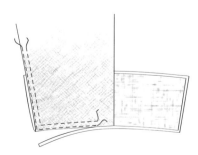

should extend out beyond the sleeve edge that much. Double-topstitch the vent, stopping 1" from the front edge. Bring thread ends to the wrong side and knot.

Lap the upper sleeve over the under sleeve seam allowance at the vent, baste and stitch. Start stitching precisely where the vent stitching stopped.

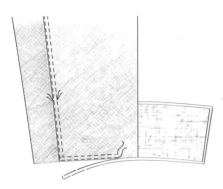

Close the remaining sleeve seam with a conventional 5/8" seam allowance. Press open. Turn right side out. Baste the partially stitched vent facing to the remainder of the sleeve and finish the two rows of topstitching. Trim off the excess facing and breathe a sigh of relief!

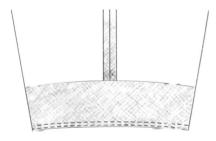

Cutting Sleeves

Whether you choose to use the conventional or lap seam method on your Ultrasuede garment, the sleeve will be sewn into the armhole with a conventional seam. This technique is easier than trying to lap the armhole seam and it gives a better look. Do not trim seam allowances from the armhole.

Check the amount of ease allowed in the sleeve cap of your pattern before cutting out the sleeve. Important: Allow only 1", adjusting the pattern as given in Chapter 4, Sleeve-Cap Ease.

Cutting Lining

Cut your lining from the lining pattern pieces or from the appropriate garment pattern pieces if separate lining patterns are not given.

Cut the underarm seam line of the sleeve lining 1/2" higher than the garment seam line. This allows for the ease needed to cover the underarm seam allowance.

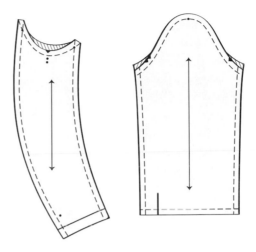

Before cutting your fabric, carefully review your pattern pieces to make sure you are lapping things correctly. A little extra time spent at this point can save you from making a costly mistake.

Cutting Skirt Pleats

Pleats in Ultrasuede skirts can be made very easily but do require a few pattern changes to reduce bulk and save fabric. Regardless of the fashion fabric, pleats always need to have the "return" extended into the waistband to support the pleat. However, to reduce bulk, the underlay needs to be under only the pleat itself. For an Ultrasuede skirt, the underlay may be cut separately.

Cut the pattern apart at the fold line of the return and the underlay. Shorten the underlay so that it is only 1" longer than the pleat itself. Turn up the hem allowance on the skirt and on the underlay. Baste. With right sides together, stitch the seam down to the pleat, change the stitch length and machine-baste the remainder of the pleat through the turned-up hem.

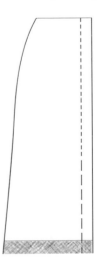

Press the pleat open. From the right side, edge-stitch each side of the seam continuing down the edge of the pleat. (Use Wash-A-Way Wonder Tape to eliminate drag when topstitching.)

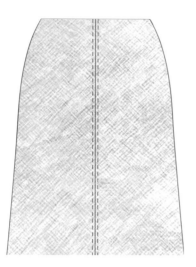

Baste and stitch the underlay to the return with a 1/4" seam allowance. Remove the basting stitches in the pleat. Now, that wasn't so hard!

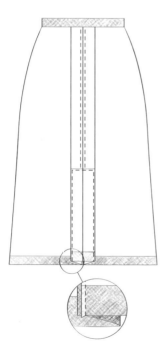

Hem Note: The hem preference for Ultrasuede and Ultraleather is the tailor's hem (see Hem Techniques in Chapter 7). However, if a sportier look is preferred, use two rows of topstitching.

CONSTRUCTION TECHNIQUES

Now that your garment is cut out, you are ready to start the fun part. Watching this fabulous fabric turn into a high-fashion garment through your sewing skills is very exciting. You will be surprised at the ease and speed of the construction, so let's get started.

DARTS

Darts in Ultrasuede garments should be long, gradually tapering to a point. Short, wide darts are difficult to stitch without getting a pucker at the point. Patterns for skirts and pants that use yokes instead of darts are better choices for this fabric than patterns with conventional darts.

There are many ways of handling darts. Try all methods on scraps of fabric to see how they work and how they look. Select the method you find most suitable for your particular fashion.

Conventional Dart

Stitch the dart, gradually tapering to the point, and then use one of the following methods to finish the dart.

- Slash open the dart along the fold and trim to 1/2". Press open and pound the seam flat. Hold the seam allowance in place with thin strips of fusible web.

- Slash the dart open and topstitch along each side catching a 1" square of fabric at the point of the dart as shown. This helps fill in the point of the dart and makes both sides equal.

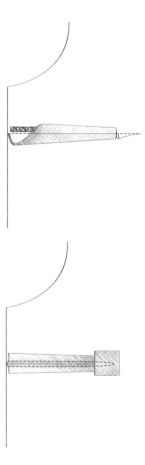

- Press the dart to one side and pound. Topstitch approximately 1/8" from the seam line. You can stitch just one side or along both sides. This method looks nice on long, double-ended darts on jacket fronts.

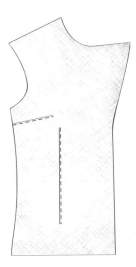

Lapped Dart

Skirt darts and darts at the back of the neck or shoulder can be cut open along one side, lapped and double-stitched in place. This method should be used only on fairly narrow darts because it is difficult to get a smooth point if the dart is very wide.

A small scrap of suede fabric added to the underside of the dart point, as previously described, makes the dart's end smoother.

Slot Dart

The slot dart method is the best choice when stitching a wide dart such as the ones found in some vest patterns. It can also be used for regular-size darts too, if you desire the slot look.

Cut out the dart along the stitching lines. Bring the cut edges together and baste them to 1"-wide strips of suede cut 1" longer than the dart opening. (Glue stick works wonders here). Topstitch along the dart edges with one or two rows of stitching, making sure the dart edges stay butted together.

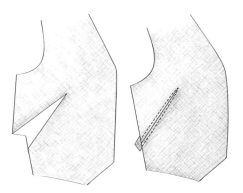

POCKETS

You will find many different types of pockets on the patterns that you may select for your Ultrasuede garment. Some are more suitable for this fabric than others. Patch pockets with or without flaps are ideal, and the welt pockets described in this chapter give a flatter appearance than do welt pockets made with traditional stitching techniques. All the pockets are made without any turned-under or faced edges for the leatherlike look.

You can easily modify the pockets given in your pattern so that they utilize the following techniques.

Patch Pocket

If a buttonhole is to be placed at the top of the pocket, make sure the pocket hem is wide enough to extend below the lower end of the buttonhole. The buttonhole needs two layers of fabric plus a patch of woven lining for support.

Cut the pocket without any seam allowances. Trim the upper edges of the patch pocket's hem as illustrated. This prevents the edge of the hem from peeking out along the side of the pocket after it has been stitched in place. It is important for a pocket without a flap to cover the top edge.

Fold over the hem allowance at the top edge of the pocket. Baste or glue in place and make two rows of topstitching across the top of the pocket. Another two rows of stitching can be stitched across the bottom edge of the hem if desired. Remember to stitch all rows of stitching from the same direction.

Baste or glue the pocket in position on the garment and stitch in place with two rows of topstitching. Reinforce the top corners of the pocket with back stitching or decorative stitching.

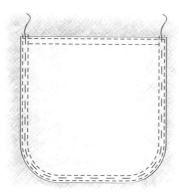

Patch Pocket With Flap

Construct and apply the pocket as directed above.

Cut the pocket flap and facing as given in the Cutting section of this chapter. Baste the facing to the pocket flap, wrong sides together, so that 1/8" of the facing extends all around the edge of the flap.

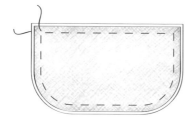

Make two rows of topstitching around the three outside edges of the flap. Trim the facing even with the flap edges.

Baste or glue the flap in position on the garment and topstitch in place.

Slash Pocket With Flap

This pocket flap has the full seam allowance left on the bottom edge of the flap and facing so that it can be sewn into the pocket slash. The pocket flap should be made before the pocket opening is cut so that the slash can be cut to fit the flap precisely. This procedure makes sure that no gaps are left at the sides of the pocket opening.

Flap Construction: Baste or glue the facing to the flap, wrong sides together, and topstitch 5/16" from the edge, around the three sides, as illustrated.

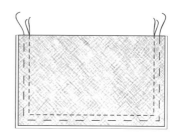

Edge-stitch only the front edge of the flap. The sides will be edge-stitched later. Trim the facing even with the edges of the flap.

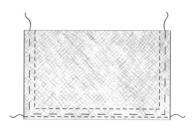

Mark the seam allowance on the right side of the flap with a strip of Wash-A-Way Wonder tape. Be sure that the edge of the tape is precisely along the seam line, and both sides of the flap below the tape are exactly the same length.

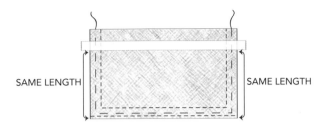

SAME LENGTH   SAME LENGTH

Pocket Construction: Cut along the pocket opening with a craft knife or a single-edge razor, placing a pin at the end of each side of the opening to prevent over cutting. Make sure that the opening is exactly the same length as the finished flap.

Slip the flap into the pocket slash so that the tape lines up with the cut edge of the slash. Baste or glue the flap in position and remove the drafting tape.

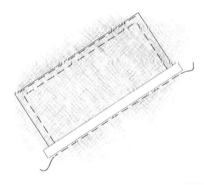

Topstitch the ends and across the width of the pocket through all the layers of the pocket flap and garment.

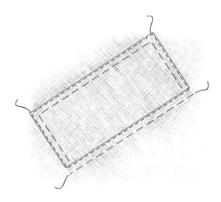

Pocket Lining: The pocket lining looks best if Ultrasuede is used rather than lining fabric, especially if you are not going to fully line the garment. If the lining pattern is one long piece, it can be cut along the fold line to facilitate the use of small scraps of fabric. You can even alter the shape of the lining pieces to take advantage of the suede scraps. Cut the pocket lining pieces without seam allowances if you use Ultrasuede.

Baste or glue, and stitch one pocket lining piece to the seam allowance of the flap.

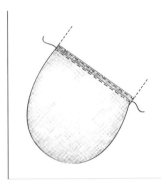

Working on the wrong side of the garment, cut two diagonal lines as shown, underneath the flap. Cut right **to** the stitching line, cutting the garment fabric only.

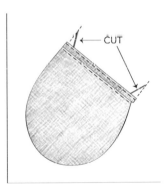

CUT

Lap the other pocket lining piece 1/4" over the free edge of fabric and baste or glue in position.

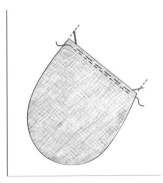

Turn the garment right side up and fold back the lower part of the garment until you see this basted seam. Machine-stitch across the top of the lining piece.

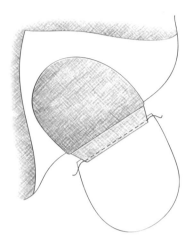

Baste or glue the pocket lining pieces together and edge-stitch.

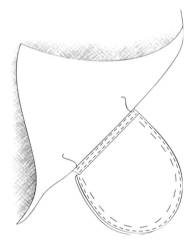

If the slash pocket is made on a garment with a front opening and facing, the pocket lining should be tucked between the facing and garment and tacked to the facing to keep it in place. Now, wasn't that easy? Make the finished flap 2" wide by 7" long.

Welt Pocket

This pocket is usually used for vests, but it can also be used as a jacket pocket or hip pocket on a skirt or dress.

Welt Construction: Delete the welt pattern piece and add 1" to the top of the pocket lining pattern. Cut this altered lining pattern from Ultrasuede making sure

the turned-down portion of the welt has the correct nap direction. Cut one pocket piece minus the added 1".

Turn down the 1" welt extension, wrong sides together, baste or glue and stitch two rows of topstitching along the fold.

Pocket Construction: Cut along the bottom and side lines of the pocket markings with a craft knife or a single-edged razor. If you are making matching pockets, you must make sure that these pocket cuts are positioned and sized identically.

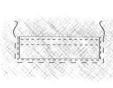

Slip the edge-stitched welt into the slash, centering it in the opening. The right side of the welt should be against the wrong side of the garment. Baste or glue the welt in position. Edge-stitch the sides and across the bottom of the welt.

RIGHT SIDE

WRONG SIDE

Baste or glue, and stitch the other pocket-lining piece to the wrong side of the flap of the garment that extends down behind the stitched welt.

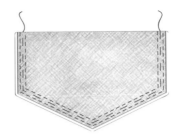

Baste or glue, and edge-stitch together the outside edges of the pocket lining pieces.

Buttonhole Pocket

See Fashion Accents in this chapter.

Single-Welt Pocket With Flap

Construct the welt pocket using the above instructions, but make sure the welt and pocket opening are just 1/2" wide.

Make the pocket flap following the instructions for the patch pocket flap. The finished flap should be 1/2" longer than the pocket opening. This extra 1/2" makes sure that the pocket opening is completely covered by the flap.

Baste or glue the flap in position above the pocket opening and topstitch in place.

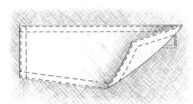

Flap Pocket in Yoke Seam

This flap pocket is a snap to make and can be used in the yoke seams of jackets, coats and dresses.

Flap Construction: The flap and flap facing should have the top seam allowance left intact. The other seam allowances are completely trimmed from the flap and trimmed to just 1/8" on the flap facing.

Baste or glue the flap and facing wrong sides together and make two rows of topstitching around the outside edge. Trim the facing edges even with the flap.

Pocket Construction: Cut two pocket lining pieces from Ultrasuede for each pocket, measuring at least 1" wider than the pocket opening. Position one pocket piece on the garment, wrong sides together, centering it over the pocket marks. Baste or glue in place. Stitch an opening 1/2" shorter than the finished measurement of the pocket flap, and 7/8" deep. Make two rows of stitching and then trim the opening close to the stitching line.

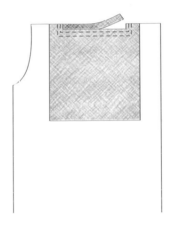

Position the other pocket piece so that the wrong side is against the right side of the first lining piece. (It looks better to have the right side of the fabric visible on the inside of the garment if it isn't going to be fully lined.) Baste or glue, and edge-stitch the pocket pieces together.

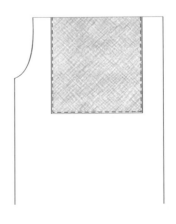

Baste or glue the flap in position, centering it over the opening. Mark the seam line, and baste the yoke over the flap. Stitch the yoke seam with two rows of topstitching.

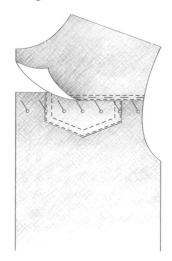

LININGS

Lining Ultrasuede garments makes them easier to slip on and off; it also prolongs the life of the garment. Coats and jackets should definitely be fully or partially lined, and dresses and skirts can be lined or not, as you desire.

If you choose to fully line dresses or skirts, attach the lining at the neckline and zipper for dresses, and at the waistline and zipper for skirts, using traditional lining techniques.

Coats look best when fully lined. Jackets can be either fully or partially lined. The type of jacket lining you choose is a matter of preference, though patterns calling for front and back yokes are more suitable to the partial lining technique than patterns without yokes.

If you are going to fully or partially line your garment and the pattern gives a back neck facing, eliminate that facing and extend the lining all the way up into the neckline. See Pattern Notes in Chapter 7. This gives a much "cleaner" finish to the inside of the garment and saves some fabric.

Stitching Tip: When stitching lining fabric to suede fabric, do so with the lining **up** and the suede next to the feed dog. Hold both layers taut as you stitch and you won't get any puckers.

Partial Lining

Partial linings consist of a full-sleeve lining and a lining at the upper portion of the back and/or front of the jacket. If your pattern has front and back yokes, it is an easy matter to line just the yokes, cutting the lining pieces from the yoke patterns. Yoke-linings are a good way to make a partial lining because the lower edges of the lining pieces are neatly enclosed in the yoke seams rather than hanging free. Follow the instructions below for yoke linings.

Patterns With Straight Yokes: Prepare the jacket for the lining by lapping the yoke over the body of the garment and basting the seam in place.

With the jacket wrong side up, place the yoke lining in position as shown so that the lining seam line is directly on top of the garment seam line. The right side of the lining is against the wrong side of the garment. Baste in place.

Turn the garment to the right side and edge-stitch the yoke to the garment.

Working on the wrong side, trim the seam allowance to 3/8"; fold the lining up into the finished position, wrong sides together, and pin.

Make the second row of topstitching on the right side of the jacket. Only one row of stitching shows on the lining and the seam is neatly enclosed.

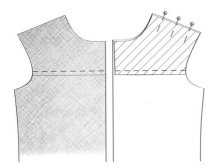

Baste the front-yoke lining to the garment at the shoulder. Overlap the back shoulder over the front, leaving the back lining free. Baste the shoulder seam and machine-stitch with two rows of topstitching.

Fold under the back lining seam allowance at the shoulder, and slip-stitch it in place at the shoulder seam. Baste the lining at the neck edge and around the armscye.

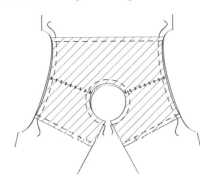

Patterns With Shaped Yokes: Baste and machine-stitch the yokes in place on the front and back of the jacket. Baste and machine-stitch the shoulder seams of the jacket.

Turn under the seam allowance at the bottom edges of the yoke linings and baste. Stitch the yoke's shoulder seams and press them open.

Position the lining inside the jacket (wrong sides together) and baste around the neck, front edge and armscye. Slip-stitch the hem of the yoke linings to the yoke seam.

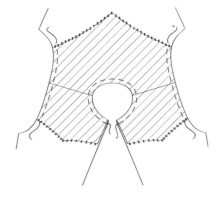

Patterns Without Yokes: Cut the pattern for the back lining so that it is 1" wider than the jacket at the center back. This allows for a pleat at the center back of the lining. This "half" lining should extend 3" below the armhole at the sides.

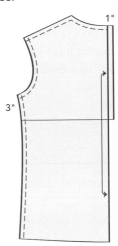

Hem the lower edge of the back lining and make a 1" wide pleat at the center back, basting across the top and bottom. Fold under the shoulder seam allowance and baste.

Position the lining in the jacket after the shoulder and side seams have been basted and machine-stitched. Baste around the armscye. Slipstitch the lining to the seam line of the garment at the shoulder and side. The lower back edge of the lining will hang free.

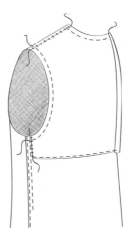

Full Lining

Fully lined jackets and coats that are hemmed at the lower edge and sleeves should have only a 1¼" hem allowance. Adjust the pattern of both the garment and lining pieces if necessary.

The lower edge of the lining can be machine-stitched to the edge of the garment's hem before the front facings are stitched in place. This technique is a good one when working with Ultrasuede because hand-catching the lining to the garment is somewhat difficult because of the characteristics of the suede.

Mark the hemline on the right side of the garment after all the vertical seams have been sewn but before the facing is applied. Use a chalk pencil or sliver of soap for this purpose.

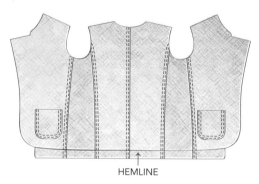

HEMLINE

Sew the vertical seams of the lining and stitch the lining to the front facings leaving the lower 2" unstitched.

Position the lining against the garment, right sides together, so the cut edges and seams are matched; pin in place. Stitch along the edges with a 1/4" seam leaving the first and last inch unstitched. If the garment has a vent you must also leave an unstitched section beside each side of the vent.

Turn the lining to the inside and position the facing against the front edge of the garment as it will be for the final stitching. Fold up the garment edge along the marked hemline and pin in place. Pin the top edge of the lining to the neckline edge of the garment. Smooth everything in place and you will see a neat fold of fabric fall into place at the lower edge of the lining. The garment's hem will be finished with one or two rows of topstitching when the facing is finally stitched in place. Hand-catch the unstitched ends of the facing in place.

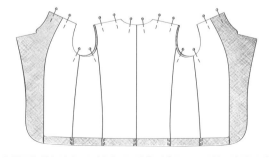

If you prefer the traditional method of hand-catching the lining in place at the lower edge of the garment, machine-stitch 1/4" from the hem edge before turning the hem up. It will be much easier to catch the lining to this line of stitching than to the suede fabric itself.

Sleeve Lining

The sleeve lining is attached to the garment at one of two points during the construction process. This is determined by the type of finish at the bottom of the sleeve. Sleeves with cuffs have the lining attached to the lower edge of the sleeve before the cuff is applied or the sleeve is sewn into the body of the garment. Sleeves without cuffs have the lining attached to the garment after the garment sleeve has been stitched in place.

Prepare the lining for either type of sleeve according to the following instructions. If the sleeve-cap ease had to be reduced for the Ultrasuede, remember to make the same alteration for the lining.

Stitch and press open the underarm seam of the sleeve lining. Easestitch the cap of the sleeve 1/8" inside the seam line, between the notches. Regular-stitch the remaining armscye right **on** the seam line. This stitching gives a guideline on which to turn and clip the sleeve's seam allowance.

With wrong sides together, slip the lining down inside the garment's sleeve. If the sleeve has a cuff finish, baste the lower edge of the sleeve and lining together. This edge will later be enclosed between the two layers of cuff fabric.

If the sleeve has a hemmed finish, the lower edge of the lining is left free at this point but then slipstitched to the sleeve hem during the finishing of the garment.

Finish the top of the sleeve lining by turning under the seam allowance all around the sleeve's edge, clipping to the seam line where necessary. Mark the notches around the edge of the sleeve with a soft pencil so that you can distinguish them from your clips. Pin the folded edge of the sleeve to the armscye seam line of the garment and slipstitch in place.

When attaching the sleeve lining to the lower edge of the sleeve, machine-stitch around the edge of the garment's hem at 1/4" before turning the hem up into position. If you are using a faced finish at the edge of

FAUX LEATHER

the sleeve, machine-stitch 1/4" from the upper edge of the facing before applying the facing to the sleeve.

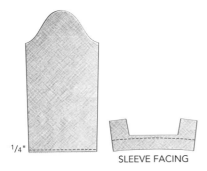

1/4"

SLEEVE FACING

Finish the lining by folding under and basting 1/4" of the sleeve lining. Position the folded edge along the line of machine stitching and hand-catch the fold just to the threads of the stitching line rather than trying to catch it to the Ultrasuede.

FRONT FACING

Baste a strip of woven interfacing or color-matched lining fabric to the wrong side of the garment, underneath the buttonhole area, before applying the front facings to coats and jackets. This stabilizes the buttonholes.

After the garment hem has been turned up, but before the shoulder seams are sewn, position the front facing against the garment front, wrong sides together. Remember, the garment front has no seam allowance but the facing has a 1/8" seam allowance remaining, so let the facing extend out beyond the garment edge 1/8". Baste in place (glue stick is a must here), and topstitch the garment fronts and hem edge with two rows of stitching. Finish the two lines of stitching at the top of the lapel as shown. Trim the facing close to the finished edge of the garment front.

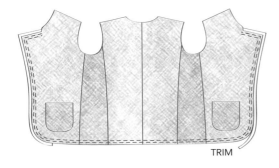

TRIM

The correct topstitching makes the difference between the expensive designer look and "loving hands at home" look. When topstitching the facing to the garment, the critical vertical rows of stitching should be on **top** of each other.

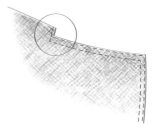

The result is the correct finished look after the collar is applied.

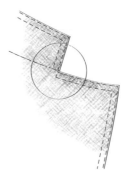

Do not back-tack on Ultrasuede to secure thread ends, as there will be an unattractive buildup of thread. Pull the thread ends to the wrong side and knot. Polyester thread easily unknots after several washings; therefore, secure the knot with a touch of a seam sealant.

FRONT BAND

Baste or glue a strip of woven interfacing or color-matched lining fabric to the wrong side of the front band in the buttonhole area. You may want to use a strip of fusible web instead. Fusible web cut 1/4" narrower the band gives crispness to bands (and cuffs) and stabilizes the buttonholes. It also eliminates any possibility of drag developing between the rows of stitching.

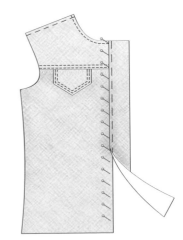

Faced Band

Mark the seam line on the front edge of the garment with pins or a sliver of soap. Lap the band piece over the front edge of the garment to the seam line. Baste or glue in place.

Pin and baste the band facing in position so that 1/8" of the facing extends beyond the edge of the top piece. Working on the right side of the garment, stitch both layers of the band to the garment with two rows of topstitching.

Pull apart the two layers of the band and trim the garment's seam allowance. This trimming must be done at this point—as you can't get to it later!

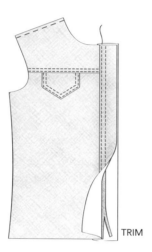

TRIM

Baste the outside edges of the band together. The topstitching along the outside edge is done after the collar has been applied.

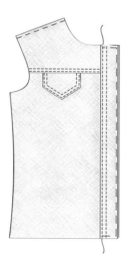

Band With Cut-On Facing

Mark the seam line on the front edge of the garment with pins or a sliver of soap. Lap the band piece over the front edge of the garment to the seam line. Baste or glue in place and stitch at 5/16". Trim the seam allowance of the garment front to 1/4".

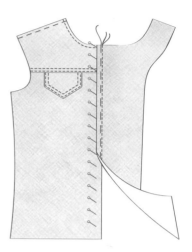

Fold the facing portion of the band back in position along the front fold line and baste again right next to the first line of basting. Edge-stitch the band and the facing to the garment front with one row of topstitching.

If fusible web is being used, position it in place; fold the facing and fuse, thus eliminating the basting along the edge.

Baste along the folded edge of the facing. This edge is topstitched after the collar has been attached.

COLLARS

Most jackets or coats made from Ultrasuede will have a collar of some kind. The two types of collars that you will find are collars with a separate band, and collars without bands or collars with a cut-on band. These two collars are applied to the garment with the same technique.

A garment having a collar with a separate band usually has a front band finish. The collar is applied after the shoulder seams have been sewn but before the garment side seams have been stitched. The garment calling for a collar without a band or with a cut-on band usually has a separate front facing. The facing should be applied after the side seams are sewn but before the shoulder seams are stitched; next, the shoulder seams are sewn and the collar is applied to the neck edge.

Collar With Separate Band

Trim the seam allowances of the collar and stand pieces as given in the Cutting section of this chapter. Interface the upper collar and the inner band for a crisp, structured look. You can even interface both band pieces for a very stiff finish. Do not apply interfacing for a soft look. Remember to trim the interfacing 1/8" smaller than the Ultrasuede pieces so that it will not "peek out" from between the layers of the finished collar.

If you are lining the garment, the lining should be basted in place around the neck edge before applying the collar. The neck edge should also be stay-stitched just inside the seam line and then trimmed to 3/8". Be sure to transfer neckline notches before trimming.

Collar Construction: Baste and double-topstitch the upper and under collar together around the three outside edges. The under collar should extend 1/8" beyond the upper collar edges at this point. Trim the under collar even with the upper collar after stitching.

Topstitching Tip: When topstitching at collar and lapel points, insert a threaded needle through the point of the collar or lapel and use this "handle" to help guide the fabric under the presser foot as you stitch around the

point. The machine tends to lose traction here and might begin to "stitch in place," ruining your topstitching. Also, do not pivot the collar around the needle until the needle is **emerging** rather than going down into the fabric. This avoids that pesky "skipped stitch" at the collar point.

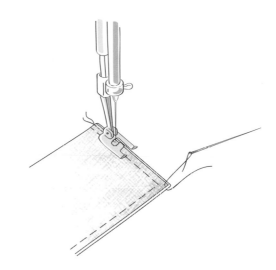

Mark the seam allowance on the lower collar edge. Pin and baste the trimmed band to the collar unit, overlapping the cut edge of the inside band to the collar seam. Baste, using a large backstitch to hold everything securely.

If fusible web is desired in the collar band, cut it 1/8" smaller around all edges than the trimmed band piece and position it on the wrong side of the band. Handle it as one with the collar band in the following steps, hand-basting if necessary.

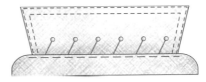

Mark the neckline seam on the wrong side of the outside band piece.

Lay the trimmed band and collar unit on top of the outside band so that the trimmed lower edge of the band is right along the marked seam line. Pin in place and baste securely across the top of the band right to the previous basting. Hand-baste in this area—glue stick is not strong enough to hold it securely for stitching. The final topstitching that joins the collar and band is done when the front edge of the jacket is topstitched.

The collar is now sandwiched between the two band pieces. Pull these two pieces apart and trim the collar seam allowance to 1/4". You will not be able to get in to trim this seam once the collar has been stitched in place.

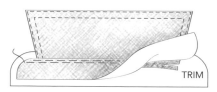

Collar Application: Clip the neckline seam to the stay stitching at regular intervals as needed, and trim to 3/8".

Pin the inside band to the neck edge so that the trimmed lower edge of the band overlaps the stay stitching 1/8". Hand-baste securely in place. Now position the outside band on the neck edge so that the wrong side of the band is against the right side of the garment. Make sure both bands lie smoothly and hand-baste in place. If fusible web has been used in the band, fuse the band layers together at this point, thus eliminating the basting step. This also eliminates any possibility of drag when the final rows of topstitching are done on the garment.

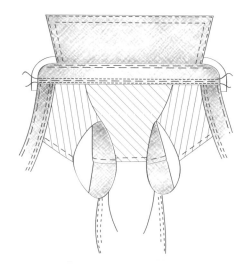

Finish the hem of the garment (see Hems section of this chapter) and then double-topstitch the front edge and the band's collar-joining seam in one operation. Trim the collar edges even and remove any basting.

Collar Without Band

The seam allowance of the two collar pieces should be trimmed as given in Cutting section of this chapter. Interface the upper collar or not, as you desire. Remember to cut the interfacing 1/8" smaller all around. Interface the under collar as shown in Interfacing section of this chapter, trimming the interfacing 1/4" smaller around the three outside finished edges.

If you are lining the garment, the lining must be basted in place around the neck edge before applying the collar. The neck edge should also be stay-stitched just inside the seam line and clipped at regular intervals. Do not trim the seam allowance at this time.

Draw a line marking the width of the neckline seam allowance on the wrong side of the lower edge of the upper collar.

Apply a thin line of glue to the wrong side of the neckline edge of the collar and position the collar against the neckline seam allowance matching up construction marks and making sure the cut edge of the neckline seam meets the drawn line. Hand-baste along the lower edge of the collar if you feel it is necessary.

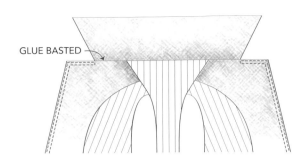

GLUE BASTED

Pin the under collar to the upper collar, wrong sides together, with 5/8" of the under collar extending beyond the edges of the upper collar. Pin and baste or glue the neck edge of the under collar securely in position. Working on the inside of the garment, edge-stitch through all layers along the lower trimmed edge of the upper collar.

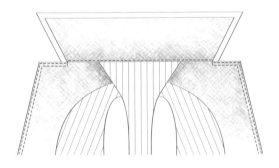

Unpin the outside edges of the collar and separate the two layers. Trim the seam allowance at the neckline.

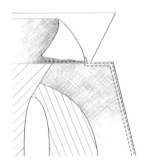

Roll the collar over your hand into the finished position and pin the two collar layers as they fall. If you have a dress form or if you have someone to help you fit the garment on yourself, you can get the proper collar roll that way. You will notice that you may have more than 5/8" of the under collar extending beyond the edge of the upper collar at this point. This is the natural shortening of the under collar and is what

creates a nice rolled collar that stays flat and neat around your neck.

While the collar is still in the rolled position, glue the edges together and finish with two rows of topstitching.

Collar With Cut-On Band

Use the above techniques for applying the collar with a cut-on band with the option of making two rows of topstitching where the collar joins the neckline edge instead of one row.

SLEEVE VENTS

The finish at the bottom of the sleeve will, of course, be determined by your pattern. Some sleeves have faced vents such as are found on men's suits, some require a vent finish combined with a cuff and some sleeves have just a simple hemmed edge. Read through these instructions and combine them with your pattern requirements for the desired finish.

Sleeve vents are constructed before the underarm seam of the sleeve is sewn, unless the vent is part of that seam.

Slash Vent

Cut a vent facing from Ultrasuede that is 3" wide and 1" longer than the vent slash. Slash the sleeve along the vent marking, rounding the top of the slash.

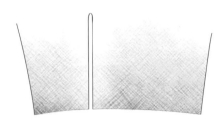

Pin and baste the facing in the proper position wrong sides together. Make two rows of stitching around the vent slash, as illustrated.

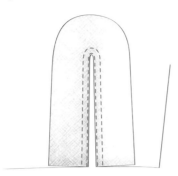

Alternate Finish: Pin and baste the facing in the proper position on the wrong side of the sleeve, but stitch the final topstitching around the vent when topstitching the edges of the cuff. This is a good way to finish the cuff and vent because you can make one continuous line of stitching up the ends of the cuff and vent. This method works only with cuffs that are cut flush with the sides of the vent.

Stitch the underarm seam using either the conventional or lapped seam method. If the garment is going to be lined, the sleeve lining should be stitched now and slipped down inside the garment's sleeve, wrong sides together. Slash the lining along the vent line cutting it 1/2" longer than the pattern indicates. Slip the lining behind the vent facing and slipstitch it in place. Baste the lower edge of the sleeve and lining together.

Tailored Vent

Slash the sleeve on the vent marking making the slash 4 1/2" long. Face the back of the vent (the edge closest to the underarm seam) with a 3/4"-wide strip of Ultrasuede that is cut 5" long. Baste and double-topstitch in place as illustrated.

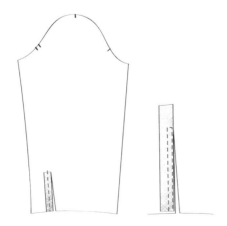

Cut a sleeve placket piece from Ultrasuede using the Ultrasuede Sleeve Placket Pattern found at the end of this chapter. Cut 3/8" into the sleeve at the top of the vent.

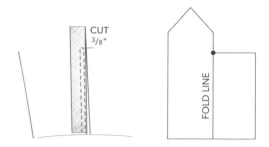

Fold the sleeve placket in half, wrong sides together. Baste and double-topstitch the folded edge to the dot. Pull the threads through to the inside of the two layers and tie.

Working on the right side of the sleeve, sandwich the edge of the sleeve slash in between the unstitched edges of the vent facing, overlapping the sleeve's edge 3/8". The lower edge of the vent facing should be even with the lower edge of the sleeve. Baste in position and double-topstitch as shown.

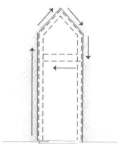

Stitch the underarm seam and apply sleeve lining as described in the previous vent section.

Vent in Seam

Some patterns have a sleeve vent constructed as part of the sleeve seam. You will find this type of con-

FAUX LEATHER

struction more often on men's than on women's garments. It is a very easy vent finish, and you can modify any sleeve pattern to use this type of vent if you wish by following the instruction below.

Draw a line up the back section of the sleeve starting where the vent slash is located. Cut the sleeve apart along this line and add a 5/8" seam allowance to both sides of the cut, plus an extra 1/2" in the vent area.

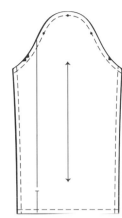

Now overlap the original underarm seam so that the seam lines are on top of each other. Tape in place and use this new pattern to cut your sleeves.

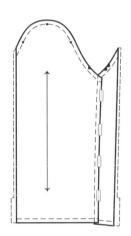

Baste, stitch and press open the underarm seam of the sleeve. Use thin strips of fusible web under the seam allowances to hold them flat, or edge-stitch on each side of the seam.

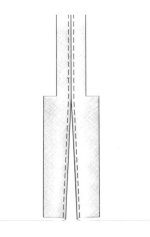

When lining this type of sleeve, you should cut the lining from the altered sleeve pattern. Stitch the underarm seam to a point 1/2" above the top of the vent opening and press the seam open. Slip the lining down inside the sleeve and baste along the lower edge. Slipstitch the edge of the lining to the vent edges.

Faced Vent

A tailored sleeve vent on a man's sport coat or woman's jacket is best handled with a facing. Cut the facing as follows or refer to the alternate method in the Cutting section of this chapter.

Overlap the pattern pieces at the front seam until the seam lines are on top of each other; pin together. Remove the hem allowance from both sleeve pattern pieces and the vent extension of the upper sleeve. Trace around this adjusted pattern for your sleeve facing, making it 1/8" larger around the three outside edges, 3" wide on the sides of the vent and 2" wide at the bottom edge.

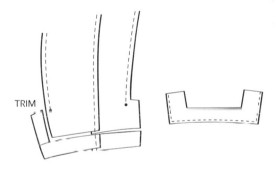

TRIM

Stitch the front seam of the sleeve using either the conventional or flat technique.

Apply interfacing to the sleeve facing if more body is desired. Cut the interfacing 1/4" smaller than the facing so that it doesn't "peek out" from the finished sleeve. Also, machine-stitch 1/4" down from the edge of the facing so that you have a line of stitching to follow to attach the lining.

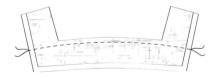

Position the facing against the lower edge of the sleeve, wrong sides together, and glue. Remember the facing is 1/8" larger than the sleeve, so it should extend out beyond the sleeve edge that much. Double-topstitch around the facing as shown. End the stitching at the construction dot marking the top of the vent. Pull the threads through to the wrong side and tie. Trim the excess facing.

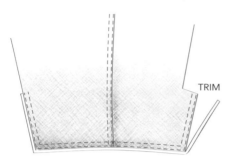

Baste and stitch the upper sleeve seam to the dot using the lapped seam method. This works best if the sleeve is turned inside out for the stitching. Hold the vent closed by sewing the vent buttons in place.

CUFFS

Directions are given for the two basic types of cuffs that you will find on patterns, the cuff with a separate facing and the one-piece fold-over cuff. Interfacing the cuff is optional. If you decide to use it, apply the interfacing to the upper cuff piece or the half of the fold-over cuff, which will form the upper cuff. Remember to trim the interfacing 1/8" smaller than the cuff so that it won't peek out around the edges.

If desired, fusible web, cut to fit the finished cuff, can be used instead of interfacing. It gives a crisp look and eliminates any chance of drag when sewing the final rows of topstitching. Glue-baste it in position before you begin the cuff application.

If you choose not to use interfacing or fusible web, then position a patch of color-matched, woven lining

fabric under the buttonhole area for support. The glue will hold the patch in place until the buttonhole is worked.

Cuff With Separate Facing

The upper cuff piece should be trimmed of all seam allowances. The cuff facing should retain the full seam allowance at the sleeve edge and just a 1/8" seam allowance around the outer three edges.

Position the lining in the sleeve and baste around the lower edge. Mark the seam line at the lower edge of the sleeve. Lap the upper cuff over the seam allowance so that the trimmed edge just meets the seam line. Baste or glue in position.

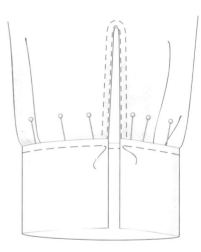

Position the cuff facing under the cuff, wrong sides together, so that 1/8" of the facing extends beyond the three outside edges of the upper cuff. Baste or glue securely at the sleeve edge. Double-topstitch through all layers at the top edge of the cuff.

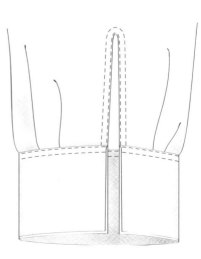

Separate the cuff pieces and trim the sleeve seam allowance. Trim away the excess seam allowance at the sleeve edge of the cuff facing also.

Baste the outer edges of the cuff and facing together. If fusible web has been used in the cuff, fuse the cuff layers together at this point, eliminating the basting step. Double-topstitch around the three outer edges.

Trim the facing even with the upper cuff edge. Do both lines of stitching from the same direction.

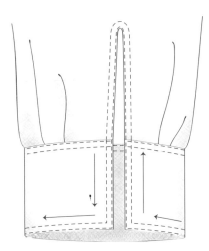

Fold-Over Cuff

This cuff piece should have three seam allowances trimmed away, leaving just one intact at the sleeve edge.

Mark the seam line on the right side of the lower edge of the sleeve. Lap the trimmed edge of the cuff over the lower sleeve seam until the edge meets the

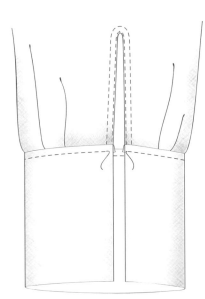

seam line. Baste or glue in place. Trim away 1/4" of the sleeve's seam allowance at the lower edge of the sleeve.

Fold the facing portion of the cuff, back into the finished position, wrong sides together. The 5/8" seam allowance will extend up into the sleeve. Baste across the top of the cuff again and then baste or glue around all three outside edges. This basting is important in order to prevent the layers of fabric from shifting during the final stitching. If fusible web has been used in the cuff, this is the time to fuse the cuff layers together, thus eliminating the basting.

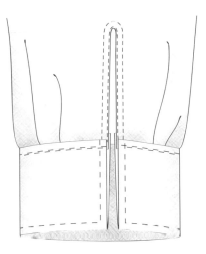

Double-topstitch across the top of the cuff. Double-topstitch around the outside edges of the cuff. It is important that these two stitching operations be done from the **same** direction so that a drag does not develop around the cuff edge. Trim away excess seam allowance at the top edge of the cuff facing.

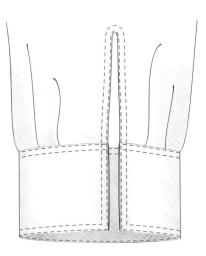

SETTING IN SLEEVES

Always set sleeves into the armhole with a conventional seam. This method is easiest and looks best when finished.

Ultrasuede and Ultraleather fabric cannot handle the cap ease found in most patterns, so you will have to make some alterations to your pattern before cutting the fabric. Follow the instructions given in Chapter 4, Sleeve-Cap Ease, for measuring and adjusting the sleeve-cap. Allow only 1" of ease in the sleeve cap.

The remaining 1" of ease must be controlled some way while you stitch the sleeve in place, and we have found this to be the easiest method.

With the suede right side up, machine-stitch from notch to notch around the top of the sleeve, keeping the stitching just short of the given seam line. Use a regular stitch length, but backstitch one stitch for every third forward stitch.

Now, working on the wrong side of the sleeve and using just the point of a pin, pull up the bobbin thread between each backstitch. This will cause the sleeve cape to curve under, and it holds the ease in place for the final stitching.

Pin the sleeve into the armhole, matching the construction marks. Place the pins directly **in** the seam line for better control of the fabric ease. Baste in place and try the garment on to check the fit.

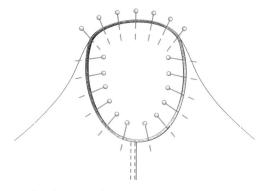

Once the fit is perfect and smooth, machine-stitch the sleeve in place. Stitch a second row 1/4" in the seam allowance. Trim to this stitching. Tailored jackets and coats need shoulder pads. They are optional for casual jackets. Refer to Chapter 7 for shoulder pad information. **Note:** *Clip the seam allowance of the lamb's wool to the stitching line around the seam cap. This releases the tension on the seam allowance and allows the sleeve seam to lie flat.*

ZIPPERS

Some Ultrasuede garments will require zippers, and these are really very easy to insert. Zippers in conventional seams will be stitched in using the traditional techniques. However, the flat method of seam construction makes it possible to easily insert zippers that have a very flat finish. Follow the instructions below for the center-slot, lapped and fly zipper.

For Ultraleather, invisible zippers, described in Chapter 6, are recommended.

Center-Slot Zipper

The simplest way to insert the center-slot zipper in an Ultrasuede garment is to use the Lapped Seam method for the zipper seam.

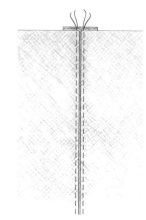

Trim the seam allowance from both sides of the seam. Cut a 1"-wide strip of fabric the same length as the seam. Butt the trimmed edges of the seam together and center them down the length of the strip. Baste in place and edge-stitch each side of the seam.

Make a slash down the center of the 1" strip the length of the zipper only! Position the zipper under the slash and baste or glue securely.

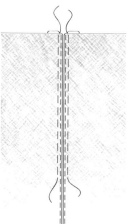

Do the second row of topstitching 1/4" away from the first, stitching from the same direction on each side. This row of stitching holds the zipper in place, and you will have four neat rows of topstitching showing down the zipper seam.

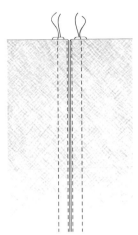

Lapped Zipper

This method is used at the sides of skirts and pants and at the center back of pants, skirts and dresses. It is also a simple way of making a fly zipper for pants. Just add two extra rows of topstitching to outline the fly.

Trim the seam allowance from the edge of the garment that laps over the zipper. Trim the other seam allowance a scant 3/8", just the length of the zipper.

TRIM

LENGTH OF ZIPPER

Zipper Tip: Use a longer zipper than necessary so it extends entirely above the waistline seam. This makes it easier to lower the back waistline seam if necessary for fitting purposes. (You won't be cutting into the metal stoppers at the top of the zipper.)

Position the zipper under the partially trimmed garment piece so the fabric edge is next to the zipper teeth.

Glue or baste it in place and edge-stitch with a zipper foot the length of the zipper teeth.

Cut a facing for the other side of the garment that is 1" wide and 1" longer than the zipper. Lay the facing along the edge of the completely trimmed seam allowance, wrong sides together. Glue or baste and double-topstitch the edge of the facing just the length of the zipper.

Mark the seam line down the length of the garment piece to which the zipper has been attached. Lap the faced side of the garment over the zipper so that the trimmed edge meets the seam line.

Baste in position. Double-topstitch the remainder of the seam below the zipper.

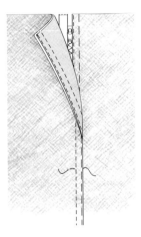

Working on the right side of the garment, fold back the left side until the zipper facing is exposed. Baste the facing to the zipper tape. Machine-stitch the facing to the zipper tape with a row of machine stitching. Stitch as close as possible to the zipper teeth. **Note:** *This row of stitching will not show on the "face" side of the garment.*

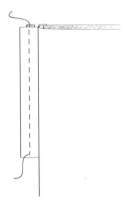

Slip a 1/4" strip of fusible web in between the facing and the garment fabric. Fuse in place from the wrong side. This keeps the facing flat and always in the correct position.

Fly Zipper

Trim away the seam allowance on the lapped-over part of the garment and leaving the seam allowance completely intact on the under part of the garment.

Position the zipper under the edge of the untrimmed seam allowance so the edge of the fabric is beside the zipper teeth. Glue or baste and edge-stitch with a zipper foot, close to the zipper teeth.

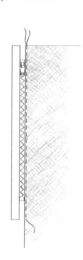

Cut a facing for the other side of the garment that is 2" wide and 1" longer than the zipper. Lay the facing along the edge of the other seam, wrong sides together. Glue or baste and double-topstitch the edge of the facing just the length of the zipper.

Mark the seam line down the length of the garment piece to which the zipper has been attached. Lay the faced side of the garment over the zipper so that the trimmed edge meets the marked seam line. Glue or

baste and double-topstitch the remainder of the seam below the zipper.

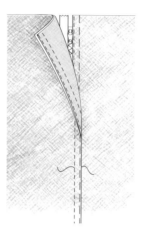

Glue the facing in position and finish the fly zipper with two rows of decorative topstitching 1 1/4" from the edge on the right side of the garment. This stitching should also catch the zipper tape. **Note:** Use a woven-fabric method for all Ultraleather zippers.

WAISTBANDS

You will find two types of waistbands on Ultrasuede garments, the faced waistband and the fold-over waistband. Fold-over waistbands use larger pieces of fabric than faced waistbands, so if you are short of large, uncut pieces of fabric, you can make the waistband into a faced one and utilize smaller pieces of fabric. Simply cut the waistband pattern apart along the fold line and use these two pieces to cut the waistband and facing.

Interface waistbands that are used at the top of pants and skirts, or, eliminate the interfacing and just don't trim the waistline seam; it will act as interfacing. Interfacing is optional for waistbands at the bottom edge of jackets, or you can use a piece of fusible web between the waistband layer for a crisp look. In either case, a piece of woven interfacing or color-matched lining fabric should be positioned on the wrong side of the band underneath the buttonhole area.

Faced Waistband

The top waistband piece should have all the seam allowances trimmed away. The waistband facing should have the three outside seam allowances trimmed to 1/8"; the seam allowance that joins the body of the garment should be left intact.

Mark the seam line on the right side of the garment piece that joins the waistband. Overlap the top waistband piece until the trimmed edge meets the seam line. Baste or glue securely in place.

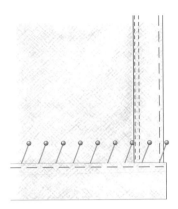

Position the waistband's facing against the top waistband, wrong sides together. The 1/8" allowance of the facing should extend beyond the edges of the top waistband. Baste or glue in place, then finish with a double row of topstitching.

Separate the two waistband layers and trim the seam allowance.

Pin and baste or glue the edges of the waistband together. Or, a piece of fusible web cut 1/4" narrower than the waistband can be fused in position between the fabric layers and all fused together at this point. Double-topstitch the remaining edges of the waistband. If the garment has a collar and front facing or band that hasn't been topstitched, then continue the topstitching through these areas at this time. Make sure that all the rows of topstitching are made in the same direction.

Fold-Over Waistband

Use the pattern piece given with the pattern, or, if you are making a waistband for pants or a skirt, cut the waistband piece 1" longer than the top edge of the garment and 2 1/2" wide.

The 1" band extension can be placed on either side of the waist opening, as you prefer.

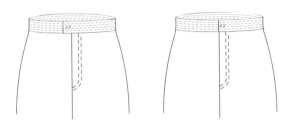

Mark the seam line at the waist of the garment and lap the waistband to the seam line. Baste or glue in position.

Fold the waistband down into the finished position so that 1/2" extends below the waistline seam on the wrong side. Baste or glue securely. **Note:** *The waistline seam is left untrimmed in the waistband to give extra body. Fusible web can also be added to the waistband also if desired.*

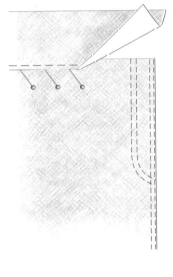

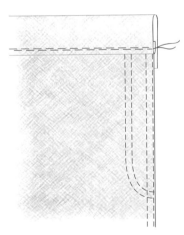

Finish the waistband by making four rows of topstitching along the length of the waistband. Make sure that all the rows of stitching are done in the same direction. Trim the front edges of the waistband even, then trim away the excess seam allowance from the back of the band.

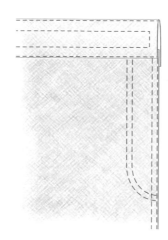

HEMS

If you look at ready-to-wear Ultrasuede garments, you will see various types of hem finishes. Some garments are just cut at the desired length and left with a raw edge. We feel this gives an unfinished look and encourages you to make conventional or faced hems.

For Ultraleather we recommend the Tailor's Hem found in Chapter 7, Hem Techniques.

Conventional Hems

Turn up the garment along the hemline. The hem width is 3/4" for unlined garments and 1 1/4" for lined garments. The hem allowance of the pattern should be trimmed to these widths before being pinned to the fabric.

Finish the hem by fusing with strips of fusible web or making a double row of topstitching along the lower edge. A word of caution here, fused hems sometimes get a "glued" look after repeated washings.

Hems can also be done by hand using the tailor's hem technique found in Chapter 7, Hem Techniques. Make a row of machine stitching 1/4" below the hem edge first, then catch the hand stitches to this stitching line instead of to the suede. Much easier!

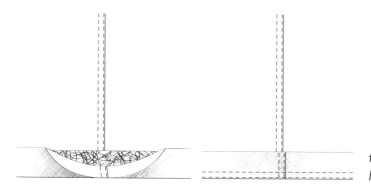

Faced Hem

Faced hems are more suitable for garments with curved edges. It is impossible to use a conventional hem finish on these garments and achieve a smooth look as Ultrasuede does not ease well.

Cut facing strips 3/4" wide, using the garment piece as a pattern so that you duplicate the curve exactly. Position the facing against the garment, wrong sides together, and baste or glue. Finish with a double row of topstitching along the lower edge.

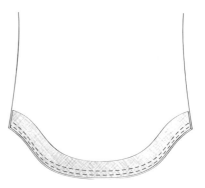

Hem at Front Facing

Garments that are hemmed and have a fold-back or separate front facing should be finished according to the following instructions.

Conventional Hem: Fold the hem up and baste or glue. Trim the front edge of the hem so that it extends only 1/2" into the facing. Fold the facing back in the finished position. Baste or glue in position and trim after it has been stitched across the lower edge.

Note: *A conventional hem can be left 2" wide— then you have the option of lowering the hemline at a later date.*

FAUX LEATHER

Finish the lower edge by fusing the hem with strips of fusible web or double-topstitching along the lower edge of the hem. If you are topstitching the hem edge, then topstitch the entire jacket at this time, going up the front, across the collar, down the other front and across the bottom edges in one operation. Make both rows of stitching from the same direction. **Note:** *This top-stitching should be done **before** setting in the sleeves. Why? It's much easier to stitch this "must be perfect" stitching without the extra bulk of the sleeves!*

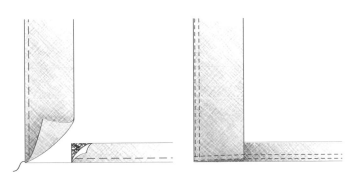

Faced Hem: The lower edge of the facing should be trimmed 1/8" wider than the lower edge of the garment.

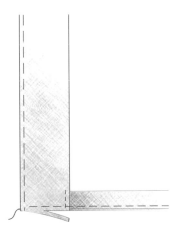

Face the hem with a 3/4"-wide strip of Ultrasuede placed wrong sides together with the facing extending 1/8" below the garment edge. The hem strip should extend just 1/2" into the facing at the front edge. Baste or glue the hem facing in place and finish by double-topstitching as above. Trim all edges even.

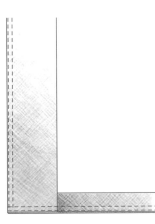

BUTTONHOLES

All buttonholes should be backed by interfacing to prevent rippling and stretching. A square or strip of woven interfacing, or better yet, a color-matched lining fabric should be used. Color-matched lining will avoid having a stripe of white showing in the buttonhole opening.

There are four methods of making buttonholes in Ultrasuede fabric. All are easy, but the bound buttonhole does require precise marking and cutting. It is suggested that you try the various buttonhole methods on scraps of fabric to see which one you prefer. You will also work out any construction problems before you begin work on the garment.

Buttonhole I

This is the easiest buttonhole and is frequently seen on designer fashions.

Using 14 stitches to the inch (or a stitch length of 2mm), stitch a rectangle the desired length and 1/8" wide at each buttonhole location. Count the stitches along each side to make sure all the buttonholes are the same size. Cut the buttonholes open using a craft knife, buttonhole cutter or a single-edged razor blade.

Buttonhole II

Make a standard machine buttonhole. These look best when corded. See your machine instruction book for cording instructions.

Buttonhole III

Here is the easiest bound buttonhole, and it gives a nice flat look. Make the front part of this buttonhole **before** the facing is attached to the garment. If the buttonholes are being made in a front band, waistband or cuff, make the front side of the buttonholes before attaching these pieces to the garment. **Note:** *Do not use this buttonhole on Ultraleather as the knit backing will show through the cut edge of the "window."*

Make a template the exact size of the buttonhole opening. (The cardboard from a bias or seam tape package makes a good template.) Cut the buttonhole 1/4" wide and the exact length of the buttonhole. The distance from the front edge of the buttonhole to the edge of the cardboard should be the same distance from the front edge of the buttonhole to the edge of the garment. This makes the positioning of the template easier.

Use the template to cut the buttonhole "window" on the garment piece. Make sure the "windows" are placed exactly where they are supposed to be before cutting. Use a craft knife, buttonhole cutter or a single-edge razor blade to cut the openings.

Cut two strips of fabric 1" x 2" for each buttonhole. (The strips should be 1" longer than the buttonhole opening.) Place the two strips right sides together and machine-baste down the center of the strips.

Press the strips open and position them under the buttonhole "windows," centering them in the opening. Baste securely around the outside edges of the "window" or glue in place.

After the facing has been attached to the garment, baste or glue around the buttonhole again, through the facing layer. Finish the buttonhole by edge-stitching around the buttonhole "window." Use a zipper foot for greater visibility.

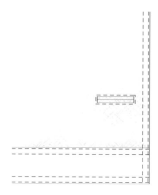

Remove any basting stitches, including the ones across the buttonhole openings. Cut a "window" or slit on the facing side just inside the stitched box.

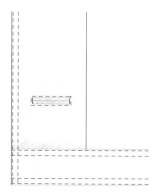

Note: *Do not baste or glue the buttonhole to the facing until after the facing has been double-topstitched in place. Sometimes the facing will shift a bit during the topstitching which would cause a wrinkling around the buttonhole.*

Buttonhole IV

Because this bound buttonhole does not have any stitches visible from the right side, it is very elegant looking. Remember that the front of the buttonhole is constructed before the facing is attached to the garment. Use this technique for Ultraleather.

Cut two strips of fabric 1" x 2" or 1" longer than each buttonhole opening.

Mark the exact position and width of each buttonhole with a fine pencil or basting thread on the right side of the garment. Double-check your marks to make sure they are accurate.

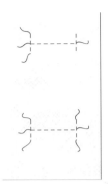

Place one buttonhole strip along the buttonhole line, right sides together, so that at least 1/2" extends beyond each end of the buttonhole. Baste and stitch 1/8" from the edge, the exact length of the buttonhole.

Position the second strip on the right side of the garment so that the cut edge butts against the cut edge of the first strip. Baste in position and stitch as for the first strip. It helps that you count stitches so the stitching lines are identical in length.

From the wrong side, cut the buttonhole open as shown leaving a good-sized wedge at each end. Do not cut the strips of fabric—just the garment fabric.

Turn the strips to the wrong side. Open the 1/8" seam and flatten it with your fingernail.

Wrap the buttonhole strips over the open seams and baste in position, as illustrated.

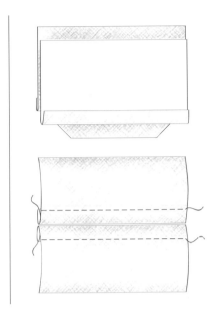

Fold back the garment at each side of the buttonhole and machine-stitch across the base of each wedge.

Baste or glue and topstitch the front facing to the garment. Baste around each buttonhole going through the facing layer at this time or glue the facing in place.

Set the machine for 16 stitches to the inch (stitch length of slightly less than 2mm) and finish the buttonhole by "stitching in the ditch" around each buttonhole. Stitch slowly, using a zipper foot for greater visibility; you don't want any of this stitching to show. Do this by hand if you can't bury stitches in the seam.

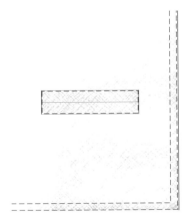

Remove all the basting and cut a "window" or a slit in the facing of the garment just inside the stitched box of each buttonhole.

SCRAP PROJECTS

Don't throw away any of those scraps of Ultrasuede. At the price you paid, they are worth lots of money. They can be used for high-fashion touches on other garments and clever craft projects. A few suggestions are given below. You'll probably think up more for yourself.

Wrap Belt

Cut a strip of Ultrasuede across the width 3" to 3 1/2" wide. Taper the ends and tie in a square knot for an instant high-fashion accent belt.

Patches

What can be more fun than Ultrasuede patches on jeans? Use various colors, cut in exciting shapes, and you will really add a touch of class to those old favorites. Little kids love the patches on their clothes, too!

Buttons

Make covered buttons and use them on other garments as well as on your Ultrasuede ones. They add interest and are machine washable to boot.

Buttonholes

Make bound buttonholes using Ultrasuede fabric for the lips. This looks especially nice on corduroy jackets. Use Buttonhole IV mentioned previously.

Piping

Use narrow strips of Ultrasuede to "pipe" collars, yokes, pockets, cuffs and anything else you can think of when making garments from other fabrics. This piping adds the look of real leather to the garment, giving none of the stitching and cleaning problems.

To make piping, cut 3/4"-wide strips of Ultrasuede on the cross-grain. Fold the strips in half, wrong sides together, and stitch 1/8" from the fold.

Baste the strip to the garment section to be piped so that the stitching on the piping lies along the seam line on the right

side of the garment. Clip the piping to the stitching when going around points, corners and curves.

Pin the garment pieces together, right side to right side, so that the suede strip is sandwiched in between. Stitch the seam and then trim, turn and press.

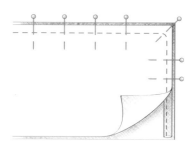

FASHION ACCENTS

Buttonhole Pocket

Use the Buttonhole Method III mentioned previously to make a buttonhole or double-welt pocket, except cut the pocket opening 1/2" wide and as long as indicated on the pattern. Cut three suede strips 2" wide and 1" longer than the pocket opening.

Prepare two strips as described for the buttonhole. Slip a pocket lining piece between the layers of the lower welt strip, after the strips have been basted together and pressed open. Baste the lining in place.

Center the prepared strips behind the pocket opening and baste in place. Edge-stitch around the pocket opening using a zipper foot, if desired, for greater visibility.

FAUX LEATHER

Stitch the remaining suede strips to the top of the other pocket-lining piece, lapping the suede 1/4" over the lining, and edge-stitch.

Position the lining/suede piece behind the pocket opening so the top of the suede strip is even with the top edge of the upper welt strip. If the lower edge of the pocket lining doesn't match, don't worry; just trim it even after the pocket is completed.

With the right side of the garment up, fold down the garment to expose the seam allowance of the upper welt strip. Hand- or glue-baste this seam allowance to the suede strip at the top of the second lining piece. Machine-stitch across the seam allowance, catching the top of the pocket piece underneath.

Fold over the side of the garment to expose the sides of the pocket lining pieces and close the pocket by stitching down the side, across the bottom and up the other side.

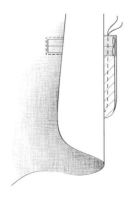

JACKET AND VEST OPTIONS

Use pieces of Ultrasuede to accent patch and welt pockets. It also gives a high-fashion look applied to the collars of sport coats. Make an Ultrasuede under collar as shown in Tailoring section. Embellish a hunting jacket by stitching Ultrasuede fabric patches to the shoulder and elbows. The shoulder patch goes on the right side unless, of course, the man is left-handed.

Make a vest with an Ultrasuede front and a sweater knit back. Or, stitch together patches of various colors of Ultrasuede for a patchwork vest.

Design a Western scene out of Ultrasuede scraps and zigzag the pieces to the back yoke of a denim jacket.

Make a braided belt from strips of suede trimmed from seams. Use the braid for a tie belt or a regular belt with a buckle. You can also hand-stitch the braid to a denim work shirt or jacket for a new look.

Wide belts and purses made from Ultrasuede are unusual. There are many patterns available for these.

Use small scraps for appliqués. Ultrasuede scraps are also excellent for cleaning glasses. They would even make a good eyeglass case or liner.

SWEATER TRIMS

Narrow strips of Ultrasuede can be used to accent the neck and sleeve trim of men's and women's sweaters. Cut the strips 3/8" or 1/2" wide across the grain of the fabric.

Turtleneck Trim

Use a regular turtleneck sweater pattern, but cut out the entire neckline 2" lower than the pattern requires. This lowering allows the sweater to slip over the head after the Ultrasuede trim-strip has been applied.

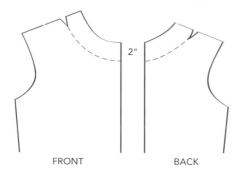

FRONT   BACK

Cut the turtleneck collar 8" wide and long enough to stretch around the head but still fit comfortably around the neck. Stitch the narrow edges of the collar, right sides together, and then finger-press the seam open. Fold the collar in half, wrong sides together; divide and mark the cut edge into four equal sections.

With the garment inside out, divide and mark the neckline into four equal sections. Slip the prepared collar down into the neckline and pin the edges together, matching up the quarter marks. The collar seam should be placed at the center back. Stitch the neckline with a 1/4" seam.

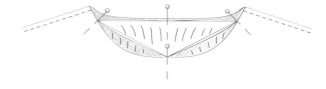

Pin the Ultrasuede strip to the neckline so that the lower edge runs right on the neckline seam.

Lap the edges of the strip at the center back and attach to the collar with two rows of topstitching.

V-Neck Trim

Topstitch one or two narrow strips of Ultrasuede fabric to the band of the V-neck before it is attached to the sweater. Baste and double-topstitch the strips to the neckband before it is folded into the finished position, then stitch it to the garment.

Cuff Trim

Stitch narrow strips of Ultrasuede fabric around the cuffs of sweaters to give a complete fashion look. Apply the strips to the cuff trim before folding and applying to the sleeve opening. Be sure cuff will go over your hand—Ultrasuede cuts down on the stretch of the cuff.

There is no end to the things you can do with all those expensive scraps. Using them up is almost as exciting as making the actual garment. Have fun!

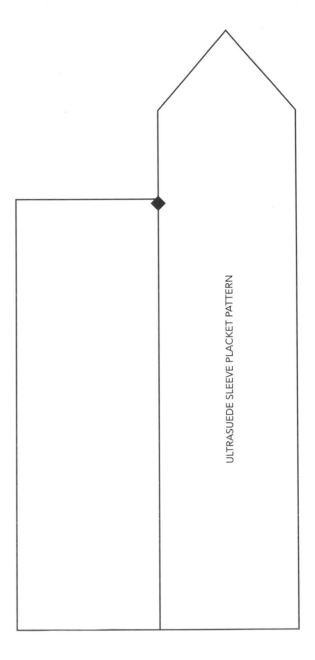

ULTRASUEDE SLEEVE PLACKET PATTERN

FAUX LEATHER

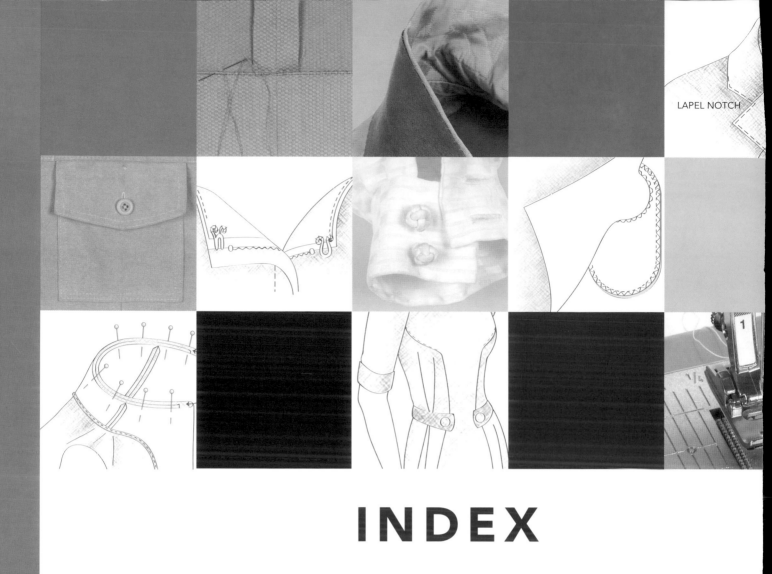

INDEX

9

INDEX

INDEX

F

Fabric glue, 1-24
Fabric marking, 1-17, 8-6
Fabrics
    checks, 1-13
    fake fur, 2-9
    knits, 1-4, 2-9
    napped, 1-10
    nonwovens, 1-5
    plaids, 1-11, 2-10
    sequined, 2-11
    Ultraleather, 1-5, 2-10,
        8-4
    Ultrasuede, 1-5, 8-3
    woven, 1-3
Faced facing, 3-22
Faced hem, 8-40
Faced-hole pocket, 5-16
Faced vents, 7-7
Facings
    adaptation, 3-14
    application, 3-16
    armhole, 3-14
    clean finish, 3-16
    edge finishes, 3-16
    finishing, 3-17
    front facing, 3-16, 7-12
    neckline, 3-15
    neckline-armhole, 3-15,
        3-20
    off-set sleeveless
        armhole, 3-18
    pressing, 3-18
    pull-through method, 3-20
    sheer fabrics, 3-23
    sleeveless, 3-18
    sleeveless, scooped-
        necked, 3-20
    stitching, 3-18
    techniques, 3-18
    tips, 3-22
    Ultrasuede fabric, 8-14
    waistline, 3-23
Fake band hem, 7-21
Fake band patch pocket, 5-9
Fake cuff hem, 7-21
Fake fly, 6-18
Fastenings
    covered snaps, 6-33
    French tack, 2-19
    frogs, 6-31
Fasturn, 1-24

Fellstitch, 2-18
Fitting tailored garments, 7-4
Flat collar, 4-3
Flat-felled seam, 2-5
Fly zipper, 6-14, 8-38
French dart, 3-7
French seam, 2-5
French tack, 2-19
Frogs, 6-31
Front facing, 7-12
Full-roll collar, 4-4
Fused hem, 7-20
Fusible interfacing, 3-3
Fusible web, 3-6

G

Glue Baste-It, 1-24
Glue stick, 1-24, 8-6
Grading, 2-6

H

Hair canvas, 3-4
Hand basting, 2-17, 8-7
Hand needles, 2-16
Hand prick stitch, 2-18
Hand stitches
    arrowhead, 2-19
    backstitch, 2-17
    basting, 2-17
    blindstitch, 2-18
    catchstitch, 2-19
    chain-stitch carriers, 2-19
    fellstitch, 2-18
    French tack, 2-19
    hemming stitch, 7-19
    hand prick stitch, 2-18
    how to, 2-17
    slip basting, 2-17
    slipstitch, 2-18
    stabstitch, 2-18
    whipstitch, 2-18
Hem finishes
    bound, 7-18
    faced, 8-40
    Hong Kong, 7-18
    overcast, 7-18
    pinked and stitched, 7-18
    turned and stitched, 7-18
Hem gauge, 1-23
Hem guide, 2-21
Hem stitches, hand
    catchstitch, 7-19
    hemming stitch, 7-19

locked blindstitch, 7-19
    slipstitch, 7-19
    tailor's hem, 7-19
Hem stitches, machine
    blind stitch, 2-18
    topstitch, 7-20
Hems, special
    fake band, 7-21
    fake cuff, 7-21
    lettuce edge, 7-23
    padded, 7-20
    rolled, 7-21
    satin-stitched, 7-24
    topstitched, 7-20
    Ultrasuede, 8-40
Hem techniques
    basic hem, 7-18
    double-stitched, 7-20
    fused hem, 7-20
    padded hem, 7-20
    tailor's hem, 7-19
    topstitched, 7-20
Hemming stitch, 7-19
Hemming tips, 7-22, 7-26
Hem widths, 7-17
Hong Kong finish, 2-4, 3-16,
    7-18

I

Interfacing
    application, 3-4, 4-5, 7-4
    collars, 4-5
    cuffs, 4-24
    facings, 3-16
    flaps, 5-8
    fusible, 3-5
    fusible web, 3-6
    garment fronts, 7-4
    hair canvas, 3-4
    hems, sleeve, 7-5
    lapels, 7-5, 8-10
    nonfusible, 3-3, 3-6
    pockets, 5-3
    selection, 3-3
    Ultrasuede, 8-10
Inside breast pocket, 5-24
Invisible zipper, 6-9
Invisibly stitched pockets, 5-7
Iron, 2-20, 8-6
Ironing board, 2-20
Iron-on interfacing, 3-3
Irons safe or iron
    shoe, 2-20

K

Knit fabrics
    expanded pattern, 1-15
    grainline, 1-4
    hemming, 7-20
    interlock, 1-4
    layout, 1-5
    problems of, 1-4, 1-14
    sleeves, 4-13
    stitching, 1-14
    tips, 1-14
    zipper application, 6-12

L

Lapels, 8-10
Lapped dart, 8-19
Lapped seam, Ultrasuede
    fabric, 8-8
Lapped zipper,
    Ultrasuede fabric, 8-37
    with facing, 6-7
    with waistband, 6-9
Lap seam, 2-5, 8-8
Layout, pattern
    border prints, 1-14
    checks, 1-13
    guidelines, 1-19
    knits, 1-14
    napped fabrics, 1-10
    plaids, 1-11
    printed fabric, 1-14
    stripes, 1-13
    tips, 1-9, 1-16
    Ultraleather, 8-10
    Ultrasuede, 8-12
Leather, 2-9
Leather needle, 1-19
Lettuce edge, 7-23
Lined patch pocket, 5-5, 5-18
Lined sleeves, 4-18, 8-26
Lining fabric, 7-11, 8-24
Lining techniques
    tailored garments, 7-11,
        7-15
    Ultrasuede garments, 8-11
Lockstitch, 2-3
Loops, button, 6-29

M

Machine basting, 2-11
Machine needles, 1-19
Machine stitching

My Notes for CLOTILDE'S SEW SMART

My Notes for CLOTILDE'S SEW SMART